CROCHET STYLE

CROCHET STYLE

Sally Harding

BALLANTINE BOOKS · NEW YORK

Crochet Style was conceived,
edited and designed by Frances Lincoln Limited,
Apollo Works, 5 Charlton Kings Road, London NW5 2SB

Library of Congress Catalog Card Number: 86-91074

ISBN: 0-345-34081-7

Manufactured in Italy

First American Edition: May 1987

10 9 8 7 6 5 4 3 2 1

CONTENTS

THE APPEAL OF CROCHET

The crocheted fabric offers a wealth of stitch textures, color and yarn combinations and fashion shapes. It is therefore surprising that, during the recent expansion of knitting design, crochet has remained a poor second cousin. This book attempts to redress the balance by uncovering the versatility of crochet and taking it into the realm of fashion. Perhaps preconceptions have played a part in stifling interest in crochet. So limited is the general concept of crochet that any crochet fabric other than that of a household doily or a bright afghan is frequently met with the incredulous response — "Is that really crochet?" To help dispel this myth and to inspire crochet enthusiasts, I have set out to illustrate some of the attractive aspects of the crocheted textile. I have used a wide range of yarns and many of the most interesting designs have resulted from effective combinations of differing yarn textures worked in simple stitches.

CROCHET YARNS

Yarn is without a doubt the most important element in crochet. Passion about the feel and look of yarns is what turns us into obsessive crocheters, knitters or weavers. So consider carefully and thoroughly the color, texture and composition of a yarn before purchasing it.

When possible, buy natural fibers or natural fibers mixed with a small proportion of synthetic. They have a better look and feel than totally synthetic yarns. They age with grace and can withstand washing and

Cotton
Mercerized cotton yarns have a lovely sheen and produce crisp textures. They are perfect for crochet openwork and for highlights and contrasts — for instance for shiny bobbles on a wool base.

Mohair
Ideal for plaids, cables and stripes, mohair yarns are a favorite for crochet. Do not be put off by the fact that the hairs slightly obscure the crochet loops when working. It only takes a little practice to overcome this.

Chenille
Usually made of cotton, chenille sometimes has a synthetic mixture in the core to hold the short cotton fibers securely in place. Crocheted cotton chenille produces a warm and supple fabric.

Textured yarns
These include many bumpy yarns which are often called fancy or novelty yarns. The examples illustrated here are more specifically known as slub, knop and snarl yarns. Slub yarns have irregular thick and thin sections produced by looser or tighter spinning. The single strands of knop yarn are spun so that the strands double up on themselves, creating lumps intermittently. Snarl yarns have a texture rather like terry. Little twists of yarn stick out from the core.

Metallic yarns
Evening wear is often attractively finished off by adding a glittery edging. Fine metallic yarns can also be worked together with a strand of mohair or wool for a more subtle glitter.

Wool

Smooth wool yarns have the advantage of being available in an extensive range of colors. Fine tweeds are especially effective for crochet. When choosing wool yarns, remember that some 100% wool yarns are softer than others. Alweays check the softness.

pressing. Unlike some synthetics, natural fibers breathe with your skin and can provide warmth, coolness and comfort.

There is a vast variety of yarns available today. The key to choosing yarns to crochet is to stick to the thinner, more lightweight yarns. This does not mean that the yarn will require a fine hook and that your garment will take weeks to make. Generally a better crochet fashion fabric is achieved by using a comparatively large hook to work the finer yarns loosely. Because of the structure of the loops, crochet creates a doubled fabric and can become stiff and unwearable when thick yarns are worked tightly. Experiment with any fine and lightweight yarns you have. Appealing crochet fabrics are also made with the fluffy or textured yarns such as mohairs, chenilles, slubs and loop yarns worked in simple single, half double or double crochet.

Some of the yarns most suitable for crochet are reproduced life-size on the previous pages. These are the weights which are the starting point for successful crochet fashion. On page 119 there are life-size photographs of the yarns used for the patterns in the book to help you choose a substitute yarn.

FASHION DESIGNS

The patterns in the book are divided into five distinct design categories covering stripes, plaids and checks, textures, color stitches and motifs and openwork. Each section is introduced by a selection of stitch variations which can be used as alternatives in the patterns or as a design guide for more advanced crocheters. Many of the sweater patterns are accompanied by alternative colorways or fashion design variations. This provides a wide range of garment shapes, fabrics and color combinations.

CROCHET TECHNIQUES

Although some of the crochet fabrics in the book may look unusual or complicated, only the simplest crochet stitches have been used. Anyone with basic crochet skills could work the designs, provided that they follow the step-by-step instructions in the last chapter for the more difficult techniques. This chapter also includes a list of crochet tips which are an invaluable guide to successful crochet. Even advanced crocheters would be wise to read these tips carefully before commencing any crochet project to ensure a good fit and a professional finish.

Sally Harding

STRIPES

STRIPES

Stripes are the simplest of all design patterns. Depending on the stripe and the colors, they can make a garment sporty, elegant or classic. Here are some samples illustrating how widely different stripes can look. They can be used as variations for the stripe patterns in the designs that follow or they may inspire the creation of original variations.

▶ SIMPLE STRIPES

The simplest stripe is made by introducing one or two rows of a contrasting color into a solid background. From this elementary beginning endless combinations follow by adding to the number of colors and varying the depth of the stripes. The stripes in samples 1 and 2 are examples of simple stripes in softly contrasting colors. Worked in half doubles, these stripes could easily be worked as an alternative design on *Stripes on stripes* (page 22) or *Checked stripes* (page 18).

▶ RANDOM STRIPES

Random stripes in single crochet (7) are a perfect way to use up leftover yarns. Yarns similar in weight should be used. It is possible to introduce textured yarn intermittently with smooth yarns provided it is introduced at random *evenly* across the piece being crocheted. If worked in only one area, it may make the crochet longer or shorter on one side. When smooth and textured yarns are being matched, the textured yarn should appear much thinner because the hairs or loops will add considerable bulk even though the threads actually look fine.

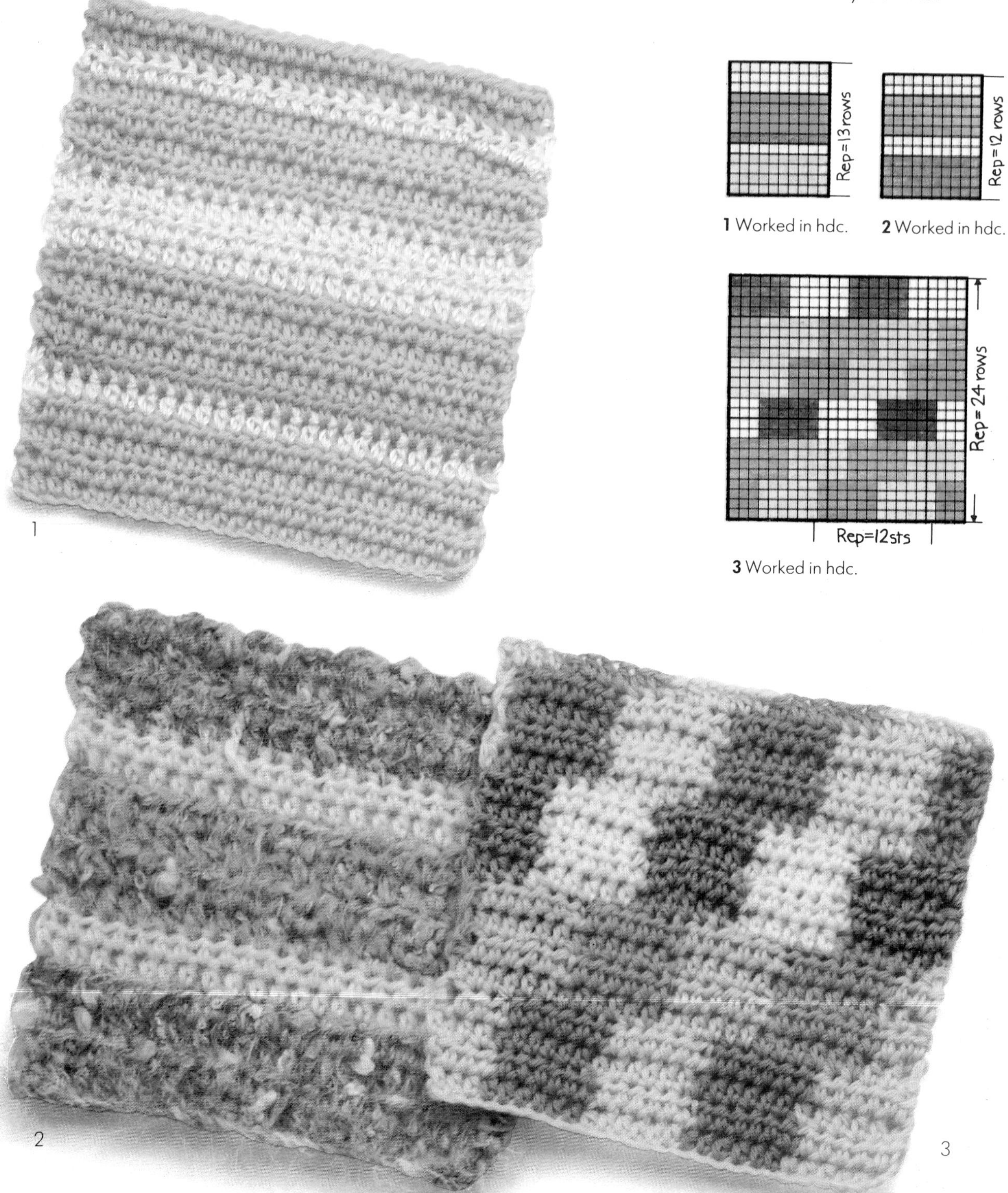

1 Worked in hdc. **2** Worked in hdc.

3 Worked in hdc.

▶ ADVANCED STRIPES

More complicated than horizontal stripes, diagonal stripes (3 and 4) use two colors in a row. If you juxtapose contrasting stripe panels you achieve an even more complicated stripe construction, but one that is still easy to work. Sample 5 would be a possible substitute for the stripes in *Stripe panels* (page 15). Irregular or wavy vertical stripes (6) soften the crisp, harder edge of straight stripes. One way of forming vertical stripes is to work the body of the garment from side seam to side seam instead of in the usual way, which is from lower edge to top.

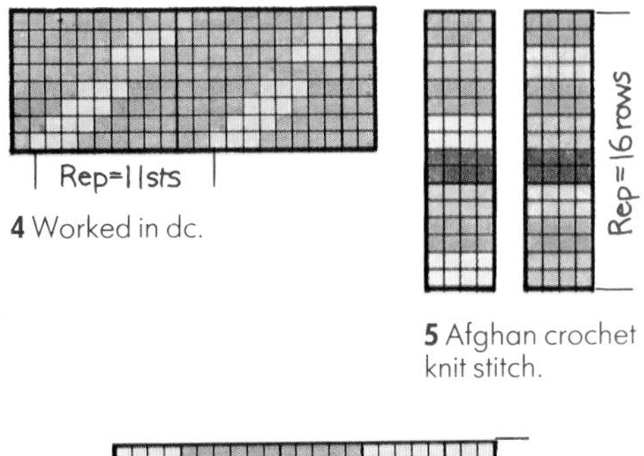

4 Worked in dc.

5 Afghan crochet knit stitch.

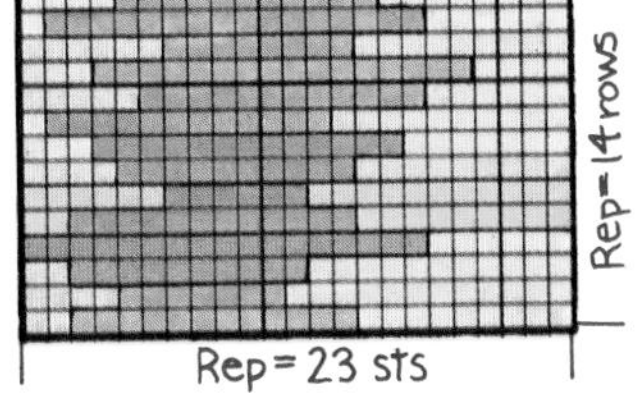

6 Worked in sc.

7 Random stripes in sc.

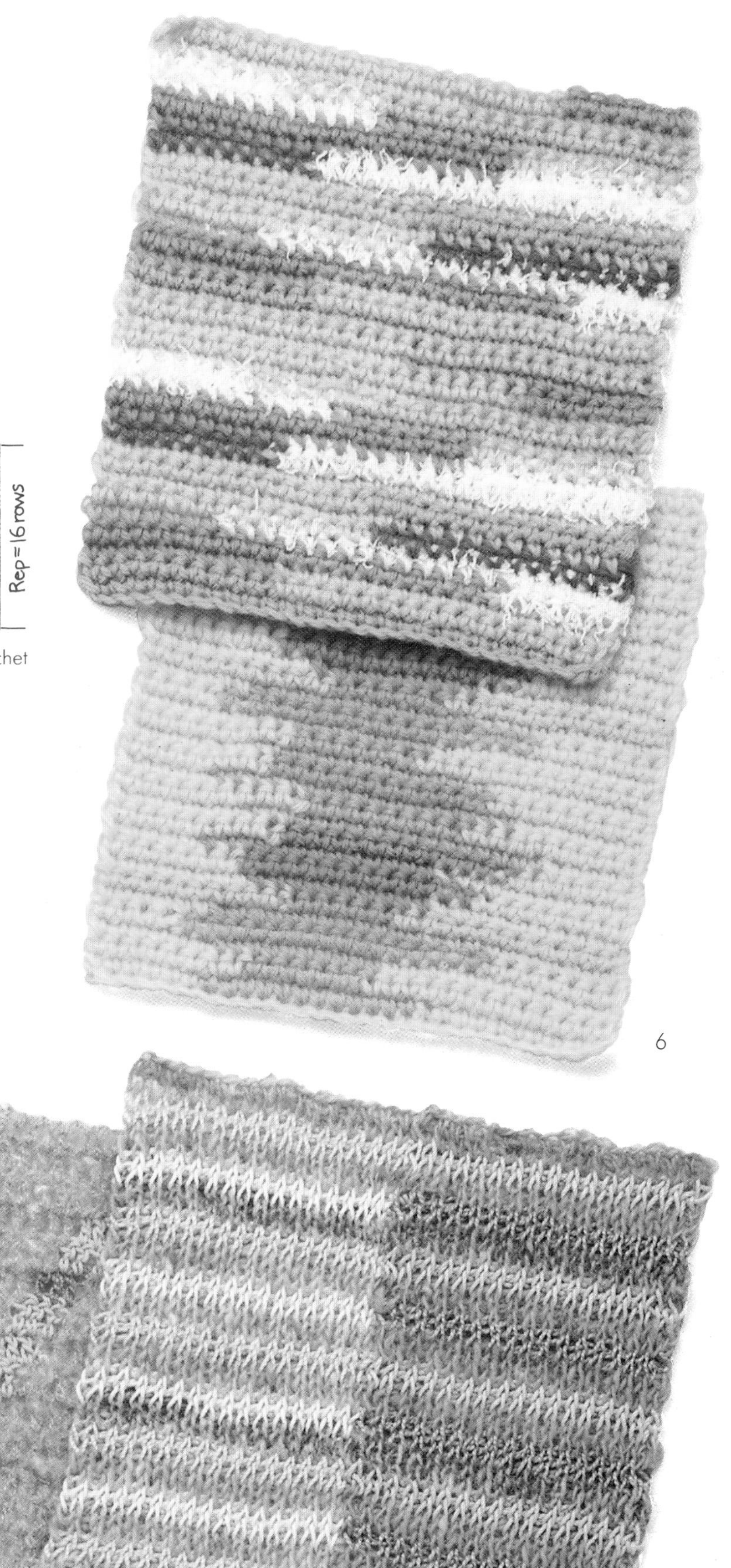

BROAD STRIPES

A mixed rayon yarn gives a subtle sheen to this classic jacket shape. The striped crochet fabric is worked in a simple pattern of single crochet and chain stitches. For a variation, create an original design with wider or narrower stripes.

▶ SIZES

To fit 34[36:38]"/86[91:96]cm bust.
Note: Figures for larger sizes are in brackets. If there is only one set of figures, it applies to all sizes.
See diagram for finished measurements.

▶ MATERIALS

See page 118 for further yarn information
Use a medium weight acrylic and rayon yarn (approx 128yd per 1¾oz):
21[23:24½]oz in main color MC (cream)
5¼oz in contrasting color A (blue)
3½oz in contrasting color B (white)
Size G crochet hook *or size to obtain correct gauge*
4 buttons
Shoulder pads (optional)

▶ GAUGE

24 sts and 23 rows to 4" over pat st using size G hook.
To save time, take time to check gauge (see Note below).

Note: Back, fronts and sleeves are worked in rows which progress from side seam to side seam instead of from lower edge to top in the usual way.
When counting sts, remember to count each sc and each ch1 space.

▶ BACK

***Using MC, ch92.
Base row 1sc in 2nd ch from hook, *ch1, skip next ch, 1sc in next ch, rep from * to end. Turn. 91 sts counting each ch sp and each sc as a st *or* 46sc.
1st row Ch1, 1sc in first sc, *ch1, 1sc in next sc, rep from * to end. Turn.
Last row forms pat st and is rep throughout. Work 4[6:6] rows more in pat st.

Armhole shaping
Next row Ch1, work (1sc, ch1, 1sc) in first sc — called "inc 2 at beg of row" —, *ch1, 1sc in next sc, rep from * to end. Turn.
Next row Ch1, 1sc in first sc, *ch1, 1sc in next sc, rep from * to last sc, end with (ch1, 1sc) twice in last sc — called "inc 2 at end of row". Turn.
Rep last 2 rows twice more.*** 103 sts.
Next row Ch45[47:49], 1sc in 2nd ch from hook, *ch1, skip next ch, 1sc in next ch, rep from * to end of ch, then cont in pat to end of row. Turn.
147[149:151] sts.
Work 4 rows without shaping.
Drop MC at edge of work but do not break off.
Using A, work one row without shaping.

Shoulder shaping
Using A, inc 2 at beg of next row.
Break off A.
Using MC, work 5 rows without shaping. Inc 2 at beg of next row.
Rep from ** to ** once more.
Using A, work 2 rows without shaping.
Break off A.
Using MC, work 3 rows without shaping.
Cont in MC, inc 2 at beg of next row.
Work 5[5:7] rows without shaping.
155[157:159] sts.

Neck shaping
Keeping to pat st, dec 2 sts at beg of next row (neck edge). 153[155:157]sts.
Note: Dec 2 sts at beg of a row by working ch1, skip first sc and work first sc in next sc.
Using MC, work 2 rows without shaping.
Using A, work 2 rows. Break off A.
*Using MC, work 12 rows.
Using A, work 2 rows. Break off A.*
Rep from * to * once more. Work 3 rows in MC.
Inc 2 at neck edge on next row.
155[157:159] sts. This completes neck shaping.
Work 2nd shoulder and armhole as for first side of back, reversing shaping and working stripe pat as set. Fasten off.

▶ LEFT FRONT

Work as for back from *** to ***. 103 sts.
Next row Ch45[47:49], using B, work 1sc in 2nd ch from hook, (ch1, skip next ch, 1sc in next ch) 10[11:11] times, using MC, *ch1, skip next ch, 1sc in next ch, rep from * to end of ch, then cont in pat to end of row. Turn.
147[149:151] sts.
Next row Using MC, ch1, 1sc in first sc, *ch1, 1sc in next sc, rep from * to within last sc in MC (not *in* last sc in MC), using B, ch1 and cont in pat to end. Turn.
Next row Using B, work over all sc in B, then using MC, ch1 and cont in pat to end. Turn.
Cont in this way for 2[2:4] rows more, moving B one st further from shoulder edge in each row.
Work one row in A.

Shoulder shaping
Work shoulder shaping as for back, keeping to stripe sequence as set on back and cont to add one more st in B with each row in between stripes in A. 155[157:159] sts.
Note: To keep an even slope formed by MC and B, remember to move B over 3 sts after each stripe in A.

Neck shaping
Keeping to pat st and stripe pat as set, shape neck as foll:
Next row With RS facing skip first 16[18:20] sts (8[9:10]sc) and rejoin B to next st with a sl st, ch1, 1sc in same sc as sl st was worked, work in pat to end of row. Turn.
Dec 2 sts at neck edge on next 4 rows, so ending with 2nd row of a stripe in A.
Note: Dec 2 sts at end of row by working to last 2sc of row, ch1 as usual, insert hook in next sc, yo and draw a loop through, insert hook in last sc, yo and draw a loop through, yo and draw through all 3 loops on hook.
Break off MC.
Dec 2 sts at neck edge on next 2 rows

ANTIC
SHOPS

[illegible] Boardwa[illegible]
Ocean City, N.J. 08226
(609) 399-9762

1208 Boardwalk
Ocean City, N.J. 08226
(609) 398-9805

255 96th St.
Stone Harbor, N.J. 08247
(609) 368-9847

1910 Boardwalk
N. Wildwood, N.J. 08260
(609) 522-9640

Boardwalk & Cresse Ave.
Wildwood, N.J. 08260
(609) 522-1127

711 Beach Ave.
Cape May, N.J. 08204
(609) 884-9742

5 Rehoboth Avenue
Rehoboth Beach, Del. 19971
(302) 227-0490

and then on every alternate row 8 times *and at the same time* work last 19 rows of left front in stripe sequence of 12 rows in B, 2 rows in A and 5 rows in B. 111 sts.

► RIGHT FRONT

Pat st is reversible so that right front is worked exactly as for left front to 4th stripe in A.
Work first row in A as for left front, then work buttonhole row as foll:
Buttonhole row Using A (and beg at neck edge), work first 9 sts (5sc) in pat st, *ch5, skip next 5 sts (ch1-1sc-ch1-1sc-ch1) and cont in pat st across next 26 sts, rep from * twice more, ch5, skip next 5 sts and cont in pat to end of row. Turn.
On next row work in pat st across ch5 of each buttonhole and complete as for left front.

► SLEEVES (make 2)

Using MC, ch10 and work base and first rows as for back. 9 sts.
Next row Ch15[13:11], 1sc in 2nd ch from hook, *ch1, skip next ch, 1sc in next ch, rep from * to end of ch, then cont in pat st to end of row. Turn.
Work one row without shaping.
Rep last 2 rows 0[1:2] times more. 23[33:39] sts.
Next row Ch15[13:11], 1sc in 2nd ch

Narrower stripes in a brighter colorway produce a more sporty jacket.

from hook, *ch1, skip next ch, 1sc in next ch, rep from * to end of ch, then cont in pat st to end of row, inc 2 in last st (top of sleeve). Turn.
Cont inc 14[12:10] sts along sleeve seam on every alternate row and 2 sts at top of sleeve on every row until 13[15:17] rows have been worked from beg (including base row). 111[111:107] sts.
Next row Using A, work in pat st, inc 2 at top of sleeve. Turn. 113[113:109] sts.
Next row Using A, work in pat st inc 10[12:18] sts along sleeve seam at beg of row. Turn. 123[125:127] sts.
Break off A. Then using MC and keeping lower sleeve edge straight, cont to shape sleeve top. Inc 2 at sleeve top on next row and then on every alternate row twice more. Work 7 rows without shaping.
Cont in stripe sequence of 2 rows A and 12 rows MC as set on back *and at the same time* inc 2 at sleeve top on next row, work 7 rows without shaping, inc 2 at beg of next row, work 13 rows without shaping (this is center of sleeve). 133[135:137] sts. Work 14 rows more in pat without shaping, then work 2nd side of sleeve shaping as for first side, reversing shaping. Fasten off.

► **POCKETS** (make 2)
Using MC, ch54[56:58]. Work base and first rows as for back. 53[55:57] sts *or* 27[28:29]sc.
Work 11 rows more in MC, 2 rows in A, 12 rows in MC, 2 rows in A, 13 rows in MC *and at the same time* shape side seam of pocket by inc 2 at side seam edge on every 10th row 3 times in all. 59[61:63] sts.

► **FINISHING**
Do not press.
Join shoulder seams. (Sew ½" wide fabric tape along shoulder seam for firmer seam if desired.) Set in sleeves. Join sleeve and side seams.
Sew on pockets overlapping 1" onto back and sewing overlapping edge parallel to side seam so that top of pocket stands out slightly from jacket. Using matching colors and with RS facing, beg at right shoulder seam and work sc evenly along back neck, down left front, along lower edge and up right front, working 2sc in lower corners. Join with a sl st to first sc and fasten off. Sew on buttons opposite buttonholes. Sew in shoulder pads if desired.

DESIGN VARIATION

► **ALTERNATIVE STRIPES**
For a simple striped jacket omit sections in B or create an original stripe design, using wider or narrower stripes or increasing number of colors.

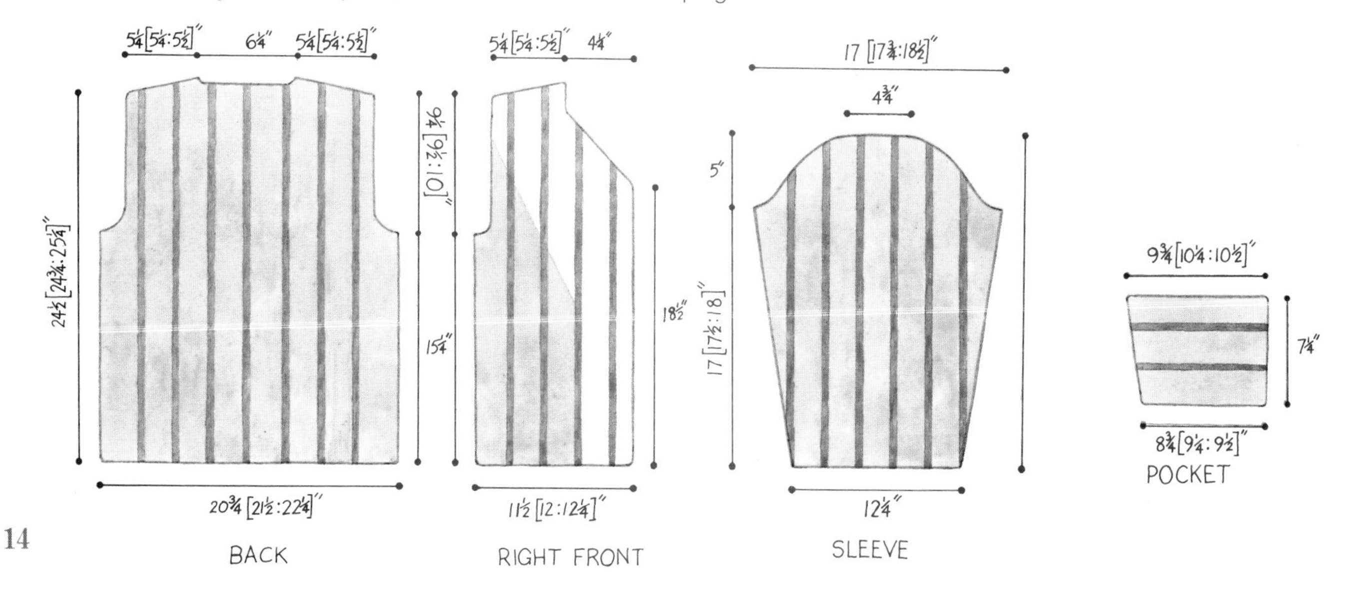

STRIPED PANELS

Panels of textured tweed stripes in Afghan crochet knit stitch have been sewn together to make this unusual sweater. The neck is finished with a roll collar and the back and front can be made with a straight lower edge as an alternative.

▶ SIZES

To fit 32-34[36-38]"/81-86[91-96]cm bust.

Note: Figures for larger size are in brackets. If there is only one set of figures, it applies to both sizes.

See diagram for finished measurements.

▶ MATERIALS

See page 118 for further yarn information

Use a fine wool tweed yarn (approx 109yd per 1oz):
4[5]oz in each of A (brown), F (rust-brown) and G (gray)
5[6]oz in B (gold-brown)
5[7]oz in D (beige)
7[8]oz in C (red)
3[4]oz in E (rose)
2[3]oz in H (white)
Size H Afghan crochet hook *or size to obtain correct gauge*
Size E crochet hook
Shoulder pads (optional)

▶ GAUGE

20 sts to 3¾" and 25 loop rows to 4" over Afghan knit st using size H Afghan crochet hook.

To save time, take time to check gauge.

Note: Back, front and sleeves are each made in vertical strips of Afghan crochet which are then sewn tog.

When changing colors work last yo of return row in new color (see page 116).

▶ BACK

Panel 1

Using Afghan hook and A, ch20[22] and beg Afghan knit st as foll:

Base row Insert hook in 2nd ch from hook, yo and draw a loop through, *insert hook in next ch, yo and draw a loop through, rep from * to end of ch. (Do not turn at end of rows.) 20[22] loops on hook.

1st row (return row) Yo and draw through first loop on hook, *yo and draw through 2 loops on hook, rep from * until there are 2 loops rem on hook, drop A at side of work but do not break off, using B, yo and draw through last 2 loops on hook (this forms first loop of next row).

2nd row (loop row) Using B, skip first vertical loop in row below and insert hook from front to back through 2nd vertical loop (under the chain), yo and draw a loop through, * insert hook through next vertical loop, yo and draw a loop through, rep from * to end.

Note: To form a firm edge, insert hook through center of last loop at the edge making sure that there are 2 vertical strands of yarn on hook at extreme left-hand edge.

3rd row Using B, as first row, changing to C with last yo of row.

4th row Using C, as 2nd row.

5th row Using C, as first row, changing to A with last yo of row.

6th row Using A, as 2nd row.

First-6th rows form dark stripe pat. Rep first-6th rows 35[37] times more, so ending with a return row in A. 109[115] loop rows worked from beg counting base row.

Break off A, B and C, but do not fasten off.

Beg with D, change to light stripe pat of one loop row in D, one in E and one in F, working return rows in matching colors as before.

Work 19 loop rows in all in lighter stripe pat as set, ending with a return row. 128[134] loop rows worked from beg counting base row. Fasten off.

Panel 2

Using G, ch20[22] and work base and first rows as for panel 1.

Beg with C, work in dark stripe pat of one loop row in C, one in F and one in G until 109[115] loop rows have been worked from beg counting base row, so ending with a return row in G.

Beg with H, change to light stripe pat of one loop row in H, one in D and one in E.

Work 28 loop rows in all in light stripe pat as set, ending with a return row.

Neck shaping

Keeping to light stripe pat, dec one st at beg of next 2 loop rows by skipping one st at beg of row. 18[20] sts.

Work one loop row more, ending with a return row. 140[146] loop rows worked from beg counting base row. Fasten off.

Panel 3

Using A, ch20[22] and work base and first rows as for panel 1.

Beg with B, work in dark stripe pat as for panel 1 until 97[103] loop rows have been worked from beg counting base row, so ending with a return row in A. Beg with D, work 61 loop rows in light stripe pat as for panel 1, ending with a return row.

Neck shaping

Break off yarn and fasten off, then keeping to light stripe pat, draw up loops in last 4 sts of row and work a return row on these 4 sts. Dec one st at

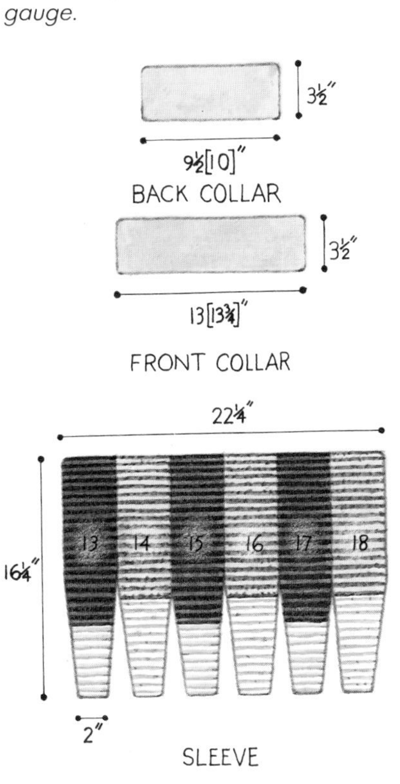

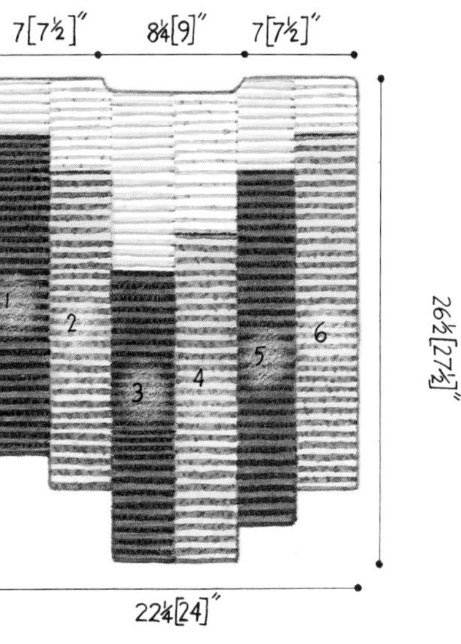

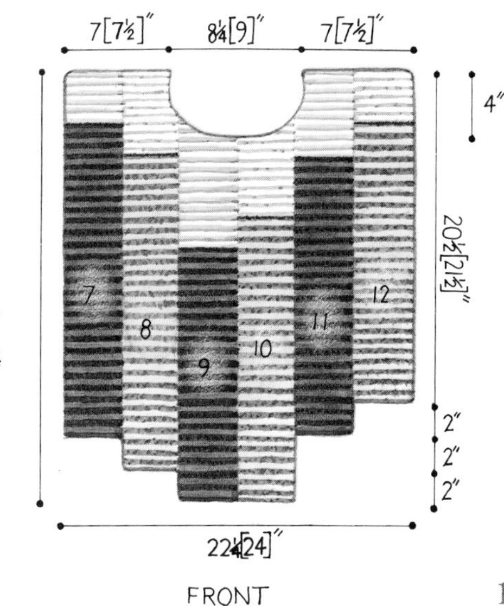

beg of next row and work a return row on hook. 3 sts.
Work a loop row and draw through all 3 loops on hook. 161[167] loop rows worked from beg. Fasten off.

Panel 4
Using G, ch20[22] and work base and first rows as for panel 1.
Beg with C, work in dark stripe pat as for panel 2 until 112[118] loop rows have been worked from beg, so ending with a return row in G.
Beg with H, work 46 loop rows in light stripe pat as for panel 2, ending with a return row.

Neck shaping
Keeping to pat, work in first 3 sts, leaving rem sts in row unworked. 4 loops on hook.
Work a return row. Dec one st at end of next row by skipping 2nd to last st in row. 3 loops on hook. Work a return row and a loop row, then draw through all 3 loops on hook. 161[167] loop rows worked from beg. Fasten off.

Panel 5
Using A, ch20[22] and work base and first rows as for panel 1.
Beg with B, work in dark stripe pat as for panel 1 until 121[127] loop rows have been worked from beg, so ending with a return row in A.
Beg with D, work 28 loop rows in light stripe pat as for panel 1, ending with a return row.

Neck shaping
Keeping to pat, dec one st at end of next 2 loop rows. Work one loop row more, ending with a return row. 152[158] loop rows worked from beg. Fasten off.

Panel 6
Using G, ch20[22] and work base and first rows as for panel 1.
Beg with C, work in dark stripe pat as for panel 2 until 121[127] loop rows have been worked from beg, so ending with a return row in G.
Beg with H, work 19 loop rows in light stripe pat as for panel 2, ending with a return row. 140[146] loop rows worked from beg. Fasten off.

▶ FRONT

Panel 7
Work as for panel 6, but using dark and light stripe pats as for panel 1.

Panel 8
Using G, ch20[22] and work base and first rows as for panel 1.
Beg with C, work in dark stripe pat as for panel 2 until 121[127] loop rows have been worked from beg, so ending with a return row in G.
Beg with H, work 16 loop rows in light stripe pat as for panel 2, ending with a return row.

Neck shaping
Keeping to pat, dec one st at beg of next loop row. Work 4 loop rows without shaping. Dec one st at beg of next loop row. Cont without shaping until 31 loop rows in all have been worked in light stripe pat, ending with a return row. 152[158] loop rows worked from beg. Fasten off.

Panel 9
Using A, ch20[22] and work base and first rows as for panel 1.
Beg with B, work in dark stripe pat as for panel 1 until 97[103] loop rows have been worked from beg, so ending with a return row in A.
Beg with D, work 42 loop rows in light stripe pat as for panel 1, ending with a return row.

Neck shaping
Break off yarn and fasten off, then keeping to stripe pat, draw up loops in last 10 sts of row and work a return row. Dec one st at beg of next 8 loop rows. Work one more loop row and draw through 2 rem loops on hook. 149[155] loop rows worked from beg. Fasten off.

Panel 10
Using G, ch20[22] and work base and first rows as for panel 1.
Beg with C, work in dark stripe pat as for panel 2 until 112[118] loop rows have been worked from beg, so ending with a return row in G.
Beg with H, work 27 loop rows in light stripe pat as for panel 2, ending with a return row.

Neck shaping
Keeping to pat, work next loop row until 10 loops are on hook, leaving rem sts in row unworked. Dec one st at end of next 8 loop rows. Work one more loop row and draw through 2 loops on hook. 149[155] loop rows worked from beg. Fasten off.

Panel 11
Using A, ch20[22] and work base and first rows as for panel 1.
Beg with B, work in dark stripe pat as for panel 1 until 109[115] loop rows have been worked from beg, so ending with a return row in H.
Beg with D, work 16 loop rows in light stripe pat as for panel 1, ending with a return row.

Neck shaping
Keeping to pat, dec one st at end of next loop row. Work 4 loop rows without shaping. Dec one st at end of next loop row. Cont without shaping until 31 loop rows have been worked in light stripe pat, ending with a return row. 140[146] loop rows worked from beg.
Fasten off.

Panel 12
Work as for panel 1, but using dark and light stripe pats as for panel 2.

▶ SLEEVES (make 2)

Panel 13
Using A, ch20 and work base and first rows as for panel 1.
Cont in dark stripe pat beg with one loop row in C, then one in B and one in A until 51 loop rows have been worked from beg counting base row and ending with a return row.

Side shaping
Dec one st at each end of next row and then at each end of every foll 12th row 4 times more *and at the same time* work 22 loop rows more in dark stripe pat, so ending with a return row in A, then work 27 loop rows in light stripe pat beg with one loop row in D, then one in F and one in E. 10 sts. Work one loop row without shaping, ending with a return row. 101 loop rows worked from beg. Fasten off.

Panel 14
Using G, ch20 and work base and first rows as for panel 1.
Cont in dark stripe pat beg with one loop row in F, then one in C and one in G until 51 loop rows have been worked from beg, so ending with a return row.

Side shaping
Shape sides as for panel 13 *and at the same time* work 10 loop rows more in dark stripe pat, so ending with a return row in G, then work 39 loop rows in light stripe pat beg with one loop row in H, then one in E and one in D. 101 loop rows worked from beg. Fasten off.

Panels 15 and 17
Work as for panel 13.

Panels 16 and 18
Work as for panel 14.

▶ COLLAR

Using Afghan hook and D, ch50[54] for back collar. Work base and first rows as for panel 1. Work 22 loop rows, ending with a return row. Collar measures approx 3½". Fasten off.
Using D, ch70[74] for front collar and work as for back collar.

▶ FINISHING

Pin all pieces (except collar) to correct measurements face down on a padded surface. Press on WS with a warm iron and damp cloth. Sew panels tog foll diagram to form back, front and sleeves. Work seam by overlapping last st of one panel over first st of adjacent panel, lining up stripes row for row and working a running st through both layers.
Join shoulder and collar seams. Sew on collar. Mark position of sleeves 11" from shoulder seams and sew sleeves in place between markers.
Using ordinary crochet hook, work a round of sc evenly around lower edge of back and front and sleeves, using D for sleeve edge and A for body and working 2sc at outside corners and skipping one st at inside corners.
Sew side and sleeve seams. Sew in shoulder pads if desired.

DESIGN VARIATION

▶ PULLOVER WITH STRAIGHT LOWER EDGE

To work a straight lower edge instead of the stepped edge inc the number of rows in dark stripe pat before beg light stripe pat as foll:

Panels 1 and 12
Work a total of 145[151] loop rows in dark stripe pat (instead of the 109[115] for stepped edge).

Panels 2 and 11
Work a total of 133[139] loop rows in dark stripe pat (instead of 109[115]).

Panels 6 and 7
Work a total of 145[151] loop rows in dark stripe pat (instead of 121[127]).

Panels 5 and 8
Work a total of 133[139] loop rows in dark stripe pat (instead of 121[127]).
Work all other panels as for stepped edge pullover.

CHECKED STRIPES

This boldly striped mohair sweater in half doubles with crochet ribbing would look effective in many color combinations. Omit the collar and the stripes for a quick and easy-to-crochet project.

▶ SIZES
To fit 32[34-36:38-40]"/81[86-91:96-102]cm bust.
Note: Figures for larger sizes are in brackets. If there is only one set of figures, it applies to all sizes.
See diagram for finished measurements.

▶ MATERIALS
See page 118 for further yarn information
Use a lightweight mohair yarn (approx 164yd per 1¾oz):
15¾[15¾:19¼]oz in main color MC (black)
3½oz in each of 2 contrasting colors A (turquoise) and B (yellow)
Size H crochet hook *or size to obtain correct gauge*

▶ GAUGE
15hdc and 12½ rows to 4" over color pat using size H hook.
16sc and 20 rows to 4" over rib using size H hook.
To save time, take time to check gauge.

Note: When working broken stripes in A and B, carry yarn not in use *loosely* across back of work. Always change to new color with last yo of previous st (see page 112). When working from chart read even-numbered rows (WS) from left to right and odd-numbered rows (RS) from right to left.

▶ BACK
Using MC, ch78[82:86].
Base row 1hdc in 3rd ch from hook, 1hdc in each ch to end. Turn. 76[80:84]hdc.
1st row (RS) Ch2, 1hdc in each hdc to end. Turn.
Last row forms hdc pat and is rep throughout.
Work 0[2:4] rows more in hdc.
Beg working from 2nd chart row as foll:
2nd chart row (WS) Ch2, 1hdc in each of first 41[43:45]hdc (changing to A with last yo of last hdc — see Note above), *using A, 1hdc in each of next 5hdc, using B, 1hdc in each of next 5hdc, rep from *, ending last rep with 0[2:4]hdc in B. Turn.
Cont foll chart, working side shaping as shown on chart, making single incs at side edges by working 2hdc in first and last sts of row until there are 98[102:106]hdc.
Cont without shaping until 59th chart row has been completed.
Neck shaping
Work neck shaping for back neck as indicated. Fasten off.

Note: For neck edge work decs at end of row by leaving number of sts required for dec unworked and at beg of row by working sl st over number of sts required for dec.

▶ FRONT
Work as for back, foll chart and working side shaping and neck shaping for front neck as indicated.

▶ SLEEVES (make 2)
Using MC, ch51.
Work base and first rows as for back. 50hdc.
Inc one st at each end of next row.
Work 2 rows without shaping. Inc one st at each end of next row. 54hdc.
Beg working from 6th row of sleeve chart, remembering to read 6th row (WS) from left to right and inc one st at each end of 7th and every foll 3rd row until there are 76hdc. Cont without shaping until sleeve measures 13" from beg or desired sleeve length. Fasten off.

▶ BACK RIB
Using MC, ch8.
Base row Ch1, 1sc in 2nd ch from hook, 1sc in each ch to end. Turn. 7sc.
1st row Ch1, working in back loop only, work 1sc in each sc to end.
Last row forms rib pat and is rep throughout.
Cont in rib pat until rib fits across lower back edge. Fasten off.

▶ **FRONT RIB**
Work as for back rib.

▶ **CUFFS** (make 2)
Using MC, ch17. Work base and first rows as for back rib. 16sc.
Cont in rib pat as for back rib until cuff measures 8".
Fasten off.

▶ **COLLAR**
Join shoulder seams.
Using MC, ch31. Work base and first rows as for back rib. 30sc.
Cont in rib pat as for back rib until collar measures 16½" and fits loosely around neck edge.
Fasten off.

▶ **FINISHING**
Do not press. Weave in all loose ends. Sew ribs to back and front. Sew on cuffs gathering in fullness at lower edge of sleeve. Sew sleeves to back and front. Join side and sleeve seams. Sew half of collar seam leaving rem seam open. Sew collar to neck edge, placing collar seam approx 2¾" from left shoulder seam.

DESIGN VARIATION

▶ **SOLID COLOR PULLOVER**
For a simple solid color pullover, follow instructions omitting stripes and collar.

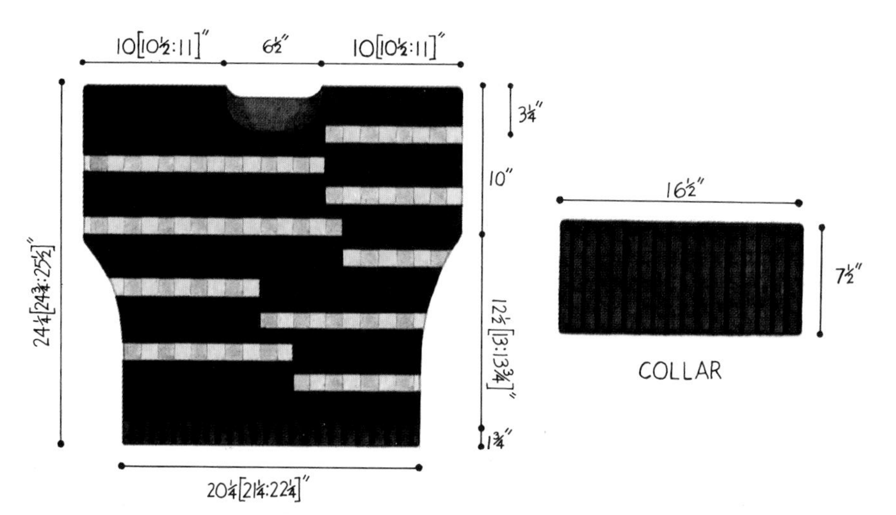

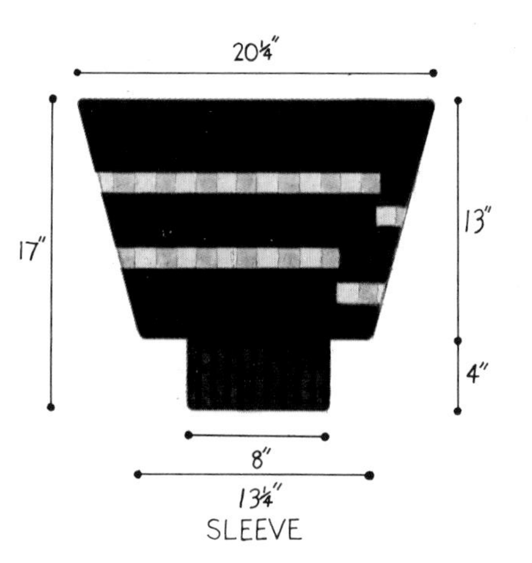

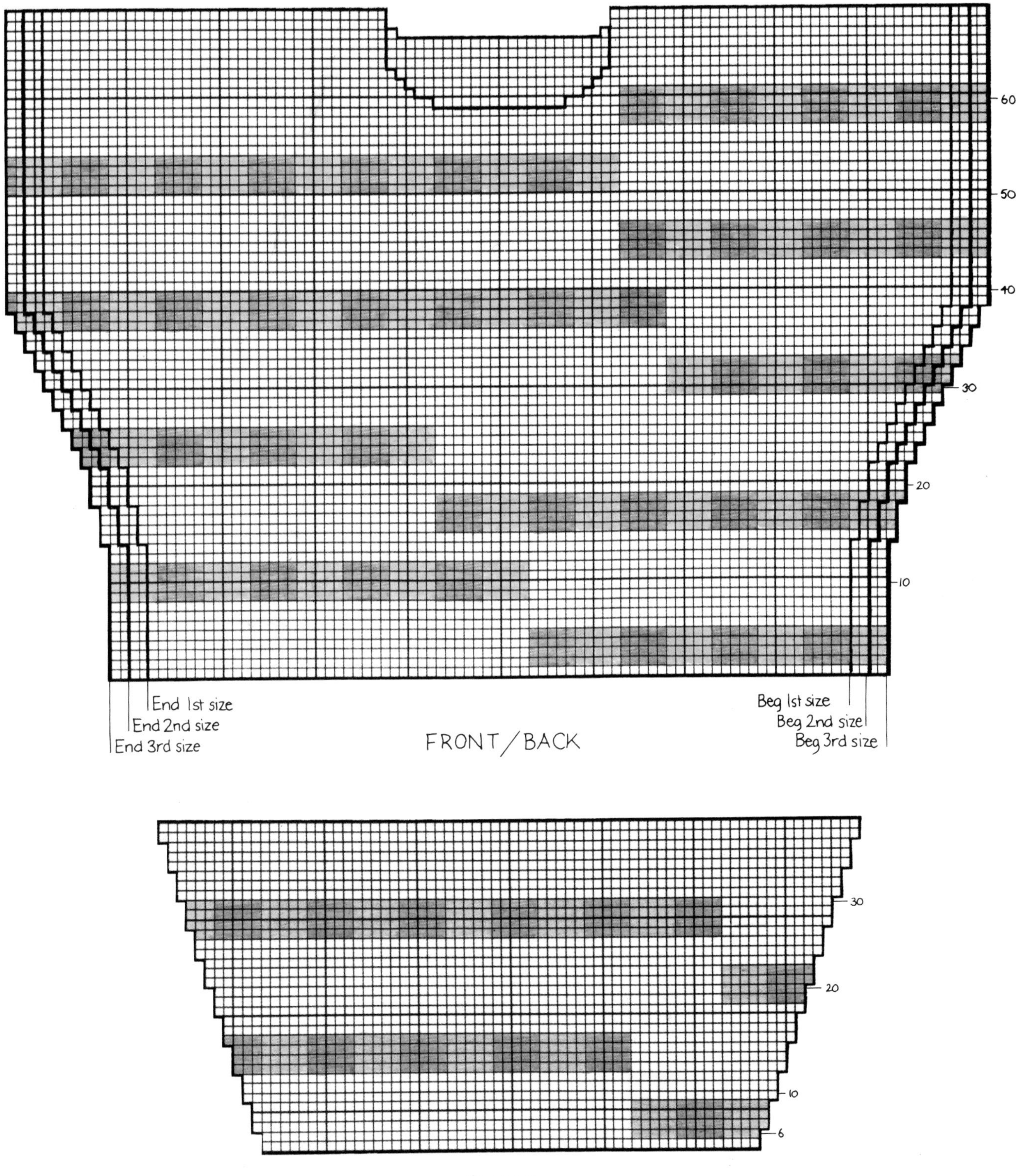

60
50
40
30
20
10
End 1st size
End 2nd size
End 3rd size
Beg 1st size
Beg 2nd size
Beg 3rd size
FRONT/BACK
30
20
10
6
SLEEVE

STRIPES ON STRIPES

Contrasting stripes combine to create triangle shapes at both sides of the front and back of this loose-fitting sweater. The cuffs and neckline are bordered by a rolled edging with a crochet rib.

▶ SIZES

To fit 32[34:36:38-40]"/ 81[86:91:96-102]cm bust.
Note: Figures for larger sizes are in brackets. If there is only one set of figures, it applies to all sizes.
See diagram for finished measurements.

▶ MATERIALS

See page 118 for further yarn information
Use a lightweight wool yarn (approx 73yd per 1oz):
17[17:18:19]oz in A (blue)
4[4:5:5]oz in B (rust)
4oz in C (pale blue)
3oz in D (yellow)
Sizes H and I crochet hooks *or size to obtain correct gauge*

▶ GAUGE

15hdc and 13 rows to 4" over stripe pat using size H hook.
To save time, take time to check gauge.

Note: When working narrow and broad stripes in the same row, do not carry yarns across the row but use a separate ball of yarn for each area of color. When changing colors, change to new color with last yo of previous hdc, keeping yarn on WS (see page 112). Read odd-numbered chart rows (RS) from right to left and even-numbered rows (WS) from left to right.

▶ BACK

Using smaller hook and A, ch11 and beg rib as foll:
Base rib row 1sc in 2nd ch from hook, 1sc in each ch to end. Turn. 10sc.
1st rib row Ch1, working in *back* loops' only, 1sc in each sc to end. Turn.
Rep last row to form rib pat. Cont in rib pat until 92[98:103:108] rows have been worked from beg, counting base row. Do not fasten off.

Turn rib sideways and work sts for back along rib row ends as foll:
Ch2, 1hdc in each of first 7[3:3:2] row ends, *skip one row end, 1hdc in each of next 5 row ends, rep from * 12[14:15:16] times more, ending with skip one row end, 1hdc in each of next 6[4:3:3] row ends, turn. 78[82:86:90]hdc.
1st row Ch2, 1hdc in each hdc to end. Turn.
Foll chart for color pat and beg with 8th[6th:4th:2nd] chart row, cont in hdc as for last row until 87th chart row has been completed. Fasten off.

▶ FRONT

Work as for back until 79th[79th:78th:78th] chart row has been completed.
Neck shaping
Next row Work first 30[32:33:35]hdc in pat foll chart. Turn, leaving rem sts unworked.
Next row Ch2, yo and insert hook in first hdc, yo and draw a loop through, yo and insert hook in next hdc, yo and draw a loop through, yo and draw through all 5 loops on hook — called 2hdc tog, work in pat to end. Turn. 29[31:32:34]hdc.

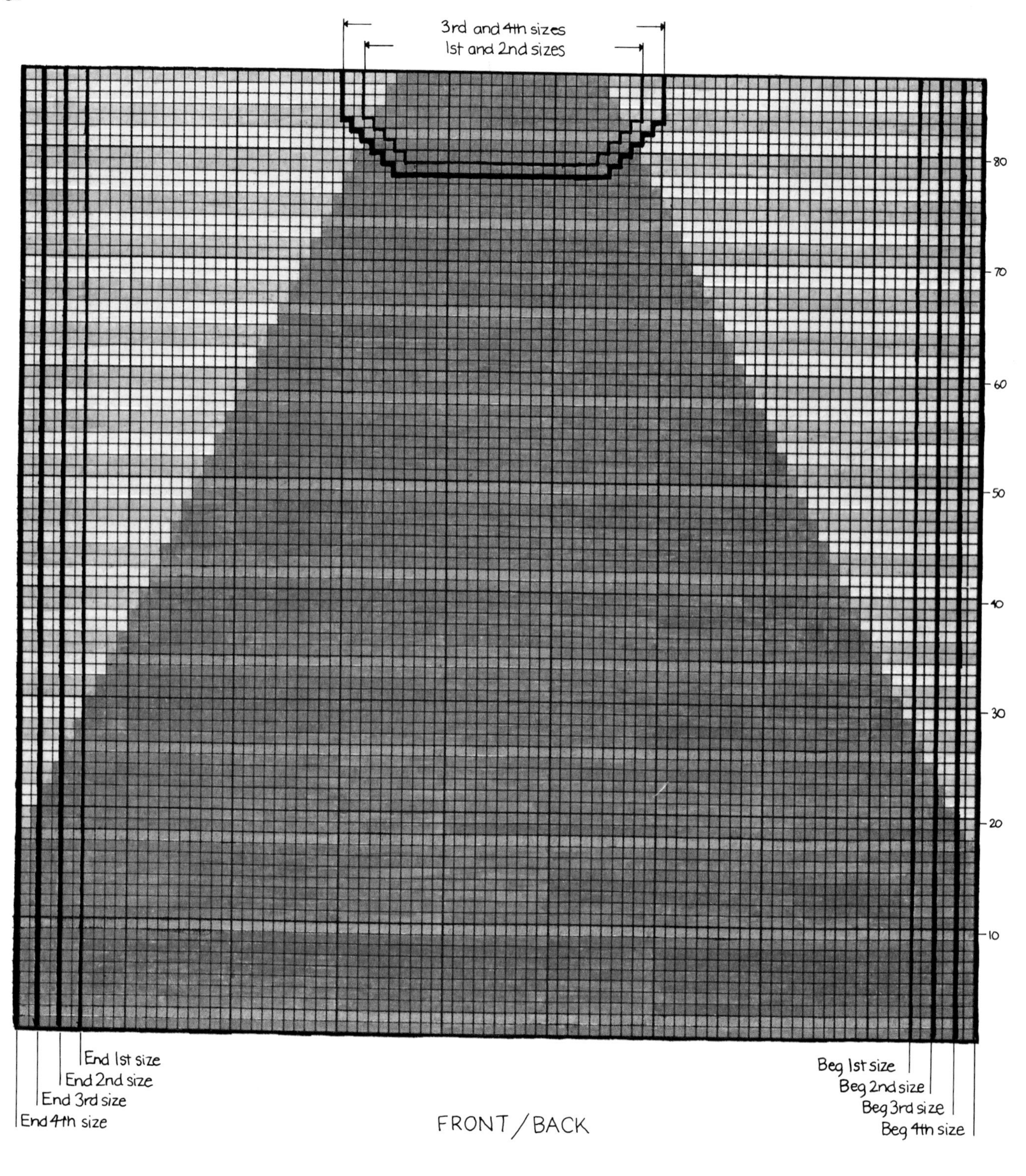
3rd and 4th sizes
1st and 2nd sizes
80
70
60
50
40
30
20
10
End 1st size
End 2nd size
End 3rd size
End 4th size
Beg 1st size
Beg 2nd size
Beg 3rd size
Beg 4th size

FRONT / BACK

Next row Ch2, work in pat to last 2hdc, 2hdc tog. Turn. 28[30:31:33]hdc.
Cont in pat, dec one st at neck edge on next 2[2:3:3] rows.
26[28:28:30]hdc.
Cont to foll chart, work last 3 rows without shaping. Fasten off.
Return to rem sts at center front. Skip next 18[18:20:20] sts and rejoin yarn to next st, work in pat to end.
Complete to match first side, reversing shaping and foll pat from chart.

▶ **SLEEVES** (make 2)
Using smaller hook and C, ch11 and work base and first rows as for back rib. Cont in rib pat as for back rib until 28[30:32:34] rows have been worked from beg, counting base row. Do not fasten off.
Turn rib sideways and work sts for sleeve along rib row ends as foll:
Ch1, 1sc in each row end, turn.
28[30:32:34]sc.
Break off C, but do not fasten off.
Next row (WS) Using A, ch2, working in *front* loop only of each sc, 1hdc in first sc, 2hdc in next sc, *1hdc in next sc, 2hdc in next sc, rep from * to end. Turn.
42[45:48:51]hdc.
Note: Cuff edging will be worked in rem loop at top of each sc left unworked in last row.
Work one row in hdc without shaping.
****Next row** Ch2, 2hdc in first hdc, 1hdc in each hdc to last hdc, 2hdc in last hdc. Turn. 44[47:50:53]hdc.
Work 2 rows without shaping.**
Rep from ** to ** once more. Break off A, but do not fasten off.
Using B, work one row (WS) in hdc inc one st at each end of row.
46[49:52:55]hdc.
Cont in stripe sequence of 7 rows A and one row B *and at the same time* inc one st at each end of every foll 3rd row until there are 70[73:76:79]hdc.
Cont in stripe pat as set without shaping until sleeve measures 18" from beg. Fasten off.

▶ **NECKBAND**
Join shoulder seams.
Edging
Using smaller hook and B and with RS facing, work a round of sc evenly around neck edge. Then change to larger hook and work 2 rounds more, working 1sc around post of each st from front (see page 114). Fasten off.
Edging will roll to RS.
Neck rib
Using smaller hook and C, ch7 and work base and first rows as for back rib. Cont in rib pat as for back until neck rib, slightly stretched, fits around neck edge. Fasten off.

▶ **FINISHING**
Do not press. Join neck rib seam. Sew neck rib to neck edge behind rolled edging. Mark positions of sleeves 9¼[9¾:10:10½]" from shoulder seams. Sew on sleeves between markers. Join side and sleeve seams.
Cuff edging
Using larger hook and B and with RS facing, hold sleeve so that cuff is at top and work a round of sc in rem loop at top of each sc left unworked in row above cuff rib. Then work 2 rounds more, working 1sc around post of each st from front as for neck edging. Fasten off.
Press seams on WS with a warm iron, omitting rib.

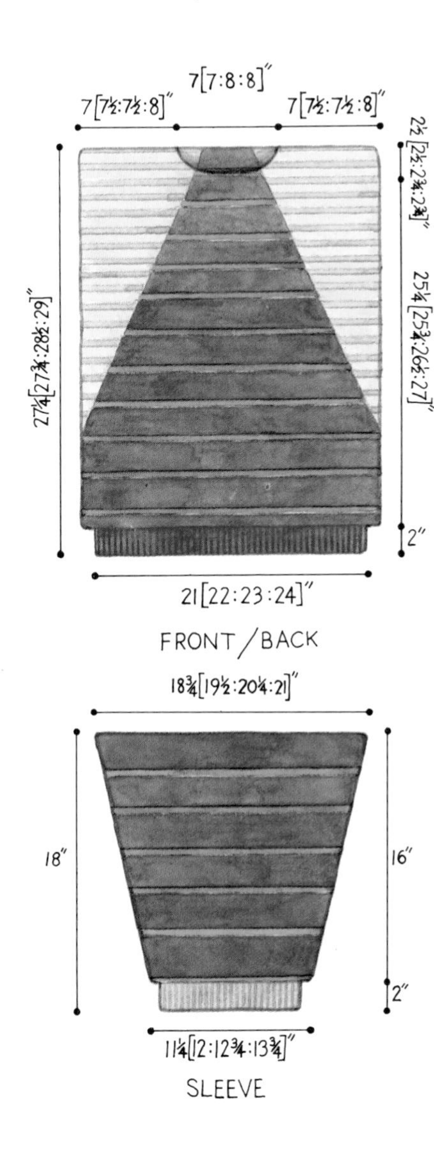

STRIPES & SQUARES

Metallic yarn sparkles in this glittery evening top which is made in single crochet with a deep knitted ribbing. You can transform this versatile design into summer daywear by working the metallic contrasting colors in cotton yarn.

▶ SIZES

To fit 32[34:36]"/81[86:91]cm bust.
Note: Figures for larger sizes are in brackets. If there is only one set of figures, it applies to all sizes.

See diagram for finished measurements.

▶ MATERIALS

See page 118 for further yarn information
Use a lightweight cotton yarn (approx 202yd per 1¾oz) and a lightweight metallic yarn (approx 175yd per ¾oz):
5[6:7]oz lightweight cotton yarn in main color MC (black)
¾oz lightweight metallic yarn in each of 3 colors A (turquoise), B (rose) and C (blue)
Small amount lightweight cotton yarn in D (pink)
Sizes D and E crochet hooks *or size to obtain correct gauge*
Size 5 circular knitting needle 24" long
Snaps

The back of this evening top crosses over at the waist to give a flattering low backline.

▶ GAUGE

23sc and 28 rows slightly stretched to 4" over rib pat using size E hook.
To save time, take time to check gauge.

Note: Crochet rib is elastic, so width of triangle on measurement diagram is approximate and is measured over only slightly stretched rib. When working with more than one color in a row, carry yarn not in use loosely across back of work, but use separate lengths of yarn for A and D for each square. When changing colors, change to new color with last yo of last sc (see page 112). When working from chart, read even-numbered rows (WS) from left to right and odd-numbered rows (RS) from right to left.

▶ BODY TRIANGLE

Using larger hook and MC, ch2.
Base row 1sc in 2nd ch from hook. Turn. 1sc.
1st row (RS) Ch1, working in *back* loops only, work 2sc in first sc. Turn. 2sc.
Cont working in *back* loops only throughout to form crochet rib pat.
2nd row Ch1, 1sc in each sc. Turn.
3rd row Ch1, 1sc in first sc, 2sc in next sc. Turn. 3sc.
4th row Ch1, 2sc in first sc, 1sc in each sc to end. Turn. 4sc.
5th row Ch1, 1sc in each sc. Turn.
6th row As 4th row. 5sc.
7th row As 5th row.
8th row As 4th row. 6sc.
9th row Ch1, 1sc in each sc to last sc, 2sc in last sc. Turn. 7sc.
10th row As 5th row.
11th row As 9th row. 8sc.
12th row As 5th row.
13th row As 9th row. 9sc.
14th-16th rows Rep 4th-6th rows. 11sc.
Set position of square motif on next row as foll:
17th row (RS) Ch1, 1sc in first sc, changing to A with last yo of st, using A, work 1sc in each of next 4sc, changing to MC with last yo of last sc, using MC, 1sc in each sc to end. Turn.
18th row Work as for 4th row, but working all sts of MC in MC and all sts of A in A. Turn. 12sc. Drop MC at side of work, but do not break off.
19th row Work as for 9th row, but working all sts of MC in B and working (1sc in A, 2sc in D, 1sc in A) over 4 sts of A. Turn. 13sc.
Cont in rib pat and beg with 20th row of chart 1, foll chart for squares and

stripes and for shaping.
When 116th[118th:120th] row of chart 1 has been completed (71[72:74]sc), foll chart 2 beg with 117th[119th:121st] row and working decs as indicated.
Note: For a dec at beg of row work ch1, insert hook in first sc, yo and draw a loop through, insert hook in next sc, yo and draw a loop through, yo and draw through all 3 loops on hook — called 2sc tog. For a dec at end of row, work 2sc tog over last 2 sts.
When 234th[237th:241st] row of chart has been completed (1sc), fasten off.

▶ STRAPS (make 2)

Using smaller hook and MC, ch2 and beg working strap in sc (not in rib as for body) as foll:
Base row 1sc in 2nd ch from hook. Turn. 1sc.
1st row Ch1, 2sc in first sc. Turn. Drop MC, but do not break off.
2nd row Using C, ch1, 1sc in first sc, 2sc in last sc. Turn.
3rd row Using C, ch1, 2sc in first sc, 1sc in each sc to end. Turn. Drop C, but do not break off.
4th row Using MC, ch1, 1sc in each sc to last sc, 2sc in last sc. Turn.
5th row Using MC, as 3rd row.
Rep last 2 rows twice more, working 2 rows C, then 2 rows MC. 10sc.
Cont in sc without shaping, working in stripe pat of 2 rows C and 2 rows MC until strap fits along one sloped edge of body triangle. Mark last row. Cont in pat until strap measures 8¾" from marker. Fasten off.

Edging
Using smaller hook and C and beg at foundation ch end of strap, work 1sc in each row end along *longer* side edge of strap. Fasten off. Using smaller hook and C and beg at same end of strap as last row, work 1 sl st *loosely* in each sc to end, inserting hook under both loops at top of each sc. Fasten off.

▶ FINISHING

Do not press. Weave in all loose ends. Sew straps to sloped sides of body triangle so that shaped end is at lower edge. Overlap body triangle to fit as required and pin tog.

Knitted rib
Using circular knitting needle and MC, pick up and K223[237:251] sts evenly around lower edge of body, working through both layers where triangle overlaps (see page 115). Do not work in rounds, but work back and forth in rows of K1, P1 rib until rib measures 4½". Using C, bind off loosely in rib. Join rib seam. Adjust strap ends if necessary, adding or subtracting rows, so that straps meet at center back neck.
Using smaller hook and C, work 1sc in each row end along other side of strap from center front to end of strap. Sew on snaps at ends of strap.

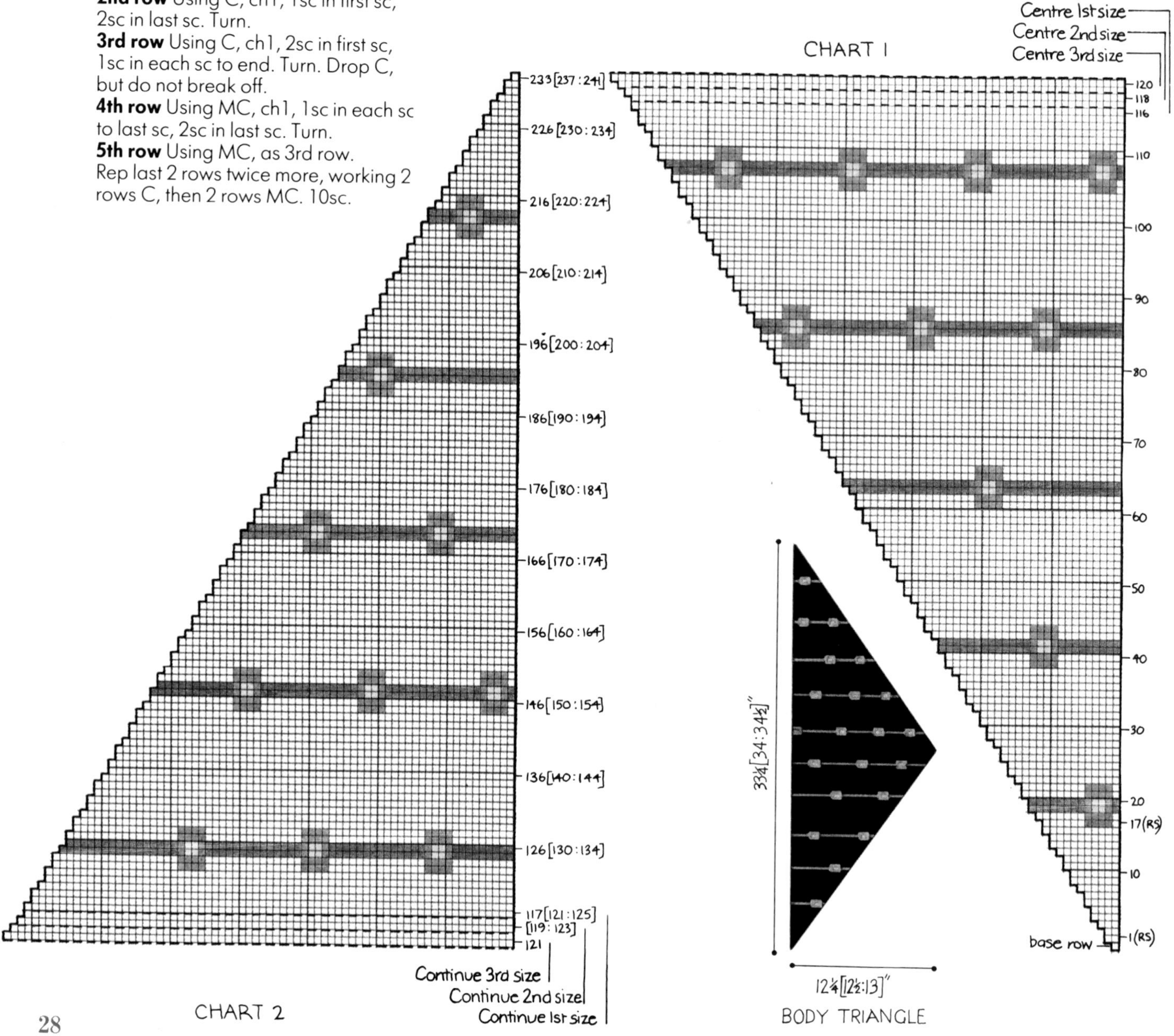

PLAIDS & CHECKS

PLAIDS & CHECKS

These samples offer simple and complicated alternatives for the plaid and check garments that follow.

▶ WINDOWPANE CHECKS

The way to understand any color design is to break it down into its basic components starting with the most elementary. For plaids or checks this would be what is called a *windowpane check*. The simple components of the windowpane check are the horizontal stripes placed at equal intervals on a solid background and crossed by regularly placed thin vertical lines. Variations are created by changing the intervals between the horizontal and vertical stripes (3).

▶ BASIC PLAIDS

Plaids begin as simple multicolored stripes. The easiest method of transforming a striped crochet fabric into a plaid is to apply the vertical stripes onto the completed crochet pieces. Embroidery techniques such as backstitch (3) or surface slip stitch (1 and 2) are suitable for the vertical stripes. Sample 2 is a possible alternative plaid for *Check and plaid* (page 41). The checks could be worked in colors to match the plaid.

▶ CHECKERED PLAIDS

More complicated plaids are made by check shapes that are crossed both horizontally and vertically by thin stripes. The more variance in check shapes and the more colors, the more complex the pattern. Samples 4, 5 and 7 are examples of this type of plaid. In sample 5 the vertical stripes are worked with separate lengths of yarn so that only 2 colors are carried across the rows (see page 112). Note how stripes of darker toned checks alternate with lighter toned checks as part of the plaid composition. In all these examples only simple stitch techniques are used. For alternative plaids for *Bold block plaid* (page 32) and *Buffalo plaid* (page 44), try samples 4 or 5.

▶ WOVEN PLAIDS

Woven plaid (6) is a combination of crochet and weaving techniques. The base is horizontal stripes of filet crochet. The completed filet is woven vertically with strands of contrasting and matching colors.

sc
dc
sc
dc
Rep= 8 rows

1 Vertical stripes worked in surface sl st.

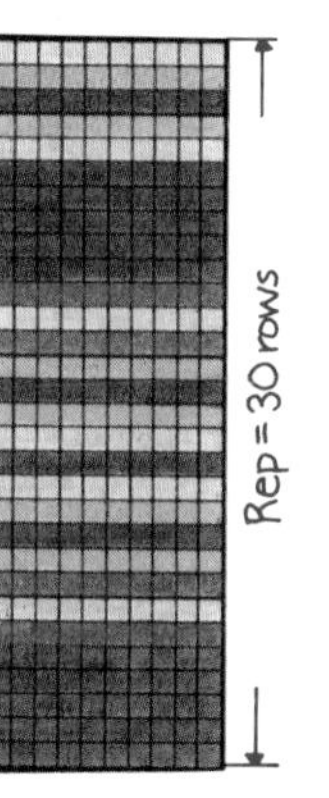

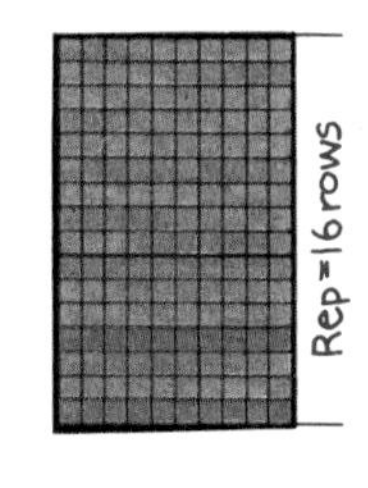

2 Afghan crochet knit stitch with vertical stripes in surface sl st.

3 Horizontal stripes in sc and vertical stripes in backstitch.

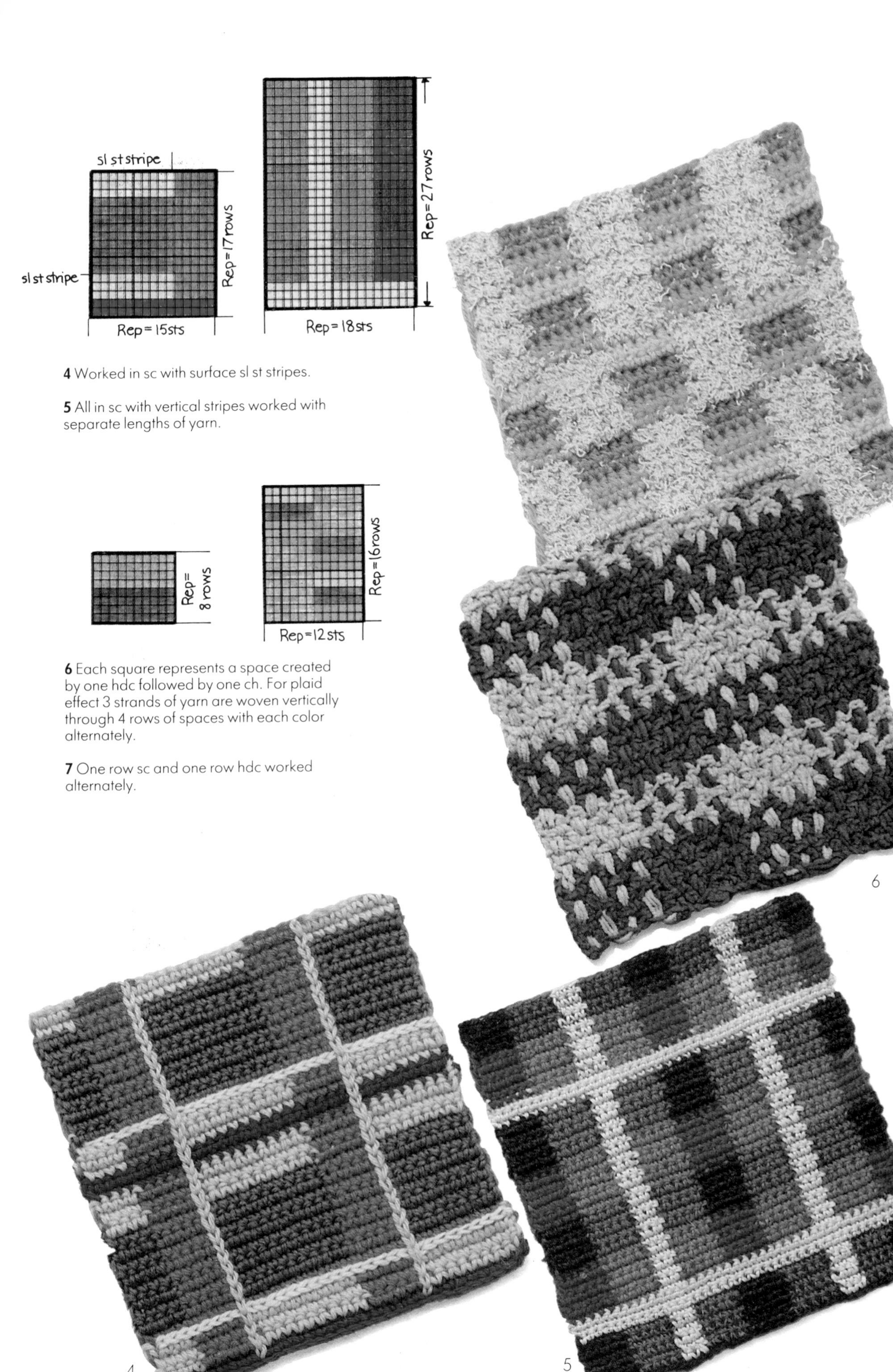

4 Worked in sc with surface sl st stripes.

5 All in sc with vertical stripes worked with separate lengths of yarn.

6 Each square represents a space created by one hdc followed by one ch. For plaid effect 3 strands of yarn are woven vertically through 4 rows of spaces with each color alternately.

7 One row sc and one row hdc worked alternately.

BOLD BLOCK PLAID

This comfortable mohair jacket with inset side pockets is crocheted in a bold plaid pattern. The jacket is worked in single crochet and a crisp knitted ribbing forms the collar, cuffs and mock front pocket flaps.

▶ SIZES
To fit 32[34-36:38-40]"/81[86-91:96-102]cm bust.
Note: Figures for larger sizes are in brackets. If there is only one set of figures, it applies to all sizes.
See diagram for finished measurements.

▶ MATERIALS
See page 118 for further yarn information
Use a lightweight mohair (approx 170yd per 1¾oz) and a lightweight wool yarn (approx 130yd per 1¾oz):
8¾[10½:12¼]oz lightweight mohair in A (sea green)
5¼[5¼:7]oz lightweight mohair in B (dark sea green)
3½[3½:5¼]oz lightweight mohair in C (beige)
Small amount of a lightweight mohair in each of D (light blue), E (light green) and F (white)
5¼oz lightweight wool yarn in G (sea green)
Size I crochet hook *or size to obtain correct gauge*
One pair of size 6 knitting needles *or size to obtain correct gauge*
7 toggle buttons
Shoulder pads (optional)

▶ GAUGE
13sc and 15 rows to 4" over block plaid pat using size I hook.
37 sts and 34 rows to 4" over rib pat using size 6 knitting needles.
To save time, take time to check gauge.

Note: When working block plaid pat with 2 colors in a row, carry yarn not in use across top of previous row, working all sts over it. Always change to new color with last yo of previous st (see page 112).

▶ BACK
Using hook and A, ch66[70:72] loosely. Beg hem as foll:
Base row 1sc in 2nd ch from hook, 1sc in each ch to end. Turn. 65[69:71]sc.
1st row Ch1, 1sc in each sc to end. Turn.
Rep last row 2 times more to complete hem.
Beg block plaid pat as foll:
1st pat row (RS) Working in *back* loop only of each sc to form turning ridge for hem and using B, ch1, 1sc in each of first 5[7:7]sc (changing to A with last yo of last sc — see Note above), using A, 1sc in each of next 11[11:12]sc, using B, 1sc in each of next 11sc, using A, 1sc in each of next 11sc, using B, 1sc in each of next 11sc, using A, 1sc in each of next 11[11:12]sc, using B, 1sc in each of last 5[7:7]sc. Turn.
Last row sets position of blocks. Rep last row 3 times more, but working in *both* loops of sc of previous row throughout.
5th row Turn hem to WS along loops left unworked in 4th row and work blocks as set, working each sc in sc of previous row and in corresponding foundation ch, thus securing hem in position. Turn.
Work 6 rows more in block plaid pat as set.
12th row Work in pat as set, inc one st at each end of row by working 2sc in first and last sc, using B. Turn. 67[71:73]sc.
Work 3 rows more in block plaid pat as set. Break off B.
16th row Working in sc and beg with A, ch1, 6[8:8]sc in A, 11[11:12] sc in C, 11sc in A, 11sc in C, 11sc in A, 11[11:12]sc in C, 6[8:8]sc in A. Turn.
Rep last row 7 times more.
24th row Work in pat as set, inc one st at each end of row. Turn. 69[73:75]sc.
Work 2 rows more in block plaid pat as set. Break off C.
27th row Working in sc and beg with B, ch1, 7[9:9]sc in B, 11[11:12]sc in A, 11sc in B, 11sc in A, 11sc in B, 11[11:12]sc in A, 7[9:9]sc in B. Turn.
Rep last row 8 times more.
36th row Work in pat as set, inc one st at each end of row. Turn. 71[75:77]sc.
Work 5 rows more in block plaid pat as set. Break off C.
42nd row Work as for 16th row, but beg and ending with 8[10:10]sc in A. Turn.
Rep last row 10 times more.
Fasten off.

Armhole shaping
53rd row With RS facing, skip first 3[4:4]sc, join B to next sc with a sl st, ch1, 1sc in same place as sl st, cont in sc across row, work all sc in A in previous row in B, and all sc in C in previous row in A, ending at last 3[4:4]sc. Turn, leaving rem sc unworked. 65[67:69]sc.
Cont in pat as set, dec one st (2sc tog) at each end of next 2 rows, then dec one st at each end of every other row 4 times. 53[55:57]sc.
Note: To work 2sc tog (insert hook in next sc, yo and draw a loop through) twice, yo and draw through all 3 loops on hook.
Work in block plaid pat as set without shaping until 15 rows have been completed from beg of armhole shaping. Break off A and B.
68th row (WS) Working in sc and beg with C, ch1, 10[11:12]sc in C, 11sc in D, 11sc in C, 11sc in D, 10[11:12]sc in C. Turn.
Rep last row 10 times more. Break off D.
79th row (RS) Working in sc and beg with E, ch1, 10[11:12]sc in E, 11sc in C, 11sc in E, 11sc in C, 10[11:12]sc in E. Turn.
Rep last row 6[8:11] times more.
Fasten off.

Shoulder and neck shaping
Keeping to block plaid pat as set in 79th row, skip first 4sc and rejoin E to next sc with a sl st, ch1 and work in pat to last 4sc. Turn, leaving rem sts unworked. 45[47:49]sc.
Fasten off.
Next row Skip first 4sc and rejoin E to next sc, ch1 and work in pat across

9[9:10]sc (including sc where E is joined). Turn, leaving rem 32[34:35]sc unworked. Break off E.
Next row Using C, ch1, work first 2sc tog, 1sc in each of next 3[3:4]sc. Fasten off.
Work 2nd side of neck as for first side, reversing shaping.

▶ LEFT FRONT

Using hook and A, ch37[39:40]. Work hem as for back. 36[38:39]sc. Beg block plaid pat as foll:
1st pat row (RS) Working in back loop only of each sc to form turning ridge and using A, ch1, 1sc in each of first 5[7:7]sc, using B, 1sc in each of next 11[11:12]sc, using A, 1sc in each of next 11sc, using B, 1sc in each of last 9sc. Turn.
Last row sets position of blocks. Work 3 rows more in pat as set, working in both loops of sc of previous row throughout.
5th row Work as for 5th row of back. Work 6 rows more in block plaid pat as set.
12th row Work in pat as set, inc one st at end of row (side edge) by working 2sc in last sc. Turn. 37[39:40]sc.
Cont in block plaid pat as set on back by working 15 rows of blocks in A and B, foll by 11 rows of blocks in A and C, inc one st at side edge on every 12th row twice more. 39[41:42]sc.
Work in block plaid pat without shaping until front has same number of rows to armhole shaping as back. Fasten off.

Armhole shaping
53rd row With RS facing, skip first 3[4:4]sc, join A to next sc with a sl st, ch1, 1sc in same place as sl st, cont in sc across row, work all sc in C in previous row in A and all sc in A in previous row in B. Turn. 36[37:38]sc.
Cont in pat as set, dec one st at armhole edge of next 2 rows, then dec one st at armhole edge on every other row 4 times. 30[31:32]sc.
Work in block plaid pat as set without shaping until 15 rows have been completed from beg of armhole shaping. Break off A and B.
68th row (WS) Working in sc and beg with D, ch1, 9sc in D, 11sc in C, 10[11:12]sc in D. Turn.
Cont in block plaid pat as set in last row, work 10 rows more.
2nd and 3rd sizes only:
79th row (RS) Working in sc and beg with C, ch1, [11:12]sc in C, 11sc in E, 9sc in C. Turn.
Cont in block plaid pat as set in last row, work [1:2] rows more.

Neck shaping
1st and 2nd sizes only:
Next row (RS) Working in sc and beg with C, ch1, 10[11]sc in C, 11[10]sc in E. Turn, leaving rem 9[10]sc unworked. 21sc.
Fasten off.
Next row (WS) Working in block plaid pat as set, skip first 2sc and rejoin E to next sc, work to end of row. Turn. 19sc.
3rd size only:
Next row (WS) Working in block plaid pat as set, skip first 10sc and rejoin E to next sc, work to end of row. Turn. 22sc.
Next row Work in block plaid pat to last 2sc. Turn. 20sc.
All sizes:
Cont in block plaid pat, dec one st at neck edge on next 3 rows. 16[16:17]sc.
Work in block plaid pat without shaping until there are same number of rows to shoulder as for back. Keeping to pat, dec 4 sts at armhole edge on next 3 rows. 4[4:5]sc. Fasten off.
Mark positions at center front for buttons, the first approx ½" below neck edge, the last on 5th row from turning ridge and the other 3 evenly spaced in between.

▶ RIGHT FRONT

Work as for left front, reversing shaping and working buttonholes to match positions of buttons. Work buttonholes 3 sts in from center front by skipping 2 sts and working ch2. On row foll buttonhole row, work 2sc in ch2 sp, catching up 2nd color which was carried across top of previous row in order to cover this loose strand.

▶ SLEEVES (make 2)

Using hook and A, ch42[44:46]. Work hem as for back. 41[43:45]sc. Beg block plaid pat as foll:
1st pat row (RS) Working in back loop only of each sc to form turning ridge and using B, ch1, 1sc in each of first 4[5:6]sc, using A, 1sc in each of next 11sc, using B, 1sc in each of next 11sc, using A, 1sc in each of next 11sc, using B, 1sc in each of last 4[5:6]sc. Turn.
Last row sets position of blocks.
Rep last row 3 times more, but working in both loops of sc of previous row throughout.
5th row Work as for 5th row of back.
Keeping to block plaid pat as set in first row, inc one st at each end of next row, then at each end of foll 5th row. Cont to shape sleeve by inc one st at each end of every 6th and 5th rows alternately 3 times more, working increased sts in same color as first and last blocks, *and at the same time* work in block plaid pat of 13[15:17] rows in

5[5:5¼]" 6½[7:7]" 5[5:5¼]"
22¾[23½:24]"
9[9:10¼]"
13¾"
20[21¼:22]"
21¾[23:23¾]"
BACK

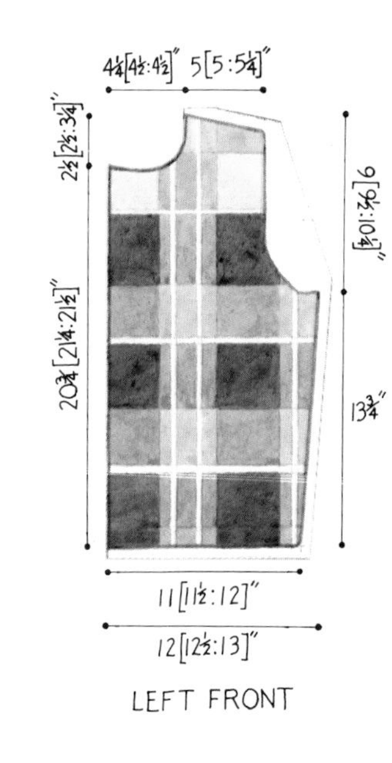

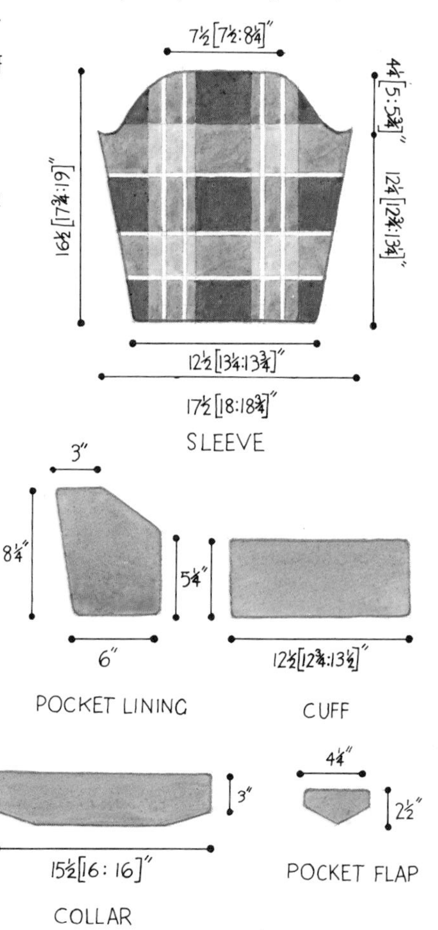

blocks of A and B as set in first pat row (counted from first pat row), *11 rows in blocks of A and C, 15 rows in blocks of A and B, rep block plaid sequence from * to end of sleeve. 57[59:61]sc.
Cont in block plaid pat as set without shaping until 46[48:50] rows have been worked from turning ridge.
Fasten off.

Cap shaping

Next row Keeping to block plaid pat as set, skip first 3[4:4]sc and rejoin yarn to next sc with a sl st, ch1, 1sc in same place as sl st, work to last 3[4:4]sc. Turn.
Cont in pat, dec one st at each end of 2nd row once, at each end of every 2nd[3rd:4th] row 3 times, at each end of every row 5 times. Dec 2 sts at each end of every row twice. 25[25:27]sc.
Fasten off.

▶ NECK AND FRONT EDGING

Using hook and with RS facing, beg at lower edge of left front and work a row of sc evenly up left front, around neck and down right front, using colors to match blocks being edged. Fasten off.
Using hook and C and with RS facing, beg at neck edge on left front and work a row of sl st around neck, easing back neck into correct width.
Fasten off.

▶ SURFACE CROCHET STRIPES

Mark the positions of horizontal surface crochet stripes on back, fronts and sleeves, the first between the first 2 horizontal rows of blocks from lower edge and the foll horizontal stripes after every 2 rows of horizontal blocks.
Mark the positions of the 2 vertical surface crochet stripes to run up the center of each vertical row of blocks in A and C with 6sc between the 2 stripes.
Working the horizontal stripes first, work the surface crochet stripes as foll:
Using hook and F and with RS facing, insert hook from front to back through edge st and, holding yarn at back of work throughout, yo and draw a loop through, *keeping loop on hook, insert hook through sp between next 2 sts, yo and draw a loop through sp and through loop on hook, rep from * to end. Fasten off.
Work horizontal and vertical surface crochet stripes in the same way, inserting hook between sts for horizontal stripes and between rows for vertical stripes and working surface crochet loosely in order to avoid pulling pieces out of shape.

▶ POCKET LININGS (make 2)

Using hook and A, ch21. Work base and first rows as for back hem. 20sc.
Work 4 rows more in sc.
Inc one st at end of next row.
Work 11 rows more without shaping.
Inc one st at end of next row. 22sc.
Dec one st at end of next row, then dec one st at beg of next row. Rep last 2 rows until 10 sts rem.
Fasten off.

▶ CUFFS (make 2)

Using knitting needles and G, cast on 115[119:125] sts and beg rib as foll:
1st row P1, *K1, P1, rep from * to end.
2nd row K1, *P1, K1, rep from * to end.
Rep last 2 rows until cuff measures 5¼" from beg.
Bind off loosely in rib.

▶ MOCK POCKET FLAPS

Using knitting needles and G, cast on 39 sts and beg rib as foll:
1st row K1, *P1, K1, rep from * to end.
2nd row Sl 1, *K1, P1, rep from * to end.
3rd row Sl 1, *P1, K1, rep from * to end.
Rep last 2 rows until flap measures ½" from beg.
Next row Sl 1, rib to last 2 sts, turn leaving last 2 sts unworked.
Next row Rib to last 2 sts, turn leaving last 2 sts unworked.
Next row Rib to last 4 sts, turn leaving last 4 sts unworked.
Cont in this way, leaving 2 more sts unworked at end of each row until there are 3 sts at center, then turn, rib 2, turn, rib 1.
Break off yarn.
Sl all sts onto one needle and bind off loosely in rib.

▶ COLLAR

Using knitting needles and G, cast on 143[149:149] sts and beg rib as foll:
1st row K1, *P1, K1, rep from * to end.
2nd row Sl 1, rib to last 45 sts, turn leaving rem sts unworked.
3rd row Rib to last 45 sts, turn leaving rem sts unworked.
4th row Rib to last 16 sts, turn leaving rem sts unworked.
5th row As 4th row.
6th row Rib to end.
7th row Sl 1, rib to end. 143[149:149] sts.
Rep last row 23 times more.
Bind off tightly in knit.

▶ FINISHING

Do not press. Weave in all loose ends.
Sew shoulder seams. Sew side seams leaving 5¼" open 4" above lower edge. Sew pocket linings into opening with straight edge along back side seam and sewing shaped edge neatly to front on WS. Sew sleeve seams and set in sleeves. Press seams lightly on WS with warm iron.
Using hook, work a row of sc evenly around pocket opening, using colors to match blocks being edged.
Mark positions of mock pocket flaps 1½" from armhole edge and then 5" from first marker just below 3rd horizontal surface crochet stripe from lower edge. Sew flap in place between markers along top edge and short sides.
Sew collar in place 1¼" from center fronts. Sew cuff seams. Sew cast-on edge of cuff to foundation row of sleeve (beg of sleeve) inside sleeve and fold cuff to outside of sleeve.
Sew on buttons opposite buttonholes.
Sew one button to each pocket flap.
If desired, sew in shoulder pads and sew small snap to corner of left front at neck edge.

TRICOLOR CHECK

Only one color is used in each row of this easy-to-make double crochet top. If you substitute a glitter yarn for one of the three contrasting colors, this top would be perfect for evening wear.

▶ SIZES

To fit 32[34:36:38-40]"/81[86:91:96-102]cm bust.

Note: Figures for larger sizes are in brackets. If there is only one set of figures, it applies to all sizes.

See diagram for finished measurements.

▶ MATERIALS

See page 118 for further yarn information

Use a lightweight cotton yarn (approx 202yd per 1¾oz):

4¼[5:5¾:6½]oz in each of 3 colors A (blue), B (apricot) and C (cerise)

Size E crochet hook *or size to obtain correct gauge*

▶ GAUGE

26 sts and 19 rows to 4" over check pat using size E hook.
To save time, take time to check gauge.

Note: When counting sts, count turning ch at beg of row as one st. To check gauge ch40 using A and work base-2nd rows of back. Cont in pat for 5".

▶ BACK

Using A, ch130[136:142:148].
Base row 1dc in 4th ch from hook, 1dc in each of next 2ch, ch3, skip next 3ch, *1dc in each of next 3ch, ch3, skip next 3ch, rep from *, ending with 1dc in last ch. Turn. 128[134:140:146] sts, counting ch3 at beg of row as one st (see Note above). Drop A at edge of work, but do not break off.
1st row Using B, ch3, 1dc in each of first 3ch skipped in last row, ch3, skip next 3dc, *1dc in each of next 3ch skipped in last row, ch3, skip next 3dc, rep from *, ending with 1sc under ch3 at end of row. Turn. Drop B at edge of work, but do not break off.
2nd row Using C, ch3, 1dc in each of first 3dc skipped in last row, ch3, skip next 3dc, *1dc in each of next 3dc skipped in last row, ch3, skip next 3dc, rep from *, ending with 1sc under ch3 at end of row. Turn.
Last row forms check pat and is rep throughout, working in sequence of one row A, one row B and one row C.
Cont in check pat until back measures 11½" from beg.
Armhole shaping
Break off all yarn and fasten off, then keeping to color sequence as set throughout, cont as foll:
Next row Rejoin yarn with a sl st to 3rd of first 3dc group of last row (i.e. ch3 and 2dc skipped at beg of row), ch1, 1dc in each of next 3dc skipped in last row, work in pat to within last 2 groups of 3dc, ch3, skip next 3dc, 1sc in next dc skipped in last row. Turn. 6 sts decreased at each end of row. 116[122:128:134] sts.
Next row Work without shaping in pat, but working last sc in ch1 at end of row. Turn.
****Next row** Ch3, skip first dc of first 3dc skipped in last row and work 1dc in each of next 2dc, work in pat to end, ending with ch2 (instead of ch3), 1sc under ch3 at end of row. Turn.
Rep last row once. One st decreased at each end of row. 114[120:126:132] sts.
Next row Ch3, skip first dc of first 2dc skipped in last row and work 1dc in next dc, work in pat to end, ending with ch1, 1sc under ch3 at end of row. Turn.
Rep last row once.** 112[118:124:130] sts.
Cont to dec one st at each end of every other row as foll:
Next 2 rows Ch3 for turning ch, ch3 for first 3 sts, 1dc in each of next 3dc skipped in last row, work in pat to end, skipping last dc and ending with 1sc under ch3 at end of row. Turn.
Next 2 rows Ch3 for turning ch, ch2 for first 2 sts, 1dc in each of next 3dc skipped in last row, work in pat to last group of 3dc, ch3, skip next 3dc, 1dc in each of next 2dc of 3dc skipped in last row, 1sc under ch3. Turn.
Next 2 rows Ch3 for turning ch, 1ch for first st, 1dc in each of next 3dc skipped in last row, work in pat to last group of 3dc, ch3, skip next 3dc, 1dc in next dc of 2dc skipped in last row, 1sc under ch3. Turn.
Next 2 rows As 2nd pat row.
Rep from ** to **. 100[106:112:118] sts.
Cont without shaping as foll:
Next row Ch3, 1dc in first dc skipped in last row, work in pat to end, ending with ch1, skip last dc, 1sc under ch3. Turn.
Rep last row until armhole measures 6¾[7:7½:7¾]".
Neck and shoulder shaping
Next row Work in pat across first 18[21:24:27] sts. Turn, leaving rem sts unworked.
Cont in pat on these sts for first side of neck, dec one st at neck edge on next 3 rows. 15[18:21:24] sts.
Next row Ch3 and work 1sc in each dc of last row and 1hdc in each dc skipped in last row. Fasten off.
Rejoin correct color to rem sts at neck edge and work across center 64 sts, working 1sc in each dc of last row and 1hdc in each skipped dc, then work in pat across last 18[21:24:27] sts.
Complete as for first side of neck, reversing shaping.

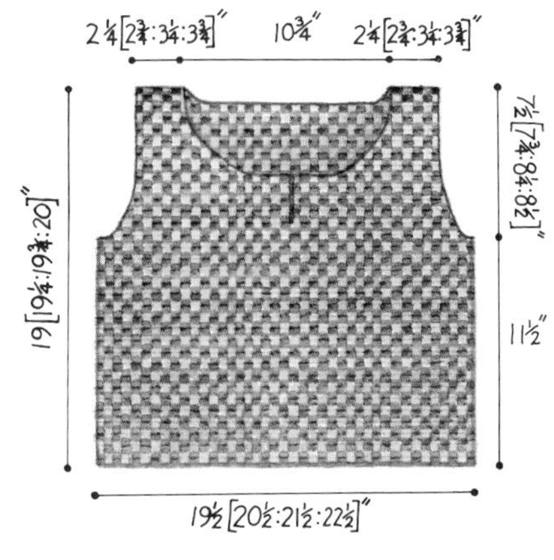

FRONT/BACK

▶ FRONT

Work as for back until armhole measures 1¼".
Divide for opening
Cont to work armhole shaping as for back *and at the same time* work in pat across next row until center is reached, then turn, leaving rem sts unworked.
Cont shaping armhole as for back, keeping center edge straight until armhole shaping is complete. 50[53:56:59] sts.
If necessary work without shaping until armhole measures approx 3½", ending at armhole edge.
Neck shaping
Next row Work in pat across first 34[37:40:43] sts. Turn, leaving 16 sts unworked.
Keeping to pat and keeping armhole edge straight, cont on these sts for first side of neck, dec 2 sts at neck edge on next and every row 5 times in all. Dec one st at neck edge on every row 9 times. 15[18:21:24] sts.
Work without shaping until front measures same as back to shoulder.
Work last row as for back. Fasten off.
Rejoin correct color to rem sts at side edge and work 2nd side of neck as for first side, reversing shaping. Using correct color, finish off center neck sts by working 1sc in each dc of last row and 1hdc in each skipped dc.

▶ FINISHING

Press pieces on WS with damp cloth and warm iron. Sew shoulder and side seams. Using A and with RS facing, work one round of sc followed by one round of sl st around neck edge, armholes and lower edge (see page 114). Press seams.

TEXTURED CHECKS

A smooth wool yarn and a nubbly cotton yarn in subtle shades combine to form an interesting textured check pattern on this casual loose-fitting sweater. The neck inset forms a collar or a polo neck.

▶ SIZES

To fit 32[34-36:38-40]"/81[86-91:96-102]cm bust.

Note: Figures for larger sizes are in brackets. If there is only one set of figures, it applies to all sizes.
See diagram for finished measurements.

▶ MATERIALS

See page 118 for further yarn information
Use a lightweight wool yarn (approx 73yd per 1oz) and a lightweight cotton knop yarn (approx 82yd per 1¾oz):
5[6:8]oz wool yarn in A (gray)
2[2:3]oz wool yarn in C (coral)
5[6:7]oz wool yarn in each of D (blue) and F (pale orange)
2oz wool yarn in G (flesh)
5[5:6]oz wool yarn in H (white)
12¼[14:15¾]oz knop yarn in B (white)
8¾[10½:12¼]oz knop yarn in E (yellow)
Sizes G and H crochet hooks *or size to obtain correct gauge*
12" zipper

▶ GAUGE

17 sts to 4" over check pat using size H hook for sl st rows and size G hook for all other pat rows.
18 sts and 26 rows (unstretched rows) to 4" over rib pat using size G hook.
To save time, take time to check gauges.

Note: When using 2 colors in a row, carry yarn not in use across top of row below and work all sts over it. When changing colors in a row, always change to new color with last yo of previous hdc (see page 112).
To check gauge ch21 and work base row as for back, then foll chart, working back and forth over first 20 sts. Read odd-numbered rows (RS) from right to left and even-numbered rows (WS) from left to right.

▶ BACK

Using smaller hook and A, ch91[95:99].
Base row 1sc in 2nd ch from hook, 1sc in each ch to end. Turn. 90[94:98]sc.
1st row (RS) Using A, ch2, 1hdc in each of first 3 sts, yo and insert hook in next st, yo and draw a loop through, then using B, yo and draw through all 3 loops on hook, carrying A across top of row below and working sts over it, work 1hdc in B in each of next 4 sts changing to A with last yo of 4th hdc, cont in this way working *4hdc in A, 4hdc in B, rep from * to last 2[6:2] sts, 1hdc in A in each st to end. Turn.
2nd row Using A, ch2, work 1hdc in A in each hdc in A and 1hdc in B in each hdc in B. Turn.
3rd row Using B, ch2, work 1hdc in B in each hdc in A and 1hdc in A in each hdc in B. Turn.
4th row Using B, ch2, work 1hdc in B in each hdc in B and 1hdc in A in each hdc in A. Turn.
5th and 6th rows As first and 2nd rows.
7th row Using C, ch1, 1sc in each hdc to end. Turn.
8th row Using larger hook and C, ch1, work 1 sl st *very loosely* in each sc to end inserting hook under *both* loops at top of each sc. Turn.
9th row Using smaller hook and D, ch2, 1hdc in each of first 2 sl st changing to E with last yo of 2nd hdc, *2hdc in E, 2hdc in D, rep from * to end. Turn.
Cont with smaller hook until next sl st row.
10th row Using E, ch2, 2hdc in E, *2hdc in D, 2hdc in E, rep from * to end. Turn.
11th and 12th rows As 9th and 10th rows.
13th and 14th rows Using A, as 7th and 8th rows.
15th row Using F, ch2, 1hdc in each of first 12 sl st changing to B with last yo of 12th hdc, *8hdc in B, 12hdc in F, rep from *, ending with 8[2:6]hdc in B and 10[0:0]hdc in F. Turn.
16th-18th rows Ch2, 1hdc in B in each hdc in B and 1hdc in F in each hdc in F. Turn.
19th and 20th rows Using G, as 7th and 8th rows.
21st and 22nd rows Using E for A and D for B, as first and 2nd rows.
23rd and 24th rows Using F, as 7th and 8th rows.
25th-38th rows As first-14th rows.
39th row Using B, ch2, 1hdc in each of first 8 sl st, changing to F with last yo of 8th hdc, *12hdc in F, 8hdc in B, rep from *, ending with 2[6:10]hdc in F. Turn.
40th-42nd rows As 16th-18th rows.
43rd-48th rows As 19th-24th rows.
First-48th rows form pat. Cont in pat until back measures approx 26¾[27¼:27½]" from beg. Fasten off.

▶ FRONT

Work as for back until front measures approx 16¾[17¼:17½]" from beg.
Neck shaping
Next row Work in pat across first 45[47:49] sts. Turn, leaving rem sts unworked.
Keeping to pat as set, dec one st at neck edge on every foll hdc row (do not dec on sc and sl st rows) 18 times in all. 27[29:31] sts.
Note: For dec (yo and insert hook in next st, yo and draw a loop through) twice, yo and draw through all 5 loops on hook — called 2hdc tog.
Work in pat without shaping

until there are same number of rows as back to shoulder. Fasten off.
Work 2nd side of neck as for first side, reversing shaping.

▶ SLEEVES (make 2)

Using smaller hook and A, ch57[61:61] and work base row as for back. 56[60:60]sc.
1st row (RS) Using A, ch2, *4hdc in A, 4hdc in B, rep from *, ending with 0[4:4]hdc in A. Turn.
Keep to check pat as set on back *and at the same time* shape sides of sleeve, inc one st at each end of next row and then at each end of every alternate hdc row (do not inc on sc and sl st rows) 18 times in all. 92[96:96] sts.
Note: For inc work 2hdc in first and last sts of row.
Cont in check pat until sleeve measures 13¾" from beg. Fasten off.

▶ CUFFS (make 2)

Using smaller hook and H, ch31 and work base row as for back. 30sc.
1st row Ch1, working in *back* loops only, 1sc in each sc to end. Turn.
Rep last row to form rib pat. Cont in rib pat until cuff measures 6¼[7:7½]" from beg unstretched. Fasten off.
Join cuff seam. Using

smaller hook and H, rejoin yarn with a sl st to one end of cuff at seam, ch3, work *1dc in next row end, 2dc in next row end, rep from * all around, join with a sl st to 3rd of ch3. Fasten off.

▶ BACK RIB

Using smaller hook and H, ch8 and work base and first rows as for cuffs. 7sc.

Cont in rib pat until rib, slightly stretched, fits across lower edge of back. Fasten off.

▶ FRONT RIB

Work as for back rib.

▶ POLO NECK COLLAR (3 pieces)

Fronts (make 2)

Using smaller hook and H, ch65 and work base and first rows as for cuffs. 64sc.

Cont in rib pat, dec 2 sts at beg of next row (neck edge), dec 2 sts at neck edge on next 2 rows, *dec one st at neck edge on next 2 rows, dec 2 sts at neck edge on next row, rep from * 3 times more. 42sc. Dec one st at neck edge on next 2 rows. 40sc.

Next row Work in rib pat, dec 10 sts at straight side (collar edge) and 2 sts at neck edge. Turn. 28sc.

Dec one st at neck edge on next 2 rows. 26sc.

*Dec 2 sts at neck edge and one st at collar edge on next row, dec one st at neck edge on next 2 rows, rep from * 3 times more. 6sc. Fasten off.

Back collar

Using smaller hook and H, ch4 and work base and first rows as for cuff. 3sc.

Work one row in rib pat. Cont in rib pat, *inc one st at beg of next row (collar edge), work 2 rows without shaping, *inc one st at collar edge on next row, work 2 rows without shaping, rep from * twice more. 7sc.

Next row Ch11, 1sc in 2nd ch from hook, 1sc in each of next 9ch, work in rib pat to end. Turn. 17sc.

Work 37 rows in rib pat without shaping.

Next row Work in sl st across first 10sc, ch1, work in rib pat to end. Turn. 7sc.

Complete 2nd side of collar as for first, reversing shaping.

▶ FINISHING

Do not press. Join shoulder seams. Mark positions of sleeves 10¾[11¼:11¼]" from shoulder seams. Sew on sleeves between markers. Sew back and front bands to lower edges of back and front. Join side and sleeve seams. Using smaller hook and H and with RS facing, work a row of sc evenly around neck edge, then work one round of sl st inserting hook under both loops at top of each sc. Fasten off.

Join collar seams, leaving center front open. Pin collar to neck, overlapping pullover body over collar approx ½" and lining shoulder seams up with collar seams. Using H, sew collar in place stitching along neck edge just below neck edging.

Sew dc end of cuffs to inside of sleeves overlapping sleeve over cuff approx 2" (adjusting length as required). Sew in zipper.

DESIGN VARIATIONS

▶ PULLOVER WITH COLLAR

For a pullover with an ordinary collar, omit zipper and turn back collar.

▶ V-NECK PULLOVER

For plain V-neck pullover omit collar.

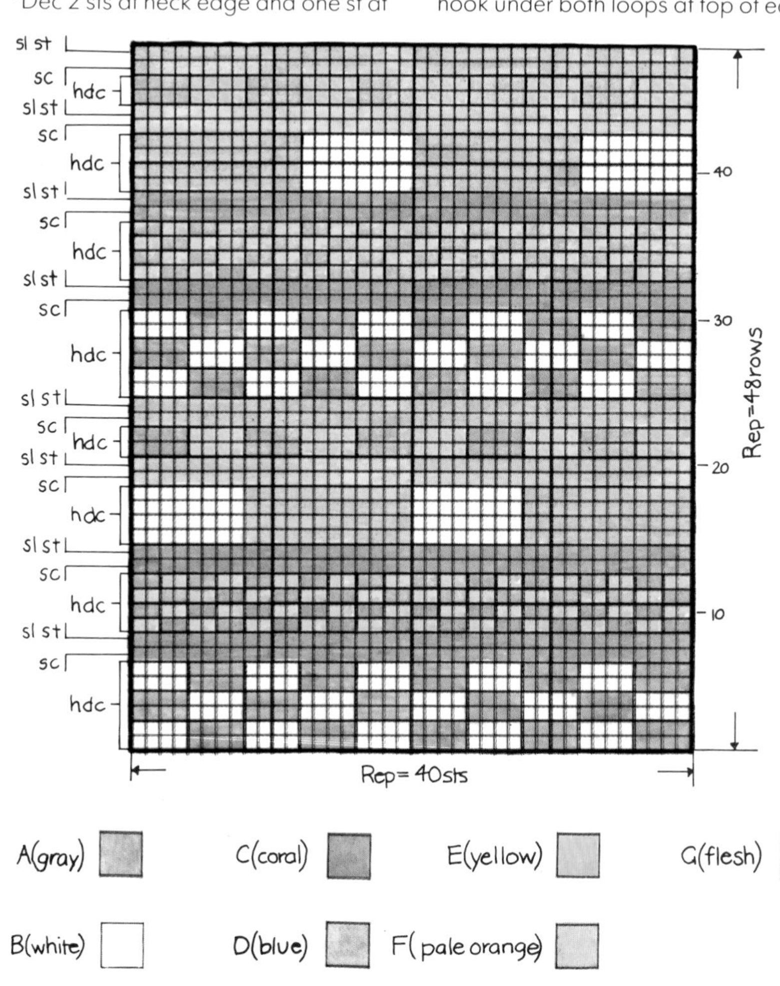

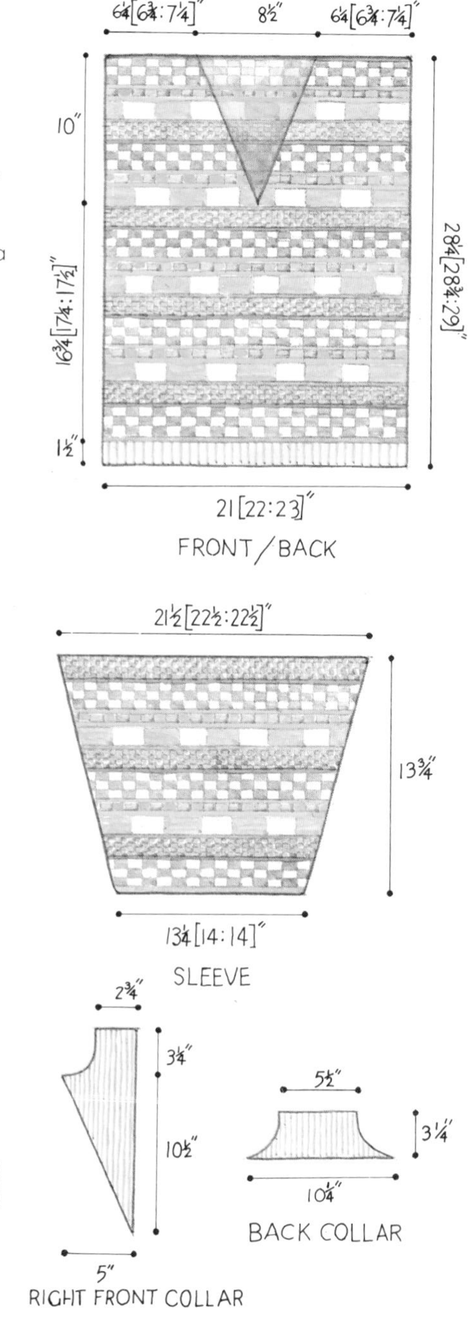

CHECK & PLAID

Sharply contrasting double crochet checks and Afghan crochet plaid produce this eyecatching sweater. The back and front are simple rectangular panels. Without sleeves, this design would make an attractive vest.

▶ SIZES

To fit 32[34:36:38]"/81[86:91:96]cm bust.

Note: Figures for larger sizes are in brackets. If there is only one set of figures, it applies to all sizes.

See diagram for finished measurements.

▶ MATERIALS

See page 118 for further yarn information

Use a fine wool tweed (approx 109yd per 1oz) and a lightweight cotton yarn (approx 202yd per 1¾oz):
6[7:8:8]oz fine wool tweed in A (black)
4[4:5:5]oz fine wool tweed in B (gray)
2[2:3:3]oz fine wool tweed in C (gray green)
1¾oz fine wool tweed in each of D (lilac) and E (turquoise)
1¾oz lightweight cotton yarn in each of F (cherry) and G (aqua green)
Size F crochet hook *or size to obtain correct gauge*
Size I Afghan crochet hook *or size to obtain correct gauge*
Shoulder pads (optional)

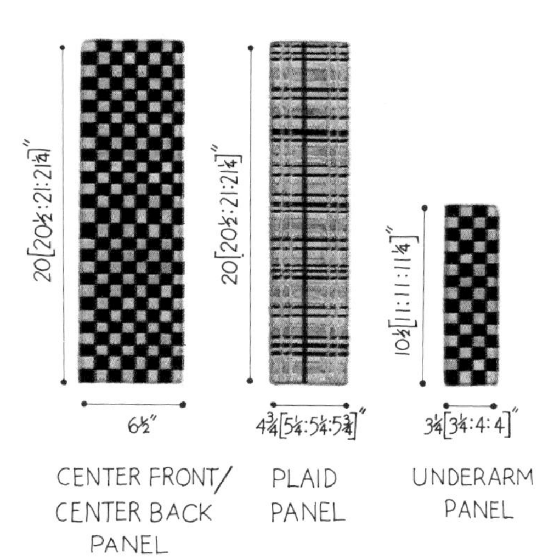

▶ GAUGE

20dc and 10½ rows to 4" over check pat using size F hook.
19 sts and 23 loop rows to 4" over Afghan knit st stripe pat using size I Afghan hook.
To save time, take time to check gauge.

Note: Front and back are each made in 3 panels which are sewn tog. When working check pat with 2 colors, carry color not in use loosely across top of row below and work all sts over it. When changing colors in a row of check pat, work last yo of previous dc in new color (see page 112). When changing colors on Afghan knit st stripes, work last yo of return row in new color (see page 116).

▶ CENTER BACK PANEL

Using crochet hook and A, ch35.

Base row Using A, 1dc in 5th ch from hook, 1dc in next ch, yo and insert hook in next ch, yo and draw a loop through, yo and draw through 2 loops on hook, change to B, yo and draw through 2 loops on hook to complete dc, carrying A loosely across top of row below and working all sts over it, work 4dc in B changing to A with last yo of 4th dc, *4dc in A, 4dc in B, rep from * to end. Turn. 32 sts, counting ch4 as first st.

1st row Using B, ch3 to count as first dc, skip first dc, 1dc in each of next 3dc changing to A with last yo of 3rd dc, 4dc in A, *4dc in B, 4dc in A, rep from *, working last dc in 4th of ch4 and changing to B with last yo of last st. Turn.

2nd row Using B, ch3, skip first dc, 1dc in each of next 3dc changing to A with last yo of 3rd dc, 4dc in A, *4dc in B, 4dc in A, rep from *, working last dc in 3rd of ch3. Turn.

3rd row Using A, ch3, skip first dc, 1dc in each of next 3dc changing to B with last yo of 3rd dc, 4dc in B, *4dc in A, 4dc in B, rep from *, working last dc in 3rd of ch3 and changing to A with last yo of last st. Turn.

4th row As 3rd row, but do not change to A at end of row.

5th row As 2nd row, but changing to C with last yo of last st at end of row.

6th row As 2nd row, using C in place of B.

7th row As 3rd row, using C in place of B and changing to A at end of row.

8th row As 4th row.

9th row As 5th row, but changing to B with last yo of last st at end of row.

2nd-9th rows form check pat. Cont in pat until panel measures 20[20½:21:21¼]" from beg. Fasten off.

▶ CENTER FRONT PANEL

Work as for center back panel.

▶ UNDERARM PANELS (make 2)

Using crochet hook and A, ch19[19:23:23].

Base row Using A, 1dc in 5th ch from hook, 1dc in each of next 2ch, 4dc in B, 4dc in A, 4dc in B, 0[0:4:4]dc in A. Turn. 16[16:20:20] sts.

This sets position of checks. Cont in check pat as for back until panel measures 10½[11:11:11¼]" from beg. Fasten off.

▶ PLAID SIDE PANELS (make 4)

Using Afghan hook and D, ch23[25:25:27]. Beg Afghan knit st as foll:

Base row Insert hook in 2nd ch from hook, yo and draw a loop through, *insert hook in next ch, yo and draw a loop through, rep from * to end of ch. Do not turn at end of rows. 23[25:25:27] loops on hook.

1st row (return row) Yo and draw through first loop on hook, *yo and draw through 2 loops on hook, rep from * until there is one loop on hook (this forms first loop of next row).

2nd row (loop row) Skip first vertical loop in row below and insert hook from front to back through 2nd vertical loop (under the chain), yo and draw a loop through, *insert hook through next vertical loop, yo and draw a loop through, rep from * to end.

Note: To form a firm edge, insert hook through center of last loop at the edge making sure that there are 2 vertical strands of yarn on hook at extreme left hand edge.

Last 2 rows form Afghan knit st and are rep throughout.

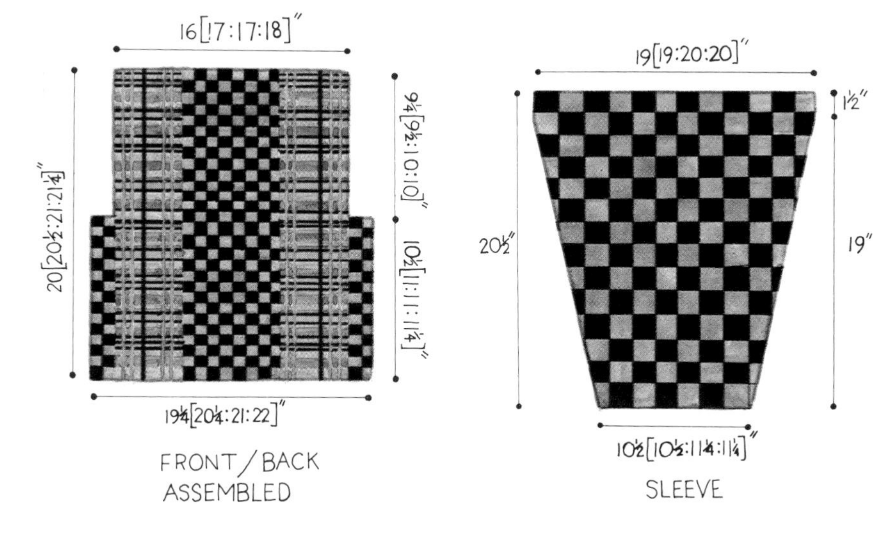

Cont in Afghan knit st until 4 loop rows have been worked from beg (counting base row), ending with a return row and changing to A with last yo of last return row. Cont in Afghan knit st working in stripe sequence of **one loop row in A, one in E, 2 in A, one in F, one in A, 2 in G, 4 in D, 2 in E, one in D, one in A, one in D, one in F, one in D, one in A, 3 in E and 3 in D** and working all return rows in same color as previous loop row. Rep from ** to ** to form stripe pat. Cont in stripe pat until panel measures 20[20½:21:21¼]" from beg, ending with a return row. Fasten off.

▶ RIGHT SLEEVE

Using crochet hook and A, ch55[55:59:59].

Base row Using A, 1dc in 5th ch from hook, 1dc in each of next 0[0:2:2]ch, 4dc in B, *4dc in A, 4dc in B, rep from *, ending last rep with 2[2:4:4]dc in B. Turn. 52[52:56:56] sts.

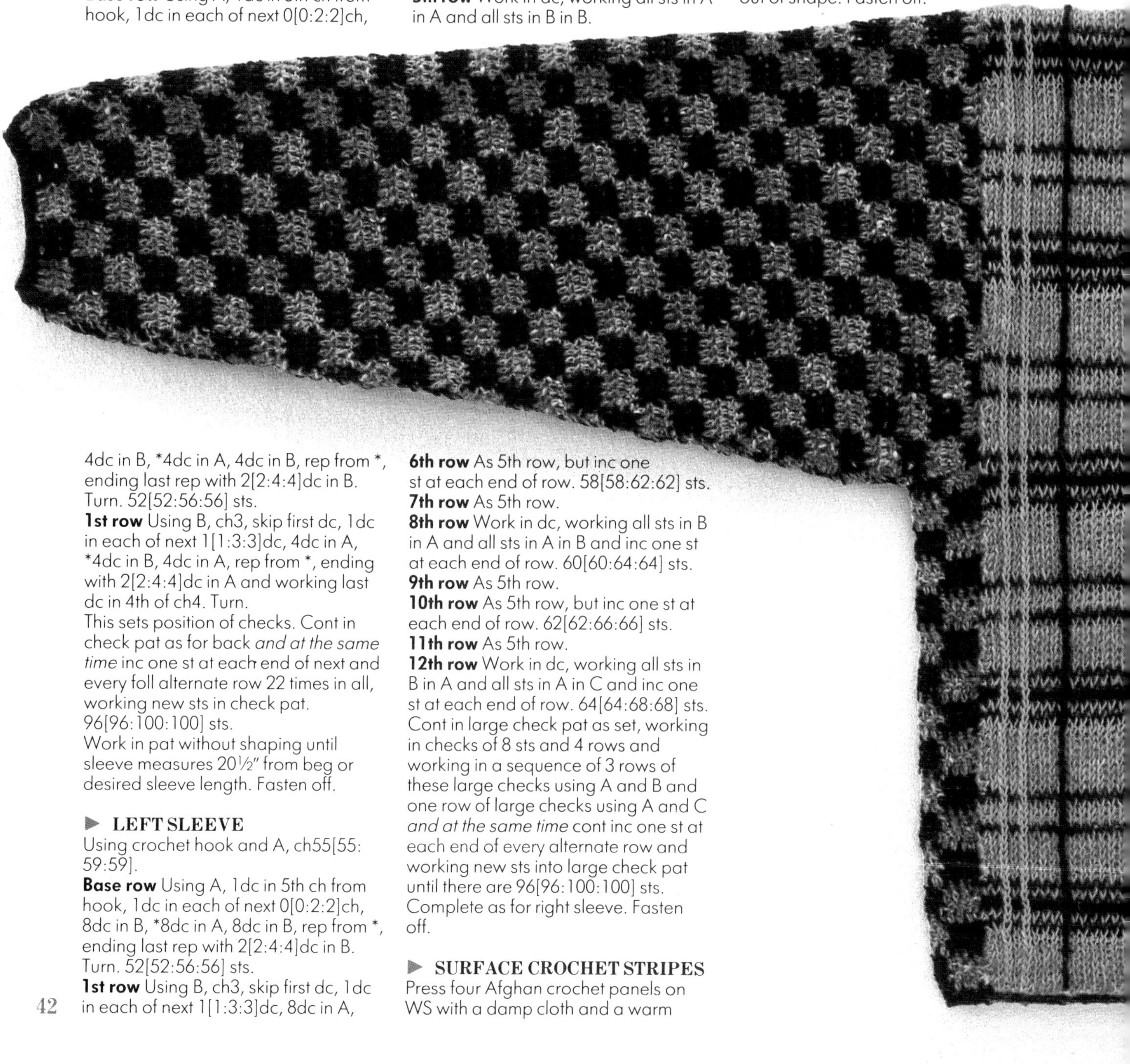

1st row Using B, ch3, skip first dc, 1dc in each of next 1[1:3:3]dc, 4dc in A, *4dc in B, 4dc in A, rep from *, ending with 2[2:4:4]dc in A and working last dc in 4th of ch4. Turn.

This sets position of checks. Cont in check pat as for back *and at the same time* inc one st at each end of next and every foll alternate row 22 times in all, working new sts in check pat. 96[96:100:100] sts.

Work in pat without shaping until sleeve measures 20½" from beg or desired sleeve length. Fasten off.

▶ LEFT SLEEVE

Using crochet hook and A, ch55[55:59:59].

Base row Using A, 1dc in 5th ch from hook, 1dc in each of next 0[0:2:2]ch, 8dc in B, *8dc in A, 8dc in B, rep from *, ending last rep with 2[2:4:4]dc in B. Turn. 52[52:56:56] sts.

1st row Using B, ch3, skip first dc, 1dc in each of next 1[1:3:3]dc, 8dc in A, *8dc in B, 8dc in A, rep from *, ending last rep with 2[2:4:4]dc in A and working last dc in 4th of ch4. Turn.

2nd row Using A, ch3, 1dc in first dc (to inc one st), 1dc in each of next 1[1:3:3]dc, 8dc in B, *8dc in A, 8dc in B, rep from *, ending last rep with 1[1:3:3]dc in B, 2dc in B in 3rd of ch3. Turn. 54[54:58:58] sts.

3rd row Using B, ch3, skip first dc, 1dc in each of next 2[2:4:4]dc, 8dc in A, *8dc in B, 8dc in A, rep from *, ending last rep with 3[3:5:5]dc in A, working last dc in 3rd of ch3 and changing to B with last yo of last dc. Turn.

4th row Using B, ch3, 1dc in first dc, 1dc in each of next 2[2:4:4]dc, 8dc in A, *8dc in B, 8dc in A, rep from *, ending last rep with 2[2:4:4]dc in A, 2dc in 3rd of ch3. Turn. 56[56:60:60] sts.

5th row Work in dc, working all sts in A in A and all sts in B in B.

6th row As 5th row, but inc one st at each end of row. 58[58:62:62] sts.

7th row As 5th row.

8th row Work in dc, working all sts in B in A and all sts in A in B and inc one st at each end of row. 60[60:64:64] sts.

9th row As 5th row.

10th row As 5th row, but inc one st at each end of row. 62[62:66:66] sts.

11th row As 5th row.

12th row Work in dc, working all sts in B in A and all sts in A in C and inc one st at each end of row. 64[64:68:68] sts.

Cont in large check pat as set, working in checks of 8 sts and 4 rows and working in a sequence of 3 rows of these large checks using A and B and one row of large checks using A and C *and at the same time* cont inc one st at each end of every alternate row and working new sts into large check pat until there are 96[96:100:100] sts. Complete as for right sleeve. Fasten off.

▶ SURFACE CROCHET STRIPES

Press four Afghan crochet panels on WS with a damp cloth and a warm iron, blocking to correct measurements.

Left front panel

Work vertical surface crochet stripes on an Afghan panel as foll:

Using crochet hook and F and with RS facing, hold panel so that base row is at top, then beg at lower edge (last row of strip), insert hook from front to back between 3rd and 4th sts from right hand edge and through sp between first 2 return rows (chains), holding yarn at back of work throughout, yo and draw a loop through, *keep loop on hook, insert hook through sp between next 2 return rows, yo and draw a loop through sp and through loop on hook, rep from * up panel to end, working surface crochet loosely to avoid pulling pieces out of shape. Fasten off.

Work 3 stripes more in F in the same way: one between 5th and 6th sts from right hand edge, one between 3rd and 4th sts from left hand edge and one between 5th and 6th sts from left hand edge.
Work one stripe in A in the same way between the 9th and 10th sts from the right hand edge.
Work 5 vertical stripes on a 2nd Afghan crochet panel in the same way for right back.

Right front panel
Work vertical stripes in F as for left front panel. Then work stripe in A between 9th and 10th sts from left hand edge.
Work a 2nd Afghan crochet panel in the same way for left back.

▶ FINISHING

Do not press check pat pieces. Weave in all loose ends. Join right and left front plaid panels to center front check panel. Join three back panels in the same way. Join shoulder seams, leaving 10½[10½:11:11]" open for neck. Sew side panels to back and front, beg seams at lower edge of pieces so that opening is left between shoulder and side panel for sleeve. Join sleeve seams, leaving 1⅝[1⅝:2:2]" open at top of sleeve. Sew sleeves to armholes joining last 1⅝[1⅝:2:2]" to top of side panel.

Edging
Using crochet hook and with RS facing, work a round of sc evenly around neck edge, using A along check pat and matching color along Afghan crochet. Then using A only, work one sc around post of each sc from front (see page 110). Fasten off. Work an edging in the same way around lower edge of back and front. Using A and crochet hook, work 36sc evenly around cuff edge and complete as for other edgings. If desired, sew in shoulder pads.

DESIGN VARIATION

▶ SLEEVELESS PULLOVER

For sleeveless pullover follow instructions omitting sleeves. Edge armholes with a row of sc or work a strip of crochet rib (see page 114).

BUFFALO PLAID

This generously shaped jacket is worked in single crochet. The two-way pockets, which button down on top, are lined with fabric and open at the sides for use as hand warmers.

▶ SIZE
One size only. To fit 34-38"/86-96cm bust.
See diagram for finished measurements.

▶ MATERIALS
See page 118 for further yarn information
Use a fine wool tweed yarn (approx 109yd per 1oz):
20oz in A (gold)
22oz in B (dark gray)
Size J crochet hook *or size to obtain correct gauge*
25" open-ended zipper
4 buttons
Small amount of matching fabric for pocket lining
Dark gray sewing thread
Shoulder pads (optional)

▶ GAUGE
14 sts and 15 rows to 4" over plaid pat using size J hook and 2 strands of yarn held tog.
To save time, take time to check gauge.

Note: Plaid pat is worked with 2 strands of yarn held tog throughout. Back, front and sleeves are worked in rows which progress from side seam to side seam instead of from lower edge to top in the usual way.
When working with 2 colors in a row, carry color not in use across top of row below, working all sts over it. Always change to new color with last yo of previous st (see page 112). For gauge sample work in sc foll chart. Read odd-numbered rows (RS) from right to left and even-numbered rows (WS) from left to right.

▶ BACK
Using 2 strands of A, ch43 and using 2 strands of each color throughout, beg at side edge as foll:
Base row 1sc in 2nd ch from hook, 1sc in each of next 9ch, *(1sc in B in next ch, 1sc in A in next ch) 5 times*, 1sc in A in each of next 10ch, rep from * to * once more, 1sc in A in each of last 2ch. Turn. 42sc.
1st row Ch1, 1sc in A in each of first 2sc, *(1sc in B in next sc, 1sc in A in next sc) 5 times, 1sc in A in each of next 10sc, rep from * once more. Turn.
2nd row Ch1, *10sc in A, (1sc in B, 1sc in A) 5 times, rep from * once, ending with 2sc in A. Turn.
3rd and 4th rows Work in sc, using B only. Turn.
Rep first and 2nd rows twice more.
Armhole shaping
9th row Using B, ch43, 1sc in A in 2nd ch from hook, cont across ch and then across sts of last row, work 1sc in B, 1sc in A, 11sc in B, (1sc in A, 1sc in B) 5 times, *10sc in B, (1sc in A, 1sc in B) 5 times, rep from * to end. Turn. 84sc.
10th row Ch1, *(1sc in A, 1sc in B) 5 times, 10sc in B, rep from *, ending with (1sc in A, 1sc in B) twice. Turn.
11th row Ch1, (1sc in A, 1sc in B) twice, *10sc in B, (1sc in A, 1sc in B) 5 times, rep from * to end. Turn.
12th row As 10th row.
13th row Work in sc, using A only.
Shoulder shaping
14th row Work in sc, using A only and inc one st at end of row by working 2sc in last st. Turn.
15th row Ch1, 1sc in B, (1sc in A, 1sc in B) twice, *10sc in B, (1sc in A, 1sc in B) 5 times, rep from * to end. Turn.
16th row Ch1, *(1sc in A, 1sc in B) 5 times, 10sc in B, rep from *, ending with (1sc in A, 1sc in B) twice, 1sc in A. Turn.
Rep last 2 rows once more.
This sets plaid pat (see plaid chart). Keeping to plaid pat throughout, inc one st at beg of next row, work 5 rows without shaping, inc one st at beg of next row, work 5 rows without shaping. 87sc.
Neck shaping
Dec one st at beg of next row (neck edge) by working 2sc tog, then dec one st at neck edge on next 2 rows. 84 sts.
Work 10 rows without shaping, so ending with first of 2 rows in B. This is center of back.
Beg with 2nd row in B, work 2nd half of back as for first, reversing shaping. Fasten off.

▶ LEFT FRONT
Using 2 strands of B, ch43 and beg at side seam as foll:
Base row 1sc in A in 2nd ch from hook, 1sc in B in next ch, (1sc in A in next ch, 1sc in B in next ch) 4 times, 1sc in B in each of next 10ch, (1sc in A in next ch, 1sc in B in next ch) 5 times, 1sc in B in each of next 11ch, 1sc in A. Turn. 42sc.
1st row Ch1, 1sc in B, 1sc in A, *10sc in B, (1sc in A, 1sc in B) 5 times, rep from * once more. Turn.
2nd row Ch1, *(1sc in A, 1sc in B) 5 times, 10sc in B, rep from * once, ending with 1sc in B, 1sc in A. Turn.
3rd and 4th rows Work in sc, using A only. Turn.
Rep first and 2nd rows twice more.
Armhole shaping
9th row Using A, ch43, 1sc in A in 2nd ch from hook, cont across ch and then across sts of last row, work 3sc in A, *(1sc in B, 1sc in A) 5 times, 10sc in A, rep from * to end. Turn. 84sc.
Cont in plaid pat as set, working shoulder shaping as for back until 31 rows to neck (counting base row) have been completed, so ending at neck edge. 87sc.
Neck shaping
Keeping to plaid pat throughout, work neck shaping as foll:
Next row Work in sl st across first 5sc,

ch1, work in pat to end. Turn. 82sc.
Next row Work in pat to last 2sc. Turn, leaving 2 sts unworked. 80sc.
Dec one st at neck edge on next 3 rows, *work one row without shaping, dec one st at neck edge on next row, rep from * once more. 75sc.
Work 4 rows more without shaping, so ending with first of 2 rows in A.
Fasten off.

► **RIGHT FRONT**
Plaid pat is reversible, so that right front is worked exactly as for left front, but adding 3 more rows at center front for overlap.

► **SLEEVES** (make 2)
Note: Incs for sleeve shaping are worked on every row so that separate lengths of ch need to be worked for every alternate row. Make 6 lengths of 4ch each in B and 3 lengths of 4ch each in A and set aside to be used during sleeve shaping.
Using 2 strands of B, ch10 and beg at sleeve seam as foll:
Base row 1sc in 2nd ch from hook, 1sc in each of next 6ch, 1sc in A in next ch, 1sc in B in last ch. Turn. 9sc.
1st row Ch1, 1sc in A in first sc, 1sc in B in each of next 8sc, then using a separate length of 4ch in B, work 1sc in B in each of 4ch. Turn. 13sc.
2nd row Ch4 in B, 1sc in A in 2nd ch from hook, then cont across rem 2ch and sts of last row work 1sc in B, 1sc in A, 11sc in B, 1sc in A, 1sc in B. Turn. 16sc.
3rd row Ch1, 1sc in A, 1sc in B, (1sc in A, 1sc in B) twice, then using a separate length of 4ch in B, work (1sc in A, 1sc in B) twice. Turn. 20sc.
4th row Ch4 in A, using A only, work in sc across ch (beg in 2nd ch from hook) and across sts of last row. Turn. 23sc.
5th row Work in sc, using A only and working 4sc in length of 4ch in A. Turn. 27sc.
6th row Ch4 in B, 1sc in 2nd ch from hook, then working across rem 2ch and sts of last row, 7sc in B, (1sc in A, 1sc in B) 5 times, 10sc in B, 1sc in A, 1sc in B. Turn. 30sc.
7th row Ch1, 1sc in A, 11sc in B, (1sc in A, 1sc in B) 5 times, 8sc in B, then using length of 4ch in B, work 2sc in B, 1sc in A, 1sc in B. Turn. 34sc.
8th row Ch4 in B, 1sc in B in 2nd ch from hook, (1sc in A, 1sc in B) twice, 10sc in B, (1sc in A, 1sc in B) 5 times, 10sc in B, 1sc in A, 1sc in B. Turn. 37sc.
9th row Ch1, 1sc in A, 11sc in B, (1sc in A, 1sc in B) 5 times, 10sc in B, (1sc in A, 1sc in B) 4 times working across length of 4ch in B, 1sc in A in last ch. Turn. 41sc.
10th row Ch4 in A, 1sc in B in 2nd ch from hook, 11sc in A, *(1sc in B, 1sc in A) 5 times*, 10sc in A, rep from * to * once, 2sc in A. Turn. 44sc.
Cont in plaid pat as set, (inc 4 sts at end of next row, inc 3 sts at beg of next row) 4 times more. 72sc.
Work without shaping until there are 54 rows along cuff edge (2 rows in A are at center of sleeve).
Work 2nd side of sleeve as for first side, but reversing shaping. Fasten off.

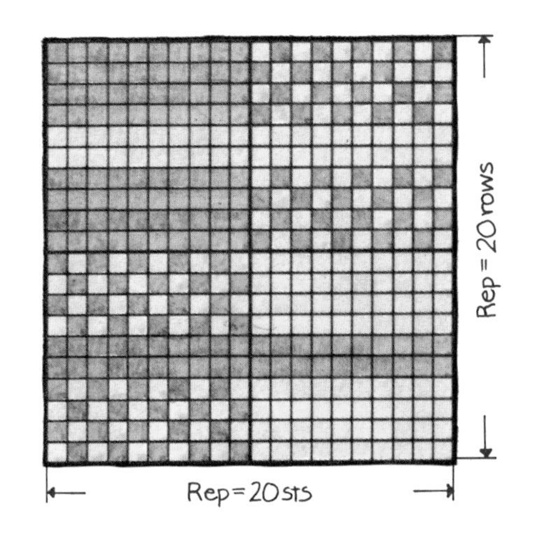

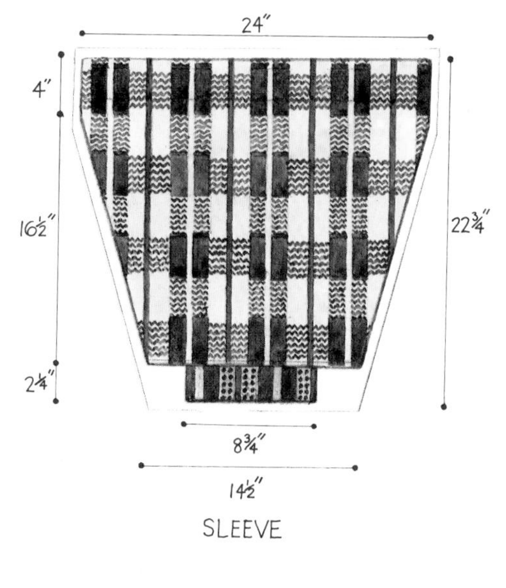

SLEEVE

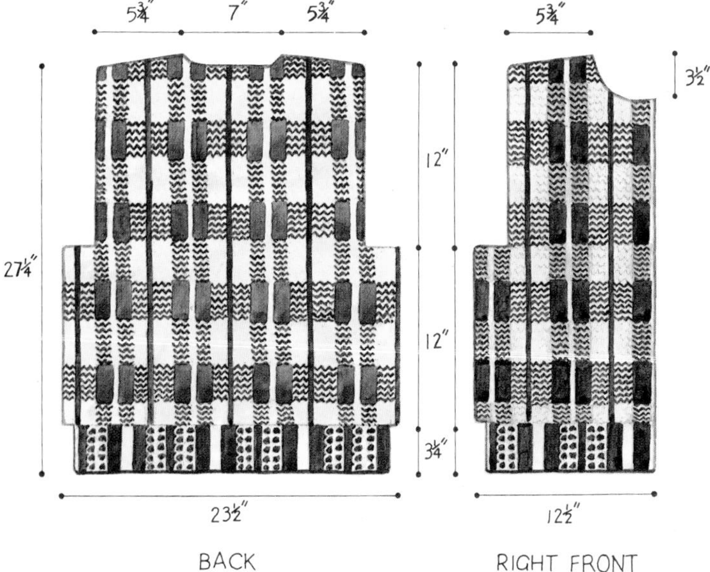

BACK

RIGHT FRONT

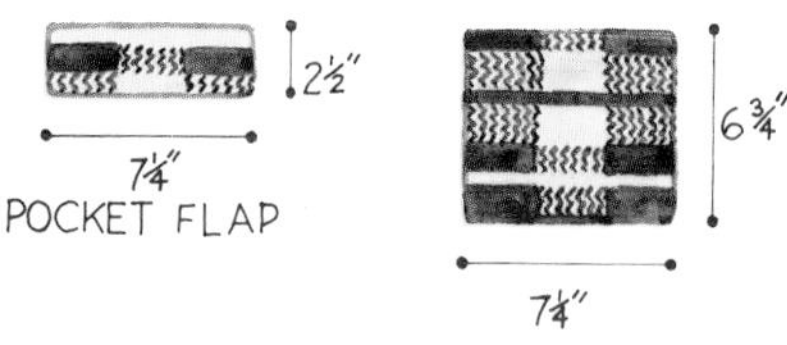

POCKET FLAP

POCKET

▶ **POCKETS** (make 2)
Using 2 strands of B, ch27.
Base row 1sc in 2nd ch from hook, 1sc in each of next 7ch, (1sc in A in next ch, 1sc in B in next ch) 5 times, 1sc in B in each of last 8ch. Turn. 26sc.
1st row Ch1, 8sc in B, (1sc in A, 1sc in B) 5 times, 8sc in B. Turn.
Rep last row twice more.
4th and 5th rows Work in sc, using A only. Turn.
Rep first row 4 times.
Cont in plaid pat as set until 25 rows have been worked from beg, counting base row. Fasten off.

▶ **POCKET FLAPS** (make 2)
Using 2 strands of A, ch27.
Base row 1sc in 2nd ch from hook, 1sc in B in next ch, *(1sc in A in next ch, 1sc in B in next ch)* 3 times, 1sc in A in each of next 10sc, rep from * to * 4 times. Turn. 26sc.
1st row Ch1, *(1sc in A, 1sc in B) 4 times*, 10sc in A, rep from * to * once. Turn.
2nd row As for first row of pocket.
3rd row (buttonhole row) Ch1, 4sc in B, ch2 in B, skip 2sc, 2sc in B, (1sc in A, 1sc in B) 5 times, 2sc in B, ch2 in B, skip 2sc, 4sc in B. Turn.
Cont in plaid pat as set, working in pat across ch2 in next row, until 9 rows have been worked from beg, counting base row. Fasten off.

▶ **HIP BAND**
Using 2 strands of B, ch13.
Base row 1sc in 2nd ch from hook, 1sc in each ch to end. Turn. 12sc.
1st-3rd rows Work in sc, using B only. Turn.
4th and 5th rows Work in sc, using A only. Turn.
6th-9th rows Work in sc, using B only. Turn.
10th-13th rows Ch1, (1sc in B, 1sc in A) 6 times. Turn.
14th-15th rows Work in sc, using B only. Turn.
16th-19th rows As 10th-13th rows.
20th-23rd rows As 6th-9th rows.
Rep 4th-23rd rows to form plaid pat.
Cont in pat until band measures 43¼" from beg. Fasten off.

▶ **CUFFS** (make 2)
Using 2 strands of B, ch9.
Work base row as for hip band. 8sc.
Work in plaid pat as for hip band until cuff measures 8¾" from beg.
Fasten off.

▶ **COLLAR**
Join shoulder seams.
Using 2 strands of B, ch7 and work base row as for hip band. 6sc.
Work in plaid pat as for hip band until collar fits around neck edge.
Fasten off.

▶ **FINISHING**
Do not press. Pin top of sleeve to armhole so that jacket body overlaps sleeve by 5 rows. With RS facing work a backstitch seam between 5th and 6th rows through both thicknesses. Sew decreased edges of armhole to sides of sleeve.
Sew on cuffs, easing in fullness of sleeves. Join side and sleeve seams. Sew on hip band, easing in fullness of back and front. Sew collar in place at neck edge.
Using 2 strands of B and with RS facing, work sc evenly around 2 side edges and lower edge (foundation row) of each pocket.
Edgings
Using 2 strands of B and with RS facing, beg at right side seam and work sc along hip band to center front, up right front, along collar edge, down left front and around hip band, working 2sc in each corner. Cont around working 1 sl st in each sc of last round and inserting hook through both loops at top of each sc.
Work an edging in the same way around cuff edges and around 2 side edges and lower edge (foundation chain) of each pocket flap.
Cut lining for pockets ½" larger all around than pocket. Turn under ¼" twice and stitch hem in place. Sew a pocket lining to back of each pocket leaving top open. Sew pockets and flaps to fronts, leaving side of pocket nearest side seam open. Sew top of fabric linings to fronts.
Sew in zipper. Sew on buttons. Sew in shoulder pads if desired.

DESIGN VARIATION

▶ **SLEEVELESS JACKET**
For a sleeveless jacket omit sleeves and work sc and sl st edging around armholes.

WOVEN PLAID

The comfortable soft feel of cotton chenille is perfect for an elegant lightweight jacket. Worked in a filet net of half doubles, the vertical stripes are woven in afterwards by hand to produce the plaid pattern.

▶ SIZES

To fit 32[34:36:38]"/81[86:91:96]cm bust.

Note: Figures for larger sizes are in brackets. If there is only one set of figures, it applies to all sizes.

See diagram for finished measurements.

▶ MATERIALS

See page 118 for further yarn information

Use a lightweight cotton chenille yarn (approx 175yd per 1¾oz):
12¼[14:14:17½]oz in A (turquoise)
12¼[14:14:15¾]oz in B (pink)
3½[3½:3½:5¼]oz in C (gray)
1¾[1¾:1¾:3½]oz in D (fuchsia)
Size E crochet hook *or size to obtain correct gauge*
Tapestry needle for weaving
2 buttons

▶ GAUGE

Before weaving: 11 sps and 13½ rows to 4" over filet pat using size E hook.

To save time, take time to check gauge.

After weaving: 11 sps and 14 rows to 4" over woven filet pat.

Note: Jacket is worked in simple stripes of filet crochet. After all pieces are completed A and B are woven through spaces to create plaid effect. Weaving will slightly shorten pieces. Lengths of pieces after weaving are given on measurement diagram.

▶ BACK

Using A, ch115[119:123:127].

Base row 1hdc in 5th ch from hook, *ch1, skip next ch, 1hdc in next ch, rep from * to end. Turn. 56[58:60:62] ch1 sps, counting first ch4 as first hdc and ch1 sp.

1st row Ch3 to count as first hdc and ch1 sp, skip first hdc, 1hdc in next hdc, *ch1, 1hdc in next hdc, rep from *, working last hdc in 2nd of ch4. Turn.

2nd row As for first row, but working last hdc in 2nd of ch3.

Rep last row to form filet pat. Work one row more in A. Cont in stripe sequence of **5 rows B, one row C, 4 rows A, one row C, 2 rows B, one row D, one row B, one row C, 4 rows A.**

Cont in filet pat, rep stripe sequence from ** to ** until 43 rows have been worked from beg, counting base row. Back measures approx 12¾".

Armhole shaping

Break off yarn, then keeping pat correct, skip first 6 sps and rejoin yarn to 7th hdc of row with a sl st, ch3 to count as first hdc and ch1 sp, 1hdc in next hdc, work in pat over next 43[45:47:49] ch1 sps, turn leaving rem 6 sps unworked. 44[46:48:50] ch1 sps.

Cont in pat without shaping until 34[36:38:38] rows have been worked from beg of armhole.

Next row Ch1, 1 sl st in first hdc, 1 sl st in ch, 1 sl st in next hdc, ch3, work in pat to last ch sp. Turn, leaving last ch sp unworked. 42[44:46:48] ch1 sps.

Rep last row once more. 40[42:44:46] ch1 sps. Fasten off. Armhole measures approx 10¾[11¼:11¾:11¾]".

▶ LEFT FRONT

Using A, ch69[71:73:75] and work base-2nd rows as for back. 33[34:35:36] ch1 sps.

Keeping to stripe pat as set on back, beg shaping center front edge as foll:

***__Next row__ Work in pat, ending with (1hdc, ch1, 1hdc) all in 2nd of ch3 (thus inc one ch1 sp at center front edge). Turn. 34[35:36:37] ch1 sps.

Work 5 rows in pat.***

Rep from *** to *** 5 times more.

Inc one ch1 sp at center front edge on next row. 40[41:42:43] ch1 sps. Work in pat without shaping until there are same number of rows as back to armhole, so ending at armhole edge.

Neck and armhole shaping

Break off yarn, then keeping pat correct, skip first 6 sps and rejoin yarn to 7th hdc of row with a sl st, ch3 to count as first hdc and ch1 sp, 1hdc in next hdc, cont in pat until 32[33:34:35] ch1 sps have been worked in all, turn leaving rem 2 sps unworked at neck edge.

Next row Ch1, sl st over first 2 sps and in 3rd hdc, ch3, 1hdc in next hdc, work in pat to end. Turn. 30[31:32:33] ch1 sps.

Cont in pat keeping armhole edge straight and dec 2 sps at neck edge on next 2 rows, then dec one sp at neck edge on every row 6 times. 20[21:22:23] ch1 sps.

Work one row without shaping. Dec one sp at neck edge on next row and then on every foll alternate row 3 times more. 16[17:18:19] ch1 sps. Work 3 rows without shaping. Dec one sp at neck edge on next row and on every foll 4th row twice more. 13[14:15:16] ch1 sps.
Cont in pat without shaping until there are same number of rows as back, dec one sp at armhole edge on each of last 2 rows as for back. Fasten off.

▶ RIGHT FRONT

Filet pat is reversible, so work right front as for left front until 41 rows have been worked from beg, so ending at armhole edge. 40[41:42:43] ch1 sps.
Next row (buttonhole row) Work in pat over first 17[18:19:20] sps, *ch5, skip 3 sps, 1hdc in next hdc*, work in pat across next 15 sps, rep from * to *, work in pat to end. Turn.
Next row Work in pat to first ch5, *(ch1, skip 1ch, 1hdc in next ch) twice, ch1, 1hdc in next hdc*, work in pat to next ch5, rep from * to *, work in pat to end. Turn.
Complete as for left front.

▶ SLEEVE AND YOKE (make 2)

Using A, ch51[55:59:59] and work base-2nd rows as for back.
24[26:28:28] ch1 sps.
Next row Ch3, 1hdc in first hdc, cont in pat to end, ending with (1hdc, ch1, 1hdc) all in 2nd of ch3. Turn.
26[28:30:30] ch1 sps.
Keeping to pat as for back, work 2 rows without shaping. Inc one sp at each end of next row and then every foll 3rd row 4 times more. 36[38:40:40] ch1 sps. Work one row without shaping. Inc one sp at each end of next row and then every foll alternate row 21 times more. 80[82:84:84] ch1 sps.
Work 8 rows without shaping.
Yoke shaping
Break off yarn, then keeping pat correct, skip first 27[28:29:29] sps and rejoin yarn to 28th[29th:30th:30th] hdc of row with a sl st, ch3 to count as first hdc and ch1 sp, 1hdc in next hdc, cont in pat until 26 sps have been worked in all, turn leaving rem 27[28:29:29] sps unworked.
Cont in pat on these center sts, dec one sp at each end of next 2 rows.
22 sps.
Work 14[15:16:16] rows without shaping.
Neck shaping
Next row Work in pat over first 10 sps. Turn, leaving rem sts unworked.
Dec one sp at beg of next row. 9 sps.
Work 9 rows in pat without shaping.
Fasten off.

▶ WEAVING

Weave in all loose ends.
Back
Using 3 strands of B and tapestry needle and with RS of back facing, beg at lower right-hand edge and weave in and out of first vertical row of ch sps working over and under chains between sps and leaving 6" of yarn loose at edge for adjusting and fastening (see page 113). When armhole edge is reached, weave back down next vertical row of ch sps working *over* chains that were worked *under* in last row and vice versa until lower edge is reached. Cont in this way until 4[5:6:7] rows in B have been completed.
Cont in vertical rows from right to left across back, ***work 5 rows in A, 3 rows in B, 3 rows in A, 5 rows in B***
rep from *** to ***, ending with 4[5:6:7] rows in A.
If necessary adjust woven strands until length is correct. Weave in all loose ends.
Left front
Work as for back from ** to **. Then work in vertical stripe sequence as for back between *** and *** until center front edge is reached. Weave in all loose ends.
Right front
Work as for left front but beg at side seam and working in rows from left to right reversing colors by working A for B and B for A.
Left sleeve and yoke
With RS of left sleeve facing and holding work so that cuff edge is at top, beg at right edge of sleeve and weave 0[1:2:2] vertical rows in A as for back. Then cont in vertical rows from right to left across sleeve and yoke, work *5 rows in B, 3 rows in A, 3 rows in B, 5 rows in A, rep from *, ending with 0[1:2:2] rows in B. Weave in all loose ends.
Right sleeve and yoke
With RS facing, work as for left sleeve and yoke.

▶ FINISHING

Do not press. Join center back yoke seam. Sew back and fronts to yoke and sleeves. Sew side and sleeve seams. Using A and with RS facing, beg at lower edge of right front and work sc evenly up right front, along back neck easing in to correct measurement, down left front and around lower edge, working 2sc in corners. Then work a round of sl st, inserting hook under *both* loops at top of each sc. Fasten off. Sew on buttons.

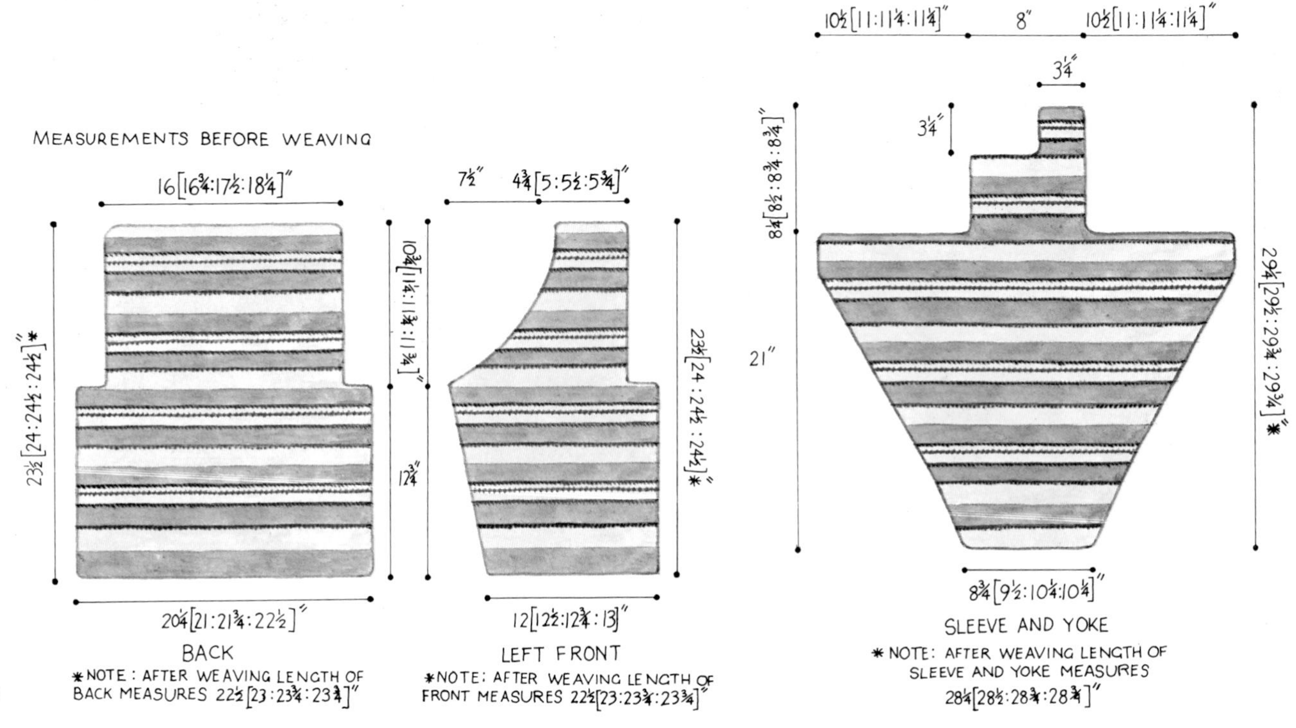

TEXTURES

TEXTURES

There are many textures to be found in books of crochet stitches — anything from subtle raised stitches to high relief. The textured stitches chosen here are ones that allow scope for making your own pattern designs. Because the basic or background stitches used are simple ones, they can also be easily increased or decreased for garment shaping.

▶ WORKING AROUND POSTS

One method of creating a textured crochet fabric is by working around the posts of stitches instead of through the tops (see page 110). Two distinct textures are achieved — one by working around a stitch from the front and another by working around a stitch from the back. Pattern shapes are formed by contrasting these two textures. For example, either diagonal stripes (1) or diamonds (4) are possible replacements for the rectangular shapes in *Basketweave* (page 64).

▶ BOBBLES

Another way to make pattern shapes is by contrasting bobbles with a smoother background surface. Sample 2 gives an idea of the versatility of designing with bobbles. Any number of solid shapes or outlines could be made with bobbles in matching or contrasting colors and yarn textures.

Instead of bobble motifs, a more solid bobble texture may be preferred. The allover bobbles (3) worked in three colors would be effective in a checkerboard pattern. Large squares of plain single crochet could be alternated with large squares of bobbles — either striped or plain.

▶ CABLES

It is possible to imitate familiar and popular knitted Aran-type textures with crochet. Cables in crossed triples are especially appealing worked in mohair (see *Cables* on page 54) which emphasizes the depth of the stitches. Bobbles allow even more scope for variations. A simple way of making crochet cables is with surface slip stitch. On a smooth background or on a background of bobbles and colored diamonds (5), intertwined surface slip stitch gives a credible cable substitute. The trick is to use a thick yarn or several strands of matching yarn for the slip stitch so that the cables gain prominence. Textured yarns also provide the bulk needed for cable shapes.

Rep=12 rows

Rep=12sts

◫ 1hdc around post from front
☐ 1hdc around post from back

1 Work first row in hdc. Then work in hdc following chart and beginning and ending each row with 1sc.

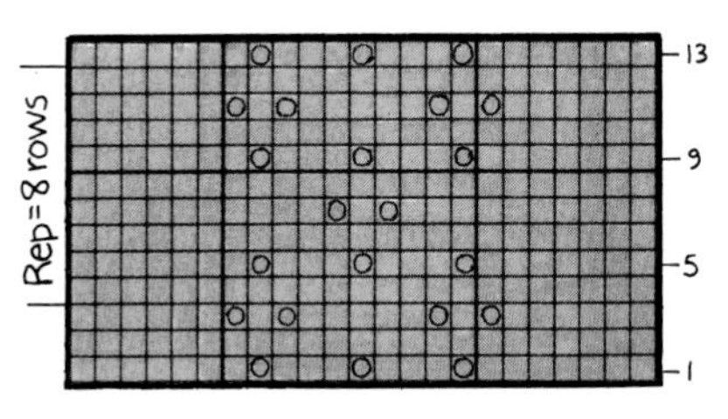

▣ bobble

2 Work odd-numbered rows in hdc and even-numbered rows in dc, placing bobbles following chart. For bobble work (1hdc, 3dc, 1hdc), remove hook. Reinsert through top of first hdc and draw loop through. Work "cable" outline in surface sl st.

3 Use 3 colors A, B and C. Using A, make a multiple of 4ch.
Base row (RS) Using A, 1sc in 2nd ch from hook, 1sc in each ch. Turn.
1st row Using B, ch1, 1sc in first sc, *leaving last loop of each st on hook work 2tr in next sc, yo and draw through all 3 loops on hook, 1sc in each of next 3sc, rep from *, ending last rep 1sc in each of next 2sc. Turn.
2nd row Using B, ch1, 1sc in each st to end. Turn.
3rd row Using C, ch1, 1sc in each of first 3sc, rep from * of first row, ending last rep 1sc in each of next 4sc. Turn.
4th row Using C, as 2nd row.
Rep first-4th rows to form pat, working in sequence of 2 rows each of C, B and A.

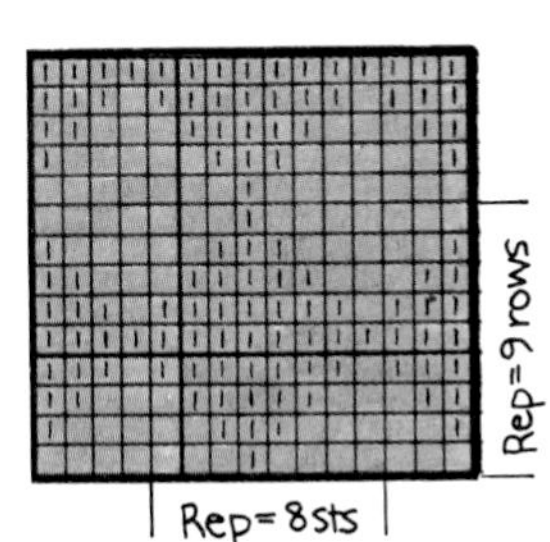

4 Follow chart and work as instructed for pat 1.

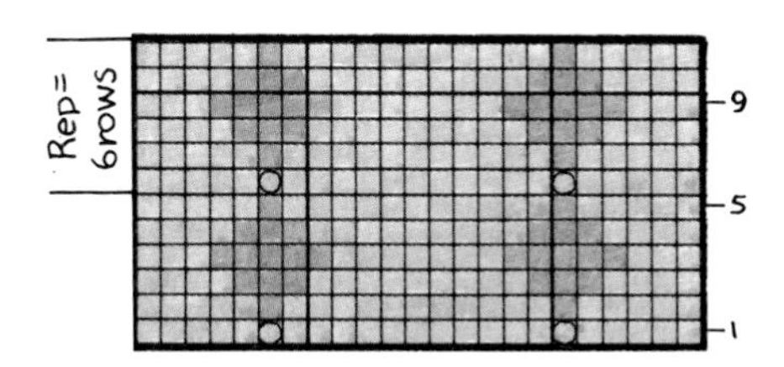

5 Follow chart and work as instructed for pat 2.

5

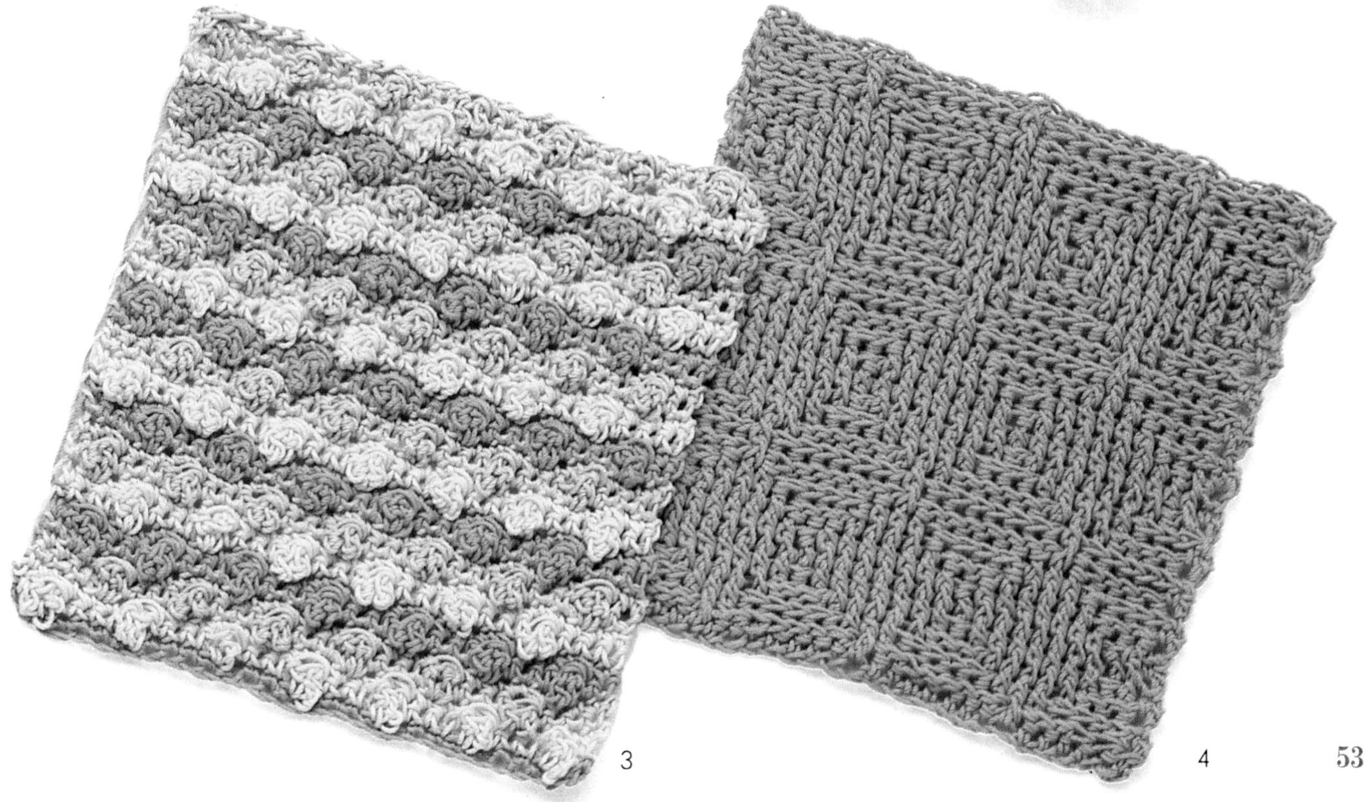
3
4

CABLES

Classic in shape, this V-neck mohair vest has a surface design reminiscent of bold knitted Aran cables. It can be easily converted to the design variation by adding long sleeves. The cables are created by simply crossing triples. More texture is added with bobbles.

► SIZES

To fit 32[34:36:38-40]"/81[86:91:96-102]cm bust.

Note: Figures for larger sizes are in brackets. If there is only one set of figures, it applies to all sizes.

See diagram for finished measurements.

Sleeves are added for the design variation. The cables and bobbles are shown here worked in white on a pale blue background.

► MATERIALS

See page 118 for further yarn information

12¼[14:14:15¾]oz of a lightweight mohair yarn (approx 170yd per 1¾oz)

Size G crochet hook *or size to obtain correct gauge*

► GAUGE

14 sts and 10 rows to 4" over pat of one row hdc and one row dc alternately using size G hook.

To save time, take time to check gauge.

► BACK

**Ch78[82:86:90].

Base row 1dc in 4th ch from hook, 1dc in each ch to end. Turn. 76[80:84:88] sts, counting turning ch as first st.

Beg rib as foll:

1st rib row Ch3 to count as first dc, skip first dc, *yo and insert hook from front to back and to front again around post of next dc, yo and draw a loop through, (yo and draw through 2 loops on hook) twice — called 1dc front —, yo and insert hook from back to front and to back again around post of next dc, yo and draw a loop through, (yo and draw through 2 loops on hook) twice — called 1dc back —, rep from *, ending with 1dc in 3rd of ch3. Turn. Last row forms rib pat. Rep last row once more.

Beg cable pat as foll:

1st pat row (RS) Ch3 to count as first dc, skip first dc, 1dc in each of next 7[9:10:12]dc, *skip next 2dc, 1tr in next dc, 2tr in next dc, then passing hook *behind* 3tr just made, work 1tr in first skipped dc and 2tr in 2nd skipped dc, skip next 2dc, 1tr in next dc, 2tr in next dc, then passing hook in *front* of 3tr just made, work 1tr in first skipped dc and 2tr in 2nd skipped dc*, 1dc in each of next 3dc, rep from * to * once, 1dc in each of next 22[22:24:24]dc, rep from * to * once, 1dc in each of next 3dc, rep from * to * once, 1dc in each of next 7[9:10:12]dc, 1dc in 3rd of ch3. Turn. 92[96:100:104] sts.

2nd row Ch2 to count as first hdc, skip first dc, 1hdc in each of next 7[9:10:12]dc, *1sc in each of next 12tr, 1hdc in each of next 3dc, 1sc in each of next 12tr*, 1hdc in each of next 22[22:24:24]dc, rep from * to * once, 1hdc in each of next 7[9:10:12]dc, 1hdc in 3rd of ch3. Turn.

3rd row Ch3, skip first hdc, 1dc in each of next 7[9:10:12]hdc, *skip next 3sc, 1tr in each of next 3sc, then passing hook in *front* of 3tr just made, work 1tr in first skipped sc, 1tr in 2nd skipped sc and 1tr in 3rd skipped sc — called front cross or FC —, skip next 3sc, 1tr in each of next 3sc, then passing hook *behind* 3tr just made, work 1tr in first skipped sc, 1tr in 2nd skipped sc and 1tr in 3rd skipped sc — called back cross or BC —, 1dc in each of next 3hdc, FC, BC*, 1dc in each of next 22[22:24:24]hdc, rep from * to * once, 1dc in each of next 7[9:10:12]hdc, 1dc in 2nd of ch2. Turn.

4th row (WS) Ch2, skip first dc, 1hdc in each of next 7[9:10:12]dc, *1sc in each of next 12tr, 1hdc in next dc, (1hdc, 3dc, 1hdc) all in next dc, remove hook from loop and reinsert in top of first hdc of group of 5 sts just made, then draw last loop through and push group of sts through to RS of work — called bobble —, 1hdc in next dc, 1sc in each of next 12tr*, 1hdc in each of next 22[22:24:24]dc, rep from * to * once, 1hdc in each of next 7[9:10:12]dc, 1hdc in 3rd of ch3. Turn.

5th row Ch3, skip first hdc, 1dc in each of next 7[9:10:12]hdc, *BC, FC, 1dc in each of next 3hdc, BC, FC*, 1dc in

each of next 22[22:24:24]hdc, rep from * to * once, 1dc in each of next 7[9:10:12]hdc, 1dc in 2nd of ch2. Turn.
2nd-5th rows form cable pat. Rep 2nd-5th rows 7 times more. Work 2nd pat row once. Back measures approx 14¾". Break off yarn and fasten off.**

Armhole shaping

Next row (RS) Skip first 7[9:10:12]hdc and rejoin yarn to 8th[10th:11th:13th]hdc with a sl st, ch3 to count as first dc, *FC, BC, 1dc in each of next 3hdc, FC, BC*, 1dc in each of next 22[22:24:24]hdc, rep from * to * once, 1dc in next hdc. Turn, leaving rem sts unworked. 78[78:80:80] sts.

Next row Ch2 to count as first hdc, skip first dc, rep from * to * of 4th pat row once, 1hdc in each of next 22[22:24:24]dc, rep from * to * once more, 1hdc in 3rd of ch3. Turn.

Next row Ch3 to count as first dc, skip first hdc, rep from * to * of 5th pat row once, 1dc in each of next 22[22:24:24]hdc, rep from * to * once more, 1dc in 2nd of ch2. Turn.

Cont in cable pat as set without shaping until 24[26:28:28] rows have been worked from beg of armhole, so ending with a 2nd[4th:2nd:2nd] pat row and working 8sc instead of 12sc across top of each of 4 cables in last row. Fasten off.

▶ FRONT

Work as for back from ** to **.

Neck and armhole shaping

Next row (RS) Skip first 7[9:10:12]hdc and rejoin yarn to 8th[10th:11th:13th]hdc with a sl st, ch3 to count as first dc, *FC, BC, 1dc in each of next 3hdc, FC, BC*, 1dc in each of next 9[9:10:10]hdc, (yo and insert hook in next hdc, yo and draw a loop through, yo and draw through 2 loops on hook) twice, yo and draw through all 3 loops on hook — called 2dc tog. Turn, leaving rem sts unworked. 38[38:39:39] sts.

Next row Ch2 to count as first hdc, skip first dc, 1hdc in each of next 9[9:10:10]hdc, rep from * to * of 4th pat row once, 1hdc in 3rd of ch3. Turn.

Next row Ch3 to count as first dc, skip first hdc, rep from * to * of 5th pat row once, 1dc in each of next 8[8:9:9]hdc, 2dc tog (working last dc of 2dc tog in 2nd of ch2). Turn. 37[37:38:38] sts.

Work one row in pat without shaping. Keeping armhole edge straight, cont in cable pat dec one st at neck edge on next row and then on every other row until 29[29:30:30] sts rem.

Cont in pat without shaping until there are same number of rows as back to shoulder, working 8sc instead of 12sc across top of each of 2 cables in last row. Fasten off.

With RS facing rejoin yarn with a sl st to first hdc (center front) of row where neck shaping was begun, ch3, 2dc tog, 1dc in each of next 8[8:9:9]hdc, *FC, BC, 1dc in each of next 3hdc, FC, BC*, 1dc in next hdc, turn, leaving rem 7[9:10:12] sts unworked. 38[38:39:39] sts.

Complete right side of neck as for left side, reversing shaping.

▶ ARMHOLE BANDS

Join shoulder and side seams. With RS facing and beg at side seam, join yarn to armhole edge with a sl st, ch3 to count as first dc, work 6[8:9:11]dc evenly along armhole shaping to corner, 1tr in corner, work 73[79:85:85]dc evenly along straight edge of armhole, 1tr in corner, 7[9:10:12]dc along armhole shaping to side seam, join with a sl st to 3rd of ch3, do not turn. 89[99:107:111] sts.

Beg rib as foll:

1st round Ch3, *1dc front, 1dc back, rep from * to end, join with a sl st to 3rd of ch3. Do not turn.

Rep last round once more and fasten off.

▶ FINISHING

Do not press. With RS facing and beg at right shoulder seam, work a round of sc evenly around neck edge, then work 2 rounds more working 1sc around post of each sc from front (see page 114). Fasten off. Edging will roll to RS.

DESIGN VARIATION

▶ PULLOVER WITH SLEEVES

For a pullover with sleeves make back and front as for sleeveless pullover. For sleeves ch28[31:34:34] and work base row as for back. 26[29:32:32] sts.

Work 2 rows in rib as for back.

Next row Ch3 to count as first dc, skip first dc, *2dc in next dc, rep from *, 1dc in 3rd of ch3. Turn. 50[56:62:62] sts.

Next row Ch2 to count as first hdc, skip first dc, *1hdc in next dc, rep from *,1hdc in 3rd of ch3. Turn.

Next row Ch3, skip first hdc, *1dc in next hdc, rep from *, 1dc in 2nd of ch2. Turn. Last 2 rows form pat.

Cont in pat inc one st at each end of next row and every foll 4th row 8 times. 68[74:80:80] sts.

Cont in pat without shaping until sleeve measures 19¼" from beg. Fasten off.

Join shoulder seams. Sew sleeves to armholes. Join side and sleeve seams. Finish as for sleeveless version.

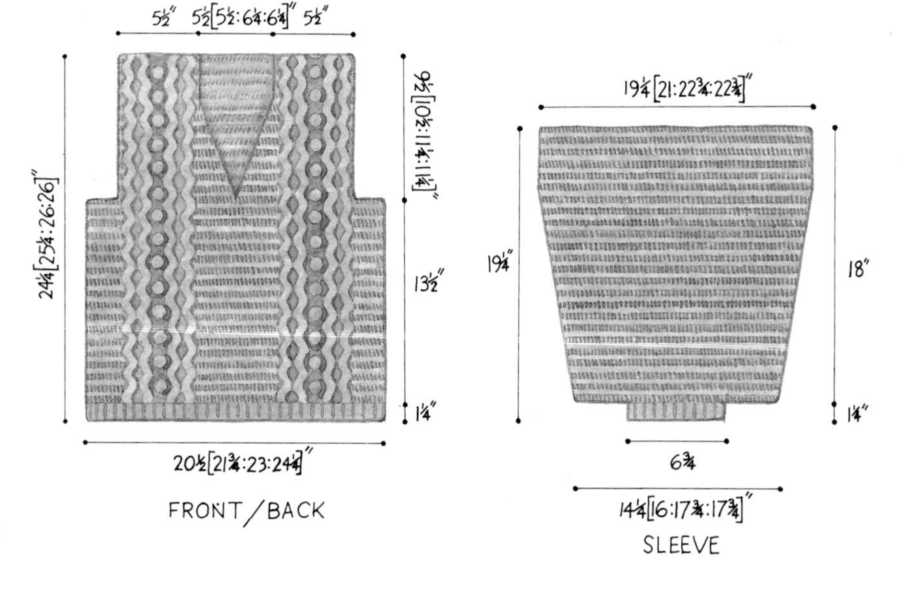

ZIGZAGS

This backless top with long sleeves is worked in half doubles. A deep crochet rib fits the waist snuggly and bobbles form zigzag panels down both sides of the front and back.

▶ SIZES

To fit 32[34:36:38]"/81[86:91:96]cm bust.

Note: Figures for larger sizes are in brackets. If there is only one set of figures, it applies to all sizes.

See diagram for finished measurements.

▶ MATERIALS

See page 118 for further yarn information

14[14:15¾:15¾]oz of a fine slubbed cotton and linen yarn (approx 186yd per 1¾oz)

Size F crochet hook *or size to obtain correct gauge*

Shoulder pads

▶ GAUGE

18hdc and 15½ rows to 4" using size F hook.

20sc and 21 rows slightly stretched over rib pat using size F hook.

To save time, take time to check gauge.

Note: Body is worked in one piece to armholes and then divided for backs and front.

▶ BODY

Ch29[31:31:33] and beg rib as foll:

Base rib row 1sc in 2nd ch from hook, 1sc in each ch to end. Turn. 28[30:30:32]sc.

1st rib row Ch1, working in *back* loops only, 1sc in each sc to end. Turn.

Rep last row to form rib pat. Cont in rib pat until 135[143:151:157] rows have been worked from beg, counting base row. Fasten off.

Turn rib sideways and work sts for body along rib row ends as foll:

Rejoin yarn with a sl st to end of foundation row, ch2, 2hdc in same place as sl st, 1hdc in each of next 2[4:5:6] row ends, (2hdc in next row end, 1hdc in each of next 5 row ends) 4 times, *2hdc in next row end, 1hdc in each of next 0[1:2:3] row ends, 2hdc in next row end, 1hdc in each of next 1[2:3:4] row ends*, (2hdc in next row end, 1hdc in each of next 2 row ends, 2hdc in next row end, 1hdc in each of next 3 row ends) 9 times, rep from * to * once, (2hdc in next row end, 1hdc in each of next 5 row ends) 4 times, 2hdc in next row end, 1hdc in each of next 1[3:4:5] row ends, turn leaving rem 13[13:15:15] row ends unworked. 154[162:168:174]hdc.

Next row Ch2, working in *both* loops throughout, 1hdc in each hdc to end. Turn.

Beg bobble pat as foll:

1st pat row (RS) Ch2, 1hdc in each of first 1[1:2:2]hdc, *(1hdc, 3dc, 1hdc) all in next hdc, remove hook from loop and reinsert in top of first hdc of group of 5 sts just made, then draw last loop through — called bobble —, (1hdc in next hdc, 1 bobble in next hdc) 3 times*, 1hdc in each of next 47[51:51:53]hdc, rep from * to * once, 1hdc in each of next 30[30:34:36]hdc, rep from * to * once, 1hdc in each of next 47[51:51:53]hdc, rep from * to * once, 1hdc in each of last 1[1:2:2]hdc. Turn. 154[162:168:174] sts.

2nd and all WS rows Ch2, 1hdc in each hdc and each bobble to end. Turn.

3rd row Ch2, 1hdc in each of first 5[5:6:6]hdc, *1 bobble in next hdc, (1hdc in next hdc, 1 bobble in next hdc) 3 times*, 1hdc in each of next 39[43:43:45]hdc, rep from * to * once, 1hdc in each of next 38[38:42:44]hdc, rep from * to * once, 1hdc in each of next 39[43:43:45]hdc, rep from * to * once, 1hdc in each of last 5[5:6:6]hdc. Turn.

5th row Ch2, 1hdc in each of first 9[9:10:10]hdc, *1 bobble in next hdc, (1hdc in next hdc, 1 bobble in next hdc) 3 times*, 1hdc in each of next 31[35:35:37]hdc, rep from * to * once, 1hdc in each of next 46[46:50:52]hdc, rep from * to * once, 1hdc in each of next 31[35:35:37]hdc, rep from * to * once, 1hdc in each of last 9[9:10:10]hdc. Turn.

7th row Ch2, 1hdc in each of first 13[13:14:14]hdc, *1 bobble in next hdc, (1hdc in next hdc, 1 bobble in next hdc) 3 times*, 1hdc in each of next 23[27:27:29]hdc, rep from * to * once, 1hdc in each of next 54[54:58:60]hdc, rep from * to * once, 1hdc in each of next 23[27:27:29]hdc, rep from * to * once, 1hdc in each of last 13[13:14:14]hdc. Turn.

9th row As 5th row.

11th row As 3rd row.

12th row As 2nd row.

First-12th rows form bobble pat. Cont in bobble pat until body measures 6¾" from rib, ending with a WS row.

Left back and armhole shaping

Next row Work in pat over first 27[29:30:31]hdc. Turn, leaving rem 127[133:138:143] sts unworked.

Next row Ch1, 1 sl st in each of first 2hdc (armhole edge), ch2, work in pat to end. Turn. 25[27:28:29]hdc.

Keeping to pat, dec one st at armhole edge on next row and on every foll row 1[2:2:3] times more. 23[24:25:25] sts.

Note: To dec one st at end of row work to last 2 sts, (yo and insert hook in next st, yo and draw a loop through) twice, yo and draw through all 5 loops on hook — called 2hdc tog. To dec one st at beg of row work 2hdc tog over first 2 sts.

Work one row without shaping. Dec one st at armhole edge on next row. Rep from ** to ** once more. 21[22:23:23] sts.

Cont in pat without shaping until armhole measures 7¾[8¼:8½:9]", ending with a WS row. Fasten off.

Front and armhole shaping

With RS facing, return to rem sts and skip next 9 sts on body (after left back), rejoin yarn to next st with a sl st, ch2,

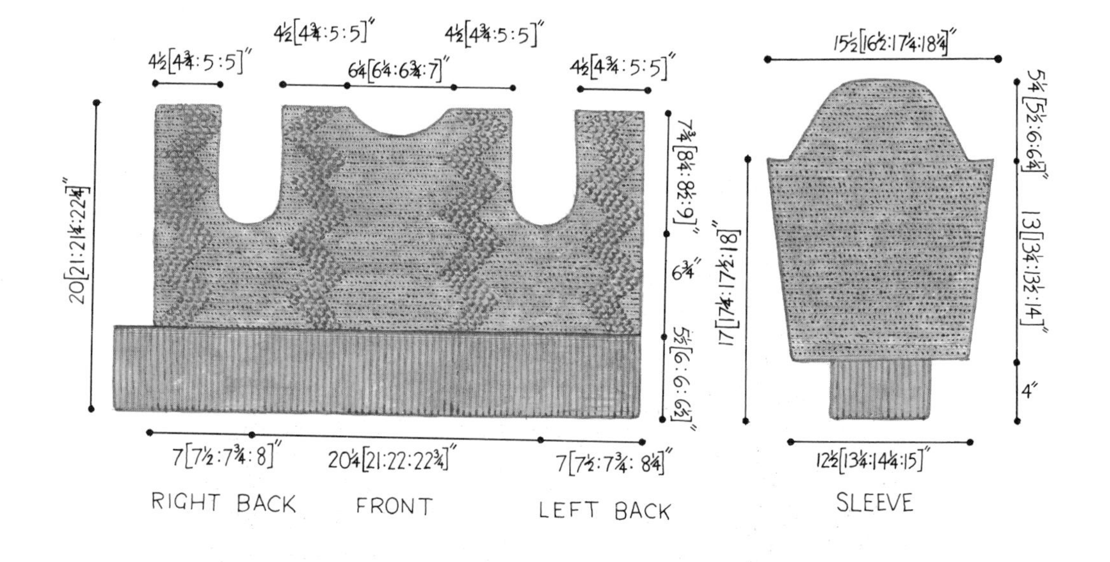

1hdc in same place as sl st, keeping to pat as set work across next 81[85:89:93]hdc, turn leaving rem 36[38:39:40]hdc unworked. 82[86:90:94]sts.
Next row Ch1, 1 sl st in each of first 2hdc, ch2, work in pat across next 78[82:86:90] sts. Turn, leaving rem 2 sts unworked.
Keeping to pat, dec one st at each end of next row and on every foll row 1[2:2:3] times more. 74[76:80:82] sts.
Work one row without shaping. Dec one st at each end of next row.
Rep from *** to *** once more. 70[72:76:78] sts.
Cont in pat until front has 7 rows less than left back, so ending with a RS row.

Front neck shaping
Next row (WS) Work in pat across first 26[27:28:28] sts. Turn, leaving rem 44[45:48:50] sts unworked.
Next row (RS) Ch1, 1 sl st in each of first 2hdc (neck edge), work in pat to end. Turn. 24[25:26:26] sts.
Keeping to pat, dec one st at neck edge on next row and on every foll row twice more. 21[22:23:23] sts.
Work 2 rows without shaping. Fasten off.
With WS facing, return to rem sts at center front and skip next 18[18:20:22] sts for center front neck, rejoin yarn to next st with a sl st, ch2, 1hdc in same place as sl st, work in pat across rem 25[26:27:27] sts, turn. 26[27:28:28] sts.
Complete 2nd side of neck as for first side, reversing shaping.

Right back and armhole shaping
With RS facing, skip next 9 sts on body (after front) and rejoin yarn to next st with a sl st, ch2, 1hdc in same place as sl st, work in pat across rem 26[28:29:30] sts, turn. 27[29:30:31] sts.
Complete right back as for left back, reversing shaping.

▶ SLEEVES (make 2)
Ch21 and work base and first rib rows as for body rib. 20sc.
Cont in rib pat as for body rib until 32[34:36:38] rows have been worked from beg, counting base row. Do not fasten off.
Turn rib sideways and work sts for sleeve along rib row ends as foll:
Ch2, 2hdc in each of first 4[5:6:7] row ends, (1hdc in next row end, 2hdc in each of next 2 row ends) 8 times, 2hdc in each of last 4[5:6:7] row ends, turn. 56[60:64:68]hdc.
Next row Ch2, working in *both* loops throughout, 1hdc in each hdc to end. Turn.
Rep last row once more.
Next row Ch2, 2hdc in first hdc, 1hdc in each hdc to last hdc, 2hdc in last hdc. Turn. 58[62:66:70]hdc.
Work 4 rows in hdc without shaping. Inc one st at each end of next row.
Rep from * to * 5 times more. 70[74:78:82] sts.
Cont in hdc without shaping until sleeve measures 17[17¼:17½:18]" from beg, including rib.

Cap shaping
Next row Ch1, 1 sl st in each of first 5hdc, ch2, 1hdc in each hdc to last 5hdc. Turn, leaving rem 5hdc unworked. 60[64:68:72]hdc.
Cont in hdc, dec one st at each end of next and every foll row 17[18:19:21] times in all. 26[28:30:30]hdc.
Dec 2 sts at each end of next and every foll row 3 times in all. 14[16:18:18]hdc. Fasten off.

▶ FINISHING
Do not press. Join shoulder seams. Join cuff and sleeve seams. Set in sleeves, easing in fullness at top. Join rib seam at back.
With RS facing, work sc evenly up left back, along front neck, down right back and along top of ribbing (easing tog ribbing slightly) to left back, cont around working 1sc around post of each sc from front (see page 114) to end of round. Fasten off.
Sew in shoulder pads.

CLUSTERS

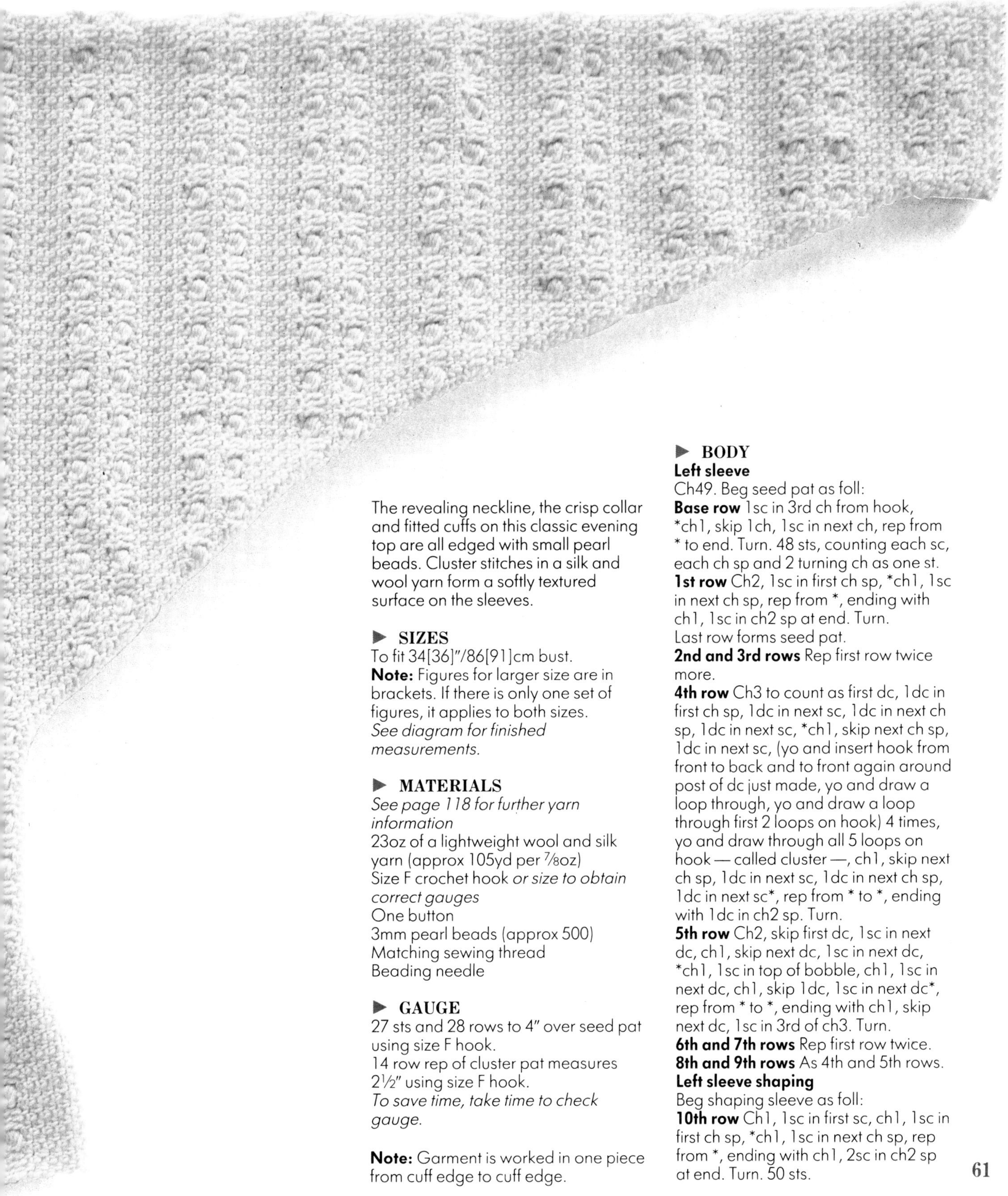

The revealing neckline, the crisp collar and fitted cuffs on this classic evening top are all edged with small pearl beads. Cluster stitches in a silk and wool yarn form a softly textured surface on the sleeves.

▶ SIZES

To fit 34[36]"/86[91]cm bust.

Note: Figures for larger size are in brackets. If there is only one set of figures, it applies to both sizes.

See diagram for finished measurements.

▶ MATERIALS

See page 118 for further yarn information

23oz of a lightweight wool and silk yarn (approx 105yd per 7/8oz)

Size F crochet hook *or size to obtain correct gauges*

One button

3mm pearl beads (approx 500)

Matching sewing thread

Beading needle

▶ GAUGE

27 sts and 28 rows to 4" over seed pat using size F hook.

14 row rep of cluster pat measures 2½" using size F hook.

To save time, take time to check gauge.

Note: Garment is worked in one piece from cuff edge to cuff edge.

▶ BODY

Left sleeve

Ch49. Beg seed pat as foll:

Base row 1sc in 3rd ch from hook, *ch1, skip 1ch, 1sc in next ch, rep from * to end. Turn. 48 sts, counting each sc, each ch sp and 2 turning ch as one st.

1st row Ch2, 1sc in first ch sp, *ch1, 1sc in next ch sp, rep from *, ending with ch1, 1sc in ch2 sp at end. Turn.

Last row forms seed pat.

2nd and 3rd rows Rep first row twice more.

4th row Ch3 to count as first dc, 1dc in first ch sp, 1dc in next sc, 1dc in next ch sp, 1dc in next sc, *ch1, skip next ch sp, 1dc in next sc, (yo and insert hook from front to back and to front again around post of dc just made, yo and draw a loop through, yo and draw a loop through first 2 loops on hook) 4 times, yo and draw through all 5 loops on hook — called cluster —, ch1, skip next ch sp, 1dc in next sc, 1dc in next ch sp, 1dc in next sc*, rep from * to *, ending with 1dc in ch2 sp. Turn.

5th row Ch2, skip first dc, 1sc in next dc, ch1, skip next dc, 1sc in next dc, *ch1, 1sc in top of bobble, ch1, 1sc in next dc, ch1, skip 1dc, 1sc in next dc*, rep from * to *, ending with ch1, skip next dc, 1sc in 3rd of ch3. Turn.

6th and 7th rows Rep first row twice.

8th and 9th rows As 4th and 5th rows.

Left sleeve shaping

Beg shaping sleeve as foll:

10th row Ch1, 1sc in first sc, ch1, 1sc in first ch sp, *ch1, 1sc in next ch sp, rep from *, ending with ch1, 2sc in ch2 sp at end. Turn. 50 sts.

11th row Ch1, 1sc in first sc, ch1, skip next sc, 1sc in first ch sp, *ch1, 1sc in next ch sp, rep from *, 1sc in last sc. Turn.
12th row Ch2, 1sc in first sc, ch1, skip next sc, 1sc in first ch sp, *ch1, 1sc in next ch sp, rep from *, ending with ch1, 1sc in last sc. Turn. 52 sts.
13th row As first row.
14th-17th rows As 10th to 13th rows. 56 sts.
18th row Ch3 to count as first dc, 1dc in first sc, 1dc in first ch sp, 1dc in next sc, rep from * to * of 4th row, working last 2dc of last rep in ch2 sp at end. Turn. 58 sts, counting each cluster, each dc and each ch sp.
19th row Ch1, 1sc in first dc, ch1, skip next dc, 1sc in next dc, rep from * to * of 5th row, ending with 1sc in 3rd of ch3. Turn.
20th and 21st rows As 12th and 13th rows. 60 sts.
22nd row Ch3, 1dc in first sc, 1dc in first ch sp, 1dc in next sc, 1dc in next ch sp, 1dc in next sc, rep from * to * of 4th row, ending with 2dc in ch2 sp at end. Turn. 62 sts.
23rd row Ch1, 1sc in first dc, (ch1, skip next dc, 1sc in next dc) twice, rep from * to * of 5th row, ending with ch1, skip next dc, 1sc in next dc, 1sc in 3rd of ch3. Turn.
Cont in this way inc one st at each end of next and every foll alternate row *and at the same time* keeping to cluster pat of 9 rows seed pat, one cluster row, 3 rows seed pat, one cluster row until 5 pairs of cluster rows have been worked from beg, then work 8 rows in seed pat still inc one st at each end of every alternate row. 112 sts.

Note: As sleeve widens add clusters, keeping pat correct and lining clusters up with clusters in previous rows.
Cont in cluster and seed pats as set, inc one st at each end of next row and every foll row until 8 pairs of cluster rows have been worked from beg, then work 7 rows in seed pat still inc one st at each end of every row. 194 sts. Break off yarn and set piece aside.

Front hip extension
Ch19[23] and work base row as for beg of cuff. 18[22] sts.
1st inc row (RS) Ch2, 1sc in first sc, ch1, 1sc in first ch sp, work in seed pat to end. Turn. 20[24] sts.
2nd inc row Work in seed pat to end, ending with 1sc, ch1, 1sc all in ch2 sp. Turn. 22[26] sts.
Rep last 2 rows 3 times more. 34[38] sts.
Break off yarn and fasten off.

Back hip extension
Ch19 and work base row as for beg of cuff. 18[22] sts.
1st inc row As 2nd inc row of front hip extension. 20[24] sts.
2nd inc row As first inc row of front hip extension. 22[26] sts.
Rep last 2 rows 3 times more. 34[38] sts.
Do not break off yarn.

Joining
Using a separate ball of yarn, make one length of 23[25]ch and one length of 25[27]ch and set aside for next row.
Join hip extensions to sleeve as foll: With RS of back hip extension facing, work in seed pat to end of piece, ch1, 1sc in first ch of length of 23[25]ch, *ch1, skip next ch, 1sc in next ch*, rep from * to * across ch, ch1, with RS of sleeve facing work 1sc in first sc, skip 2nd of first 2sc at beg of row, ch1, 1sc in first ch sp, cont in seed pat to end of sleeve, ch1, skip 1sc at end of row, 1sc in first ch of length of 25[27]ch, rep from * to * across ch, with RS of front hip extension facing work 1sc in first ch sp, work in seed pat to end. Turn. 312[324] sts.
Work one row in seed pat.
Work one cluster row, 3 seed pat rows and one cluster row.
Cont in seed pat only, work 25[27] rows more, so ending with a WS row.

Back neck shaping
Next row (RS) Work in seed pat across first 154[160] sts. Turn, leaving rem sts unworked.
Cont on these sts only, dec one st at beg of next row (neck edge). Dec one st at neck edge on next row and then on every foll alternate row twice more. 150[156] sts.
Work 26 rows without shaping, so ending with a RS row.
Inc one st at beg of next row (neck edge). Work one row without shaping.
Rep last 2 rows once more.
Inc one st at neck edge on next 2 rows. 154[160] sts.
Break off yarn and fasten off.

Front neck shaping
With RS facing, skip 11 sts on row where back neck shaping began and rejoin yarn to next st (a ch sp) with a sl st, ch1, 1sc in same place as sl st was worked, work in pat to end of row, turn. 147[153] sts.
Dec 2 sts at end of next row (front neck edge), dec one st at neck edge on next 5 rows. Work one row without shaping, so ending with a WS row.

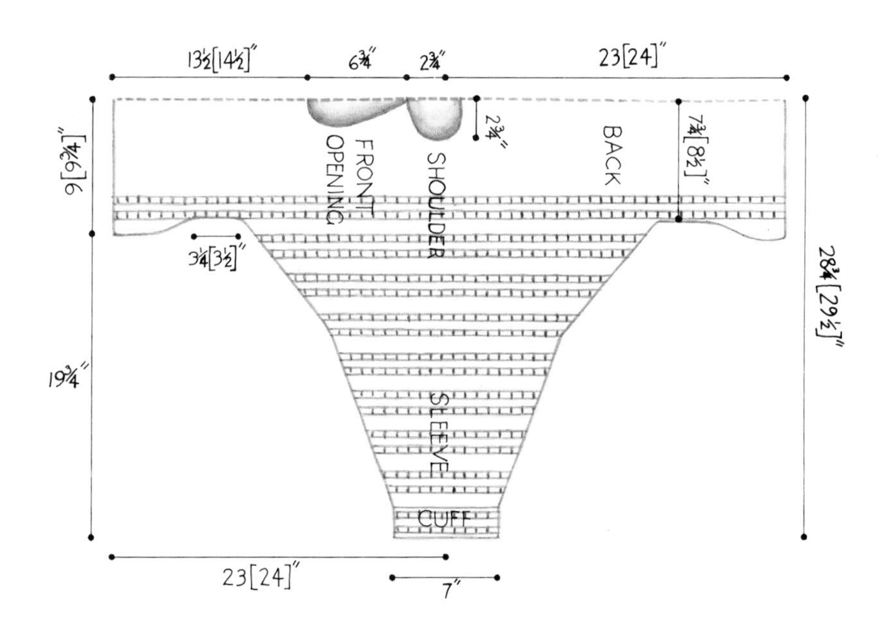

Lower neckline shaping
Dec one st at beg of next row (RS) and work in pat until there are 23 sts, turn leaving rem sts unworked.
Cont on these sts only, dec 2 sts at beg (lower neckline edge) of next row.
Dec one st at beg (neck edge) of next row and 2 sts at end of row.
Keeping neck edge straight, dec 2 sts at lower neckline edge on every row until 2 sts rem. Fasten off.
To complete lower neckline edge, return to row where lower neckline shaping began and with RS facing skip next 19 sts, rejoin yarn with a sl st to next st (ch sp), ch1, 1sc in same place as sl st, work in pat to end of row, turn. 100[106] sts.
Dec one st at end of next row (neckline edge). Dec one st at neckline edge on next 3 rows.
Work one row without shaping. Dec one st at neckline edge on next row. 92[98] sts.
Work 10 rows without shaping.
Inc one st at neckline edge on next row. Work one row without shaping.
Inc one st at neckline edge on next 4 rows, so ending with a RS row. 100[106] sts. Do not break off yarn.
Beg shaped piece for right front neck as foll:
Using a separate ball of yarn, ch3 and work base row in sc. 2sc.
Next row (WS) Ch2, 1sc in first sc, ch1, 1sc in next sc. Turn. 4 sts.
Cont in seed pat inc 2 sts at end (neckline edge) of next row. Inc 2 sts at neckline edge on next 6 rows, so ending with a RS row. 18 sts.
Inc 2 sts at beg (neckline edge) of next row and one st at end (neck edge) of row. Inc 2 sts at neckline edge on next row. 23 sts.
Break off yarn and fasten off.
Make a length of 19ch and set aside for next row.
Return to last row worked on body and with WS facing work from lower edge of front to neckline edge, work across 19ch, then cont in pat across shaped piece for right front neck, inc one st at end of row (neck edge). 140[146] sts.
Work one row without shaping.
Inc one st at neck edge on next 5 rows.
Inc 2 sts at neck edge on next row, so ending with a RS row. 147[153] sts.
Do not break off yarn.
Joining front and back
Using a separate ball of yarn, make a length of 11ch and set aside for next row.
With WS facing, beg at lower front edge and work in pat to front neck edge, work in pat across 11ch, then with WS of back facing work in pat across back. 312[324] sts.
Work 24[26] rows in seed pat, so ending with a WS row. Work one cluster row, work 3 rows in seed pat, work one cluster row, work 2 rows in seed pat, so ending with a RS row.
Right front hip shaping
Next row Work in pat across first 34[38] sts. Turn, leaving rem sts unworked.
Dec 2 sts at beg of next row. Then keeping lower edge of front straight, dec 2 sts at same edge as last dec on next 7 rows. 18[22] sts. Fasten off.
Right back hip shaping
With WS facing, rejoin yarn to back and work across last 34[38] sts of row.
Dec 2 sts at end of next row. Then keeping lower edge of back straight, complete shaping as for right front hip shaping. Fasten off.
Right sleeve
With WS facing, return to last row of body where hip shaping began, skip first 25[27] sts and work in pat across center 194 sts.
Keeping to pat as set for left sleeve, dec one st at each end of every row 42 times.
Work one row without shaping. Dec one st at each end of next row.
Rep last 2 rows 30 times more. 48 sts.
Work 9 rows without shaping. Fasten off.

▶ **COLLAR**
Ch121 and work base and first rows as for beg of left cuff. 120 sts.
Cont in seed pat until 10 rows have been worked from beg, counting base row.
Next row Ch1, skip first sc, 1sc in next ch sp, *skip next sc, 1sc in next ch sp, rep from * to end.
Fasten off.

▶ **FINISHING**
Do not press.
Neck edging
With RS facing, work a row of sc evenly around neck edge and neckline edge, join with a sl st to first sc. Fasten off.
Join collar to neck edge. Join side and sleeve seam.
Using a beading needle, string pearl beads onto a matching thread. Couch thread in place between each pearl bead around cuffs, neckline and collar.
Sew button to left side of front at neckline. Sew a buttonhole loop to right side of front opposite button.

BASKETWEAVE

Worked in a smooth, shiny mercerized cotton, this basketweave top with half sleeves can also be made into a sleeveless top. A bobbled edging and knitted ribbing trim the neckline and sleeves.

▶ SIZES

To fit 34[36:38]"/86[91:96]cm bust.
Note: Figures for larger sizes are in brackets. If there is only one set of figures, it applies to all sizes.
See diagram for finished measurements.

▶ MATERIALS

See page 118 for further yarn information
25[26¼:28]oz (approx 202yd per 1¾oz) of a lightweight cotton yarn
Size G crochet hook *or size to obtain correct gauge*
One pair of size 5 knitting needles

▶ GAUGE

20 sts and 19 rows to 4" over pat using size G hook.
To save time, take time to check gauge.

Note: When decreasing for neck, work one st dec by inserting hook around last 2 or first 2 hdc of row, keeping edge st in sc. When increasing for sleeve, work one st inc by working 2 sts around first or last hdc of row, keeping edge st in sc.

▶ BACK

Using hook, ch114[118:122].
Base row 1hdc in 3rd ch from hook, 1hdc in each ch to end. Turn. 112[116:120]hdc.
1st row (WS) Ch1, 1sc in first hdc, yo and insert hook from back to front and to back again around post of next hdc, yo and draw a loop through, yo and draw through all 3 loops on hook — called 1hdc back —, 1hdc back around each of next 0[2:4]hdc, yo and insert hook from front to back and to front again around post of next hdc, yo and draw a loop through, yo and draw through all 3 loops on hook — called 1hdc front —, 1hdc front around each of next 11hdc, *1hdc back around each of next 12hdc, 1hdc front around each of next 12hdc, rep from *, ending with 1hdc back around each of next 1[3:5]hdc, 1sc in last hdc. Turn. 112[116:120] sts.
2nd row (RS) Ch1, 1sc in first sc, 1hdc front around each of next 1[3:5]hdc, 1hdc back around each of next 12hdc, *1hdc front around each of next 12hdc, 1hdc back around each of next 12hdc, rep from *, ending with 1hdc front around each of next 1[3:5]hdc, 1sc in last sc. Turn.
3rd row Ch1, 1sc in first sc, 1hdc back around each of next 1[3:5]hdc, 1hdc front around each of next 12hdc, *1hdc back around each of next 12hdc, 1hdc front around each of next 12hdc, rep from *, ending with 1hdc back around each of next 1[3:5]hdc, 1sc in last sc. Turn.
4th row Ch1, 1sc in first sc, 1hdc front around each hdc to last sc, 1sc in last sc. Turn.
5th row As 2nd row.
6th row As 3rd row.
7th row As 2nd row.
8th row As 4th row.
9th row As 3rd row.
Rep 2nd-9th rows to form pat. Cont in pat until back measures 13" from beg, ending with a WS row.

Armhole shaping
Break off yarn and fasten off.
Keeping pat correct and with RS facing, skip first 14[15:16] sts and rejoin yarn to top of next st with a sl st, 1sc in same place as sl st, work in pat to last 15[16:17] sts, 1sc in top of next st. Turn, leaving rem 14[15:16] sts unworked. 84[86:88] sts.
Work in pat without shaping until armhole measures 9½[10:10½]", ending with a WS row.

Shoulder and neck shaping
Break off yarn and fasten off. Keeping pat correct, and with RS facing, skip first 4[5:6] sts, rejoin yarn to top of next st with a sl st, 1sc in same place as sl st, work in pat over next 21hdc, 1sc in top of next st, turn leaving rem 57[58:59] sts unworked. 23 sts.
Work first side of neck on these sts, dec one st at neck edge on next row (see Note above) and on every foll row 3 times in all *and at the same time* dec 5 sts at armhole edge on every row 3 times in all. 5 sts. Fasten off.
With RS facing, skip center 30 sts for center back neck and rejoin yarn to top of next st with a sl st, 1sc in same place as sl st, work in pat over next 21hdc, 1sc in top of next st, turn leaving rem 4[5:6] sts unworked. 23 sts.
Complete 2nd side of neck as for first side, reversing shaping.

▶ FRONT

Work as for back until armhole measures 6½[7:7½]", ending with a WS row.

Neck shaping
Keeping pat correct and with RS facing, work in pat across first 32[33:34] sts, 1sc in top of next st, turn leaving rem 51[52:53] sts unworked. 33[:34:35] sts.
Work first side of neck on these sts, dec one st at neck edge on next row and on every foll row 6 times in all, then on every alternate row 3 times. 24[25:26] sts.
Work without shaping until there are same number of rows as back to shoulder. Work shoulder shaping as for back.
With RS facing, skip 18 sts for center front neck and rejoin yarn to top of next st with a sl st, 1sc in same place as sl st, work in pat over last 32[33:34] sts, turn. 33[34:35] sts.

The sleeveless variation still retains the bobbled neck edging and ribbing.

Complete 2nd side of neck as for first side, reversing shaping.

▶ **SLEEVES** (make 2)
Using hook, ch86[90:94].
Work base row as for back. 84[88:92] sts.
1st row (WS) Ch1, 1sc in first hdc, 1hdc back around each of first 0[1:3]hdc, 1hdc front around each of next 11[12:12]hdc, *1hdc back around each of next 12hdc, 1hdc front around each of next 12hdc, rep from *, ending last rep 1hdc front around each of next 11[12:12]hdc, 1hdc back around each of next 0[1:3]hdc, 1sc in last hdc. Turn.
Cont in pat as set on back, inc one st at each end of every 5th row 6 times in all (see Note above), incorporating extra sts into pat. 96[100:104] sts.
Work without shaping until sleeve measures 9½" from beg. Fasten off.

▶ **BOBBLE EDGING**
Join left shoulder seam.
Using hook and with RS facing, beg at right shoulder and work 44sc evenly along back neck, work 56sc evenly along front neck. 100sc.
Break off yarn and fasten off.
Using hook and with RS facing, rejoin yarn to first sc with a sl st, ch2, 1hdc in same place as sl st, 5hdc in next sc, remove hook from loop and reinsert in top of first hdc of 5hdc group, then draw last loop through — called bobble —, *1hdc in each of next 3sc, 1 bobble in next sc, rep from *, ending with 1hdc in each of last 2sc. Fasten off.
Work 84sc along lower edge of sleeves and work bobble edging as for neck.

▶ **NECKBAND**
Using knitting needles and with RS facing, beg at right shoulder and pick up and K57 sts evenly along bobble edging of back neck, pick up and K66 sts evenly along front neck edge. 123 sts.
Work in K1, P1 rib (beg and ending first row with P1) for 2¼". Bind off loosely in rib.

▶ **CUFFS**
Using knitting needles and with RS facing, pick up and K105[111:117] sts evenly along bobble edging at lower edge of sleeve. Work rib as for neckband for 2¼". Bind off loosely in rib.

▶ **FINISHING**
Press pieces very lightly on WS with a damp cloth and warm iron. Join right shoulder and neckband seam. Sew top of sleeve to vertical edge of armhole. Sew horizontal edge of armhole to side of sleeve. Join side and sleeve seams. Using hook and with RS facing, work 2 rounds of sc evenly along lower edge of back and front. Fasten off.

DESIGN VARIATION

▶ **SLEEVELESS TOP**
For sleeveless top omit sleeves. Work neckband as for version with sleeves. Join right shoulder seam and work 96[100:104]sc evenly along vertical edge of each armhole. Work bobble edging along these sc as for neck. Using knitting needles and with RS facing, pick up and K129[135:141] sts evenly along bobble edging. Work in rib as for neckband for 2¼". Bind off loosely in rib. Sew sides of ribbing to horizontal edges of armhole. Join side seams.

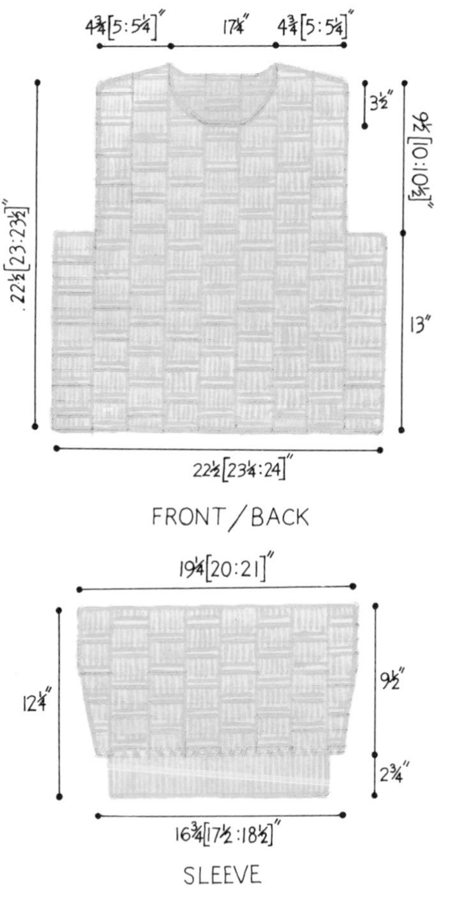

MOTIFS & PATTERNS

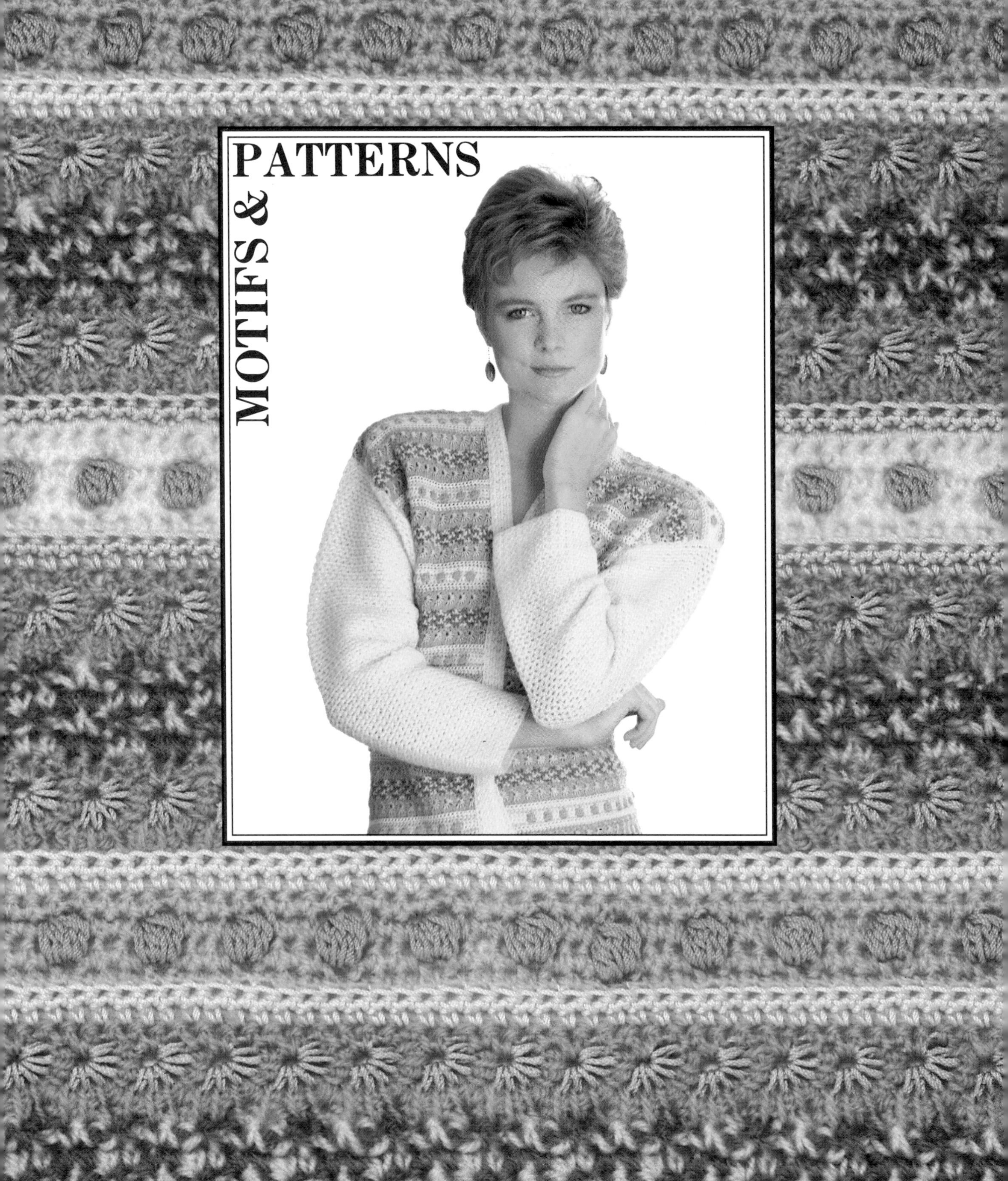

MOTIFS & PATTERNS

Color patterns are probably the most neglected area of crochet, so creative crocheters would do well to apply their talents to charted designs — from pictorial to *trompe l'oeil* to motifs and Fair Isle type patterns. The samples shown here, which include only a few of the various types of charted colorwork motifs, patterns and color stitches, give a hint of the hidden scope of simple crochet.

▶ FAIR ISLE CROCHET

Although Fair Isle is the technical term used for a specific type of knitting pattern originating in the Fair Isles of Scotland, the term has come to describe a particular type of design which is composed of detailed color patterns worked alternately and repeated in stripes. Fair Isle denotes a delicacy rather than a boldness of pattern and color. Used broadly it can be used to describe the colorwork on sample 5 or on *Bobbled Fair Isle* on page 90. The simple formula for composing original Fair Isle crochet designs is to make up three or more patterned stripes in contrasting colors, then combine and repeat these stripes.

▶ COLOR STITCHES

Some crochet stitch patterns, which are constructed by combining different types of basic stitches, are worked in two or three colors. Elongated stitches (6, 7 and 8 — see page 70) and the diamond patterns (1 and 2) are examples of this method of colorwork. There are many other crochet color stitch patterns, but these two types are interesting because of their flexibility. By working some of the diamonds or half diamonds in a contrasting color, horizontal or vertical stripes, circles, large Argyll-type diamonds and triangles can be formed. Any of these would be attractive substitutes for *Diamonds* on page 80. Elongated stitches look striking worked in a yarn which contrasts in texture with the background. Samples 6, 7 and 8 have repeating motifs which are worked over nine stitches like the motif on *Fans* on page 72. They could therefore be used instead of the fans on the sweater.

1 See page 80 for diamond stitch symbol chart. Work diamonds in colors as above.

2 See page 80 for diamond stitch symbol chart. Using separate lengths of contrasting yarn, work random diamonds into a solid background as indicated here.

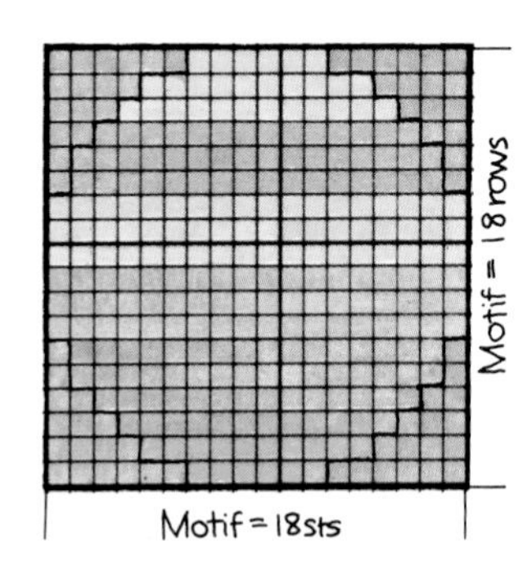

3 Afghan crochet knit stitch.

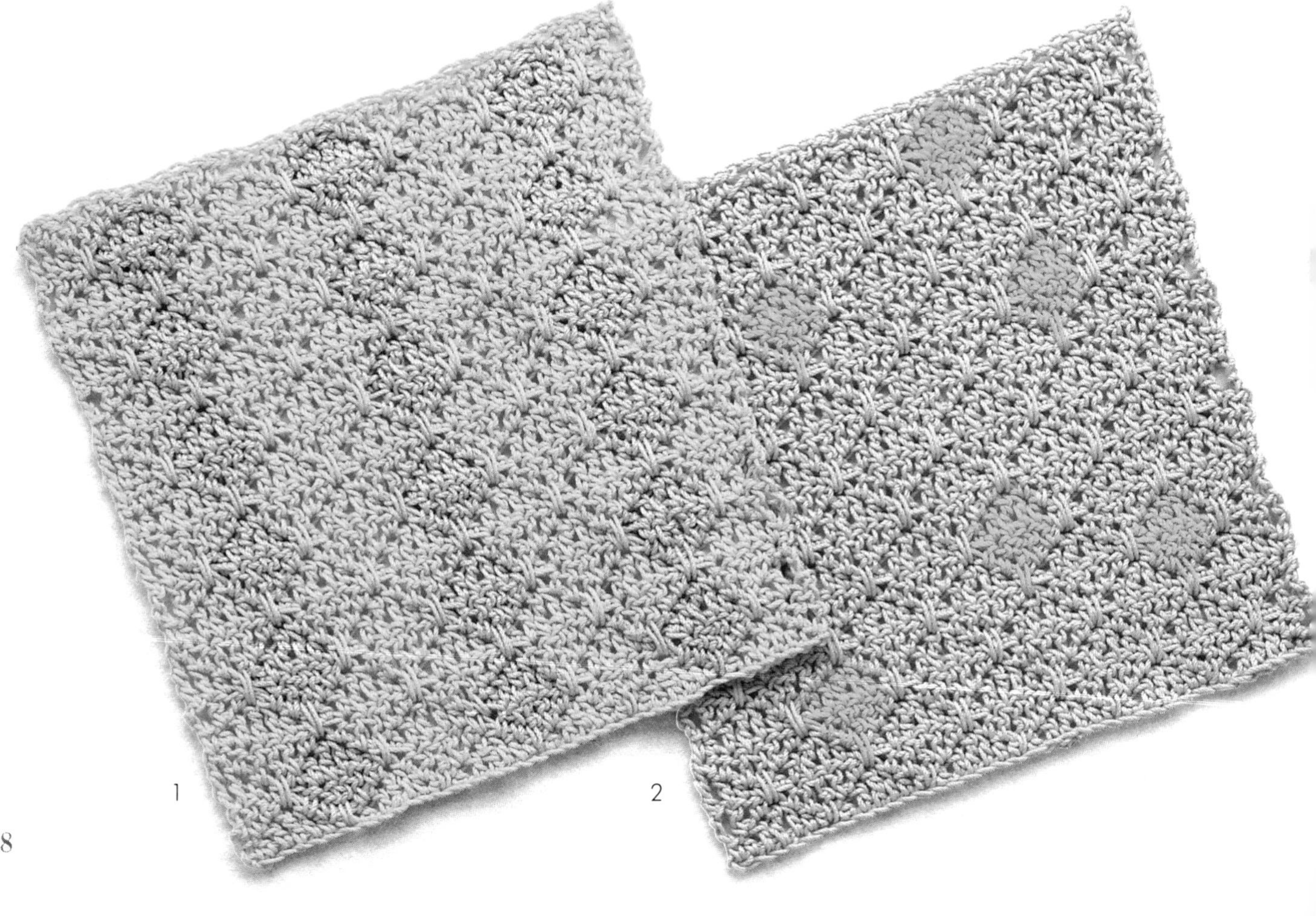

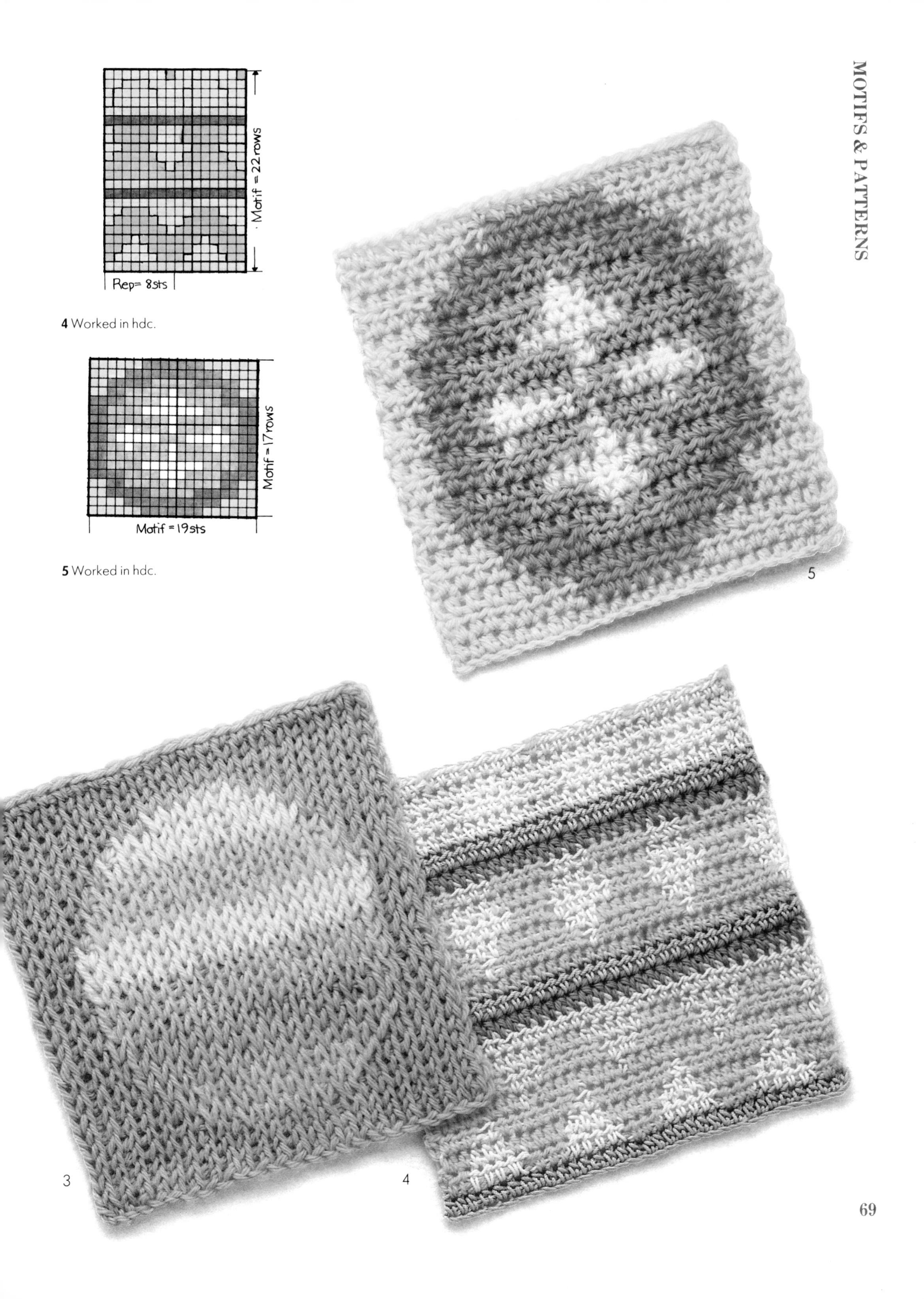

4 Worked in hdc.

5 Worked in hdc.

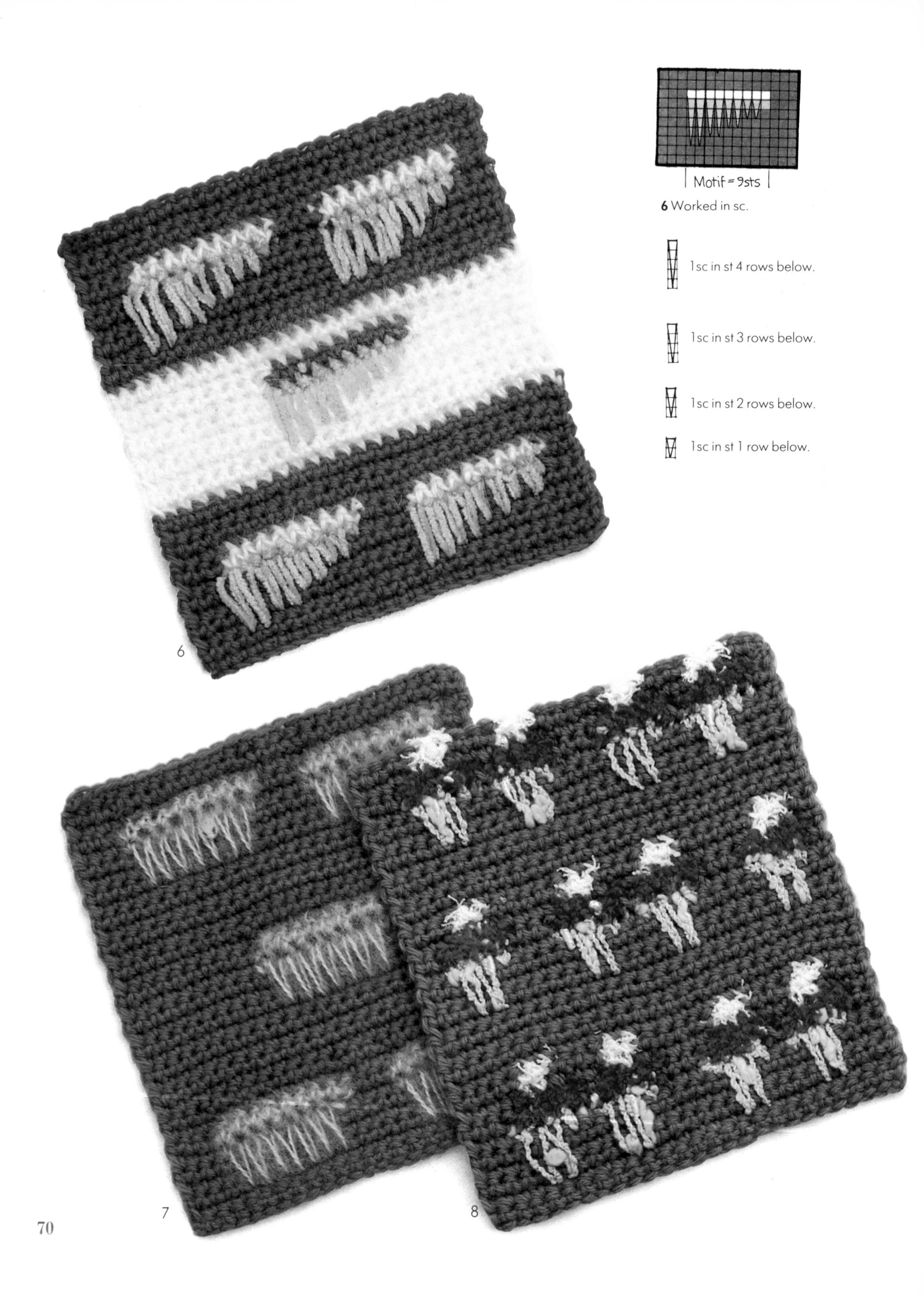
Motif = 9sts
6 Worked in sc.
1sc in st 4 rows below.
1sc in st 3 rows below.
1sc in st 2 rows below.
1sc in st 1 row below.
6
7
8

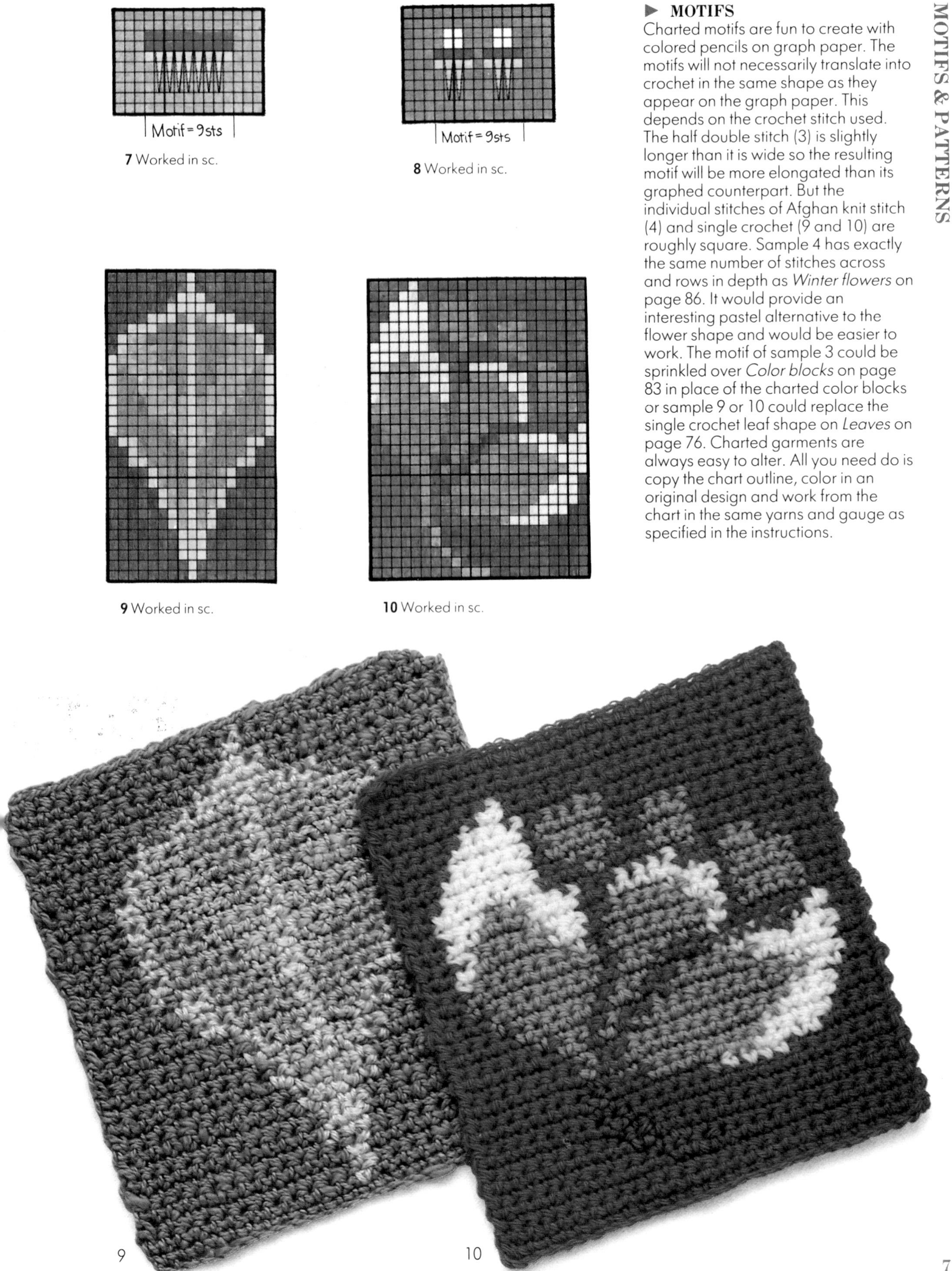

7 Worked in sc.

8 Worked in sc.

9 Worked in sc.

10 Worked in sc.

▶ MOTIFS

Charted motifs are fun to create with colored pencils on graph paper. The motifs will not necessarily translate into crochet in the same shape as they appear on the graph paper. This depends on the crochet stitch used. The half double stitch (3) is slightly longer than it is wide so the resulting motif will be more elongated than its graphed counterpart. But the individual stitches of Afghan knit stitch (4) and single crochet (9 and 10) are roughly square. Sample 4 has exactly the same number of stitches across and rows in depth as *Winter flowers* on page 86. It would provide an interesting pastel alternative to the flower shape and would be easier to work. The motif of sample 3 could be sprinkled over *Color blocks* on page 83 in place of the charted color blocks or sample 9 or 10 could replace the single crochet leaf shape on *Leaves* on page 76. Charted garments are always easy to alter. All you need do is copy the chart outline, color in an original design and work from the chart in the same yarns and gauge as specified in the instructions.

FANS

Sprinkled with tiny fans, this chenille top is worked in a simple single crochet background with the motifs in elongated single crochet. The edgings on the crocheted cuffs and collar are knitted so that they roll back to give a neat finish.

▶ SIZES

To fit 32[34-36:38-40]"
81[86-91:96-102]cm bust.

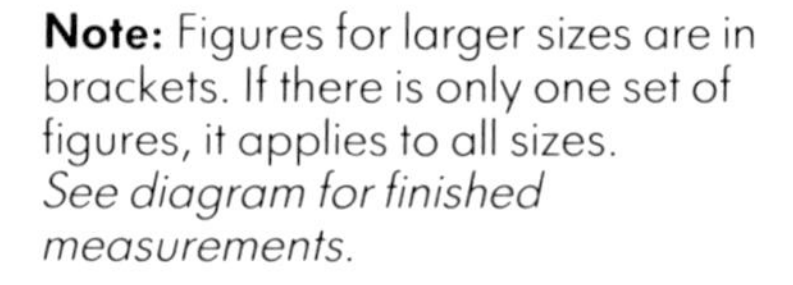

Note: Figures for larger sizes are in brackets. If there is only one set of figures, it applies to all sizes.
See diagram for finished measurements.

▶ MATERIALS

See page 118 for further yarn information
Use a lightweight cotton chenille (approx 160yd per 1¾oz), a shiny lightweight yarn (approx 93yd per 1¾oz) and a medium weight wool yarn (approx 125yd per 1¾oz):
15¾[17½:21]oz lightweight cotton chenille yarn in main color MC (black)
7[7:8¾]oz lightweight cotton yarn in contrasting color A (cream)
1¾oz medium weight wool yarn in B (black)
Size F crochet hook *or size to obtain correct gauge*
One pair of size 5 knitting needles
3 buttons
Millinery wire for collar (optional)

▶ GAUGE

12 sts to 2¾" and 20 rows to 4" over fan pat using size F hook.
To save time, take time to check gauge (see Note below).

Note: To check gauge ch28 and work base row as for back. 27sc. Work 6 rows in sc, then beg fan pat as for *1st pat row* of back, foll instructions for largest size. Work at least 18 rows in fan pat before measuring gauge. Make sure that elongated sc sts are worked *loosely* so that they do not pull tog the fabric. When working with 2 colors in a row, carry color not in use across the top of previous row and work all sts over it (see page 112).

▶ BACK

Using hook and MC, ch94[96:100].
Base row 1sc in 2nd ch from hook, 1sc in each ch to end. Turn. 93[95:99]sc.
1st row Ch1, 1sc in each sc to end. Turn.
Rep last row 3[5:7] times more.

Beg fan pat as foll:
1st pat row (RS) Ch1, 1sc in each of next 0[1:3]sc changing to A with last yo of last st, *(work fan over next 9sc as foll) using A, 1sc in next sc, skip next 7sc and work next 7 sts in rows below, insert hook from front to back through top of sc one row below next st, yo and draw a loop through pulling loop up to height of previous row so that fabric is not pulled tog, yo and draw through 2 loops on hook — called 1sc in next sc one row below —, 1sc in next sc 2 rows below, 1sc in each of next 3sc 3 rows below, 1sc in next sc 2 rows below, 1sc in next sc 1 row below, 1sc in next sc in previous row changing to MC with last yo of last sc — called 1 fan —, using MC, 1 sc in each of next 3sc changing to A with last yo of last sc, rep from *, ending last rep with 0[1:3]sc in MC. Turn.
2nd row Ch1, using MC, 1sc in each of next 0[1:3]sc changing to A with last yo of last st, *using A, 1sc in each of next 9sc of fan changing to MC with last yo of last sc, using MC, 1sc in each of next 3sc changing to A with last yo of last sc, rep from *, ending last rep with 0[1:3]sc in MC. Turn.
3rd-14th rows Using MC, ch1, 1sc in each sc to end. Turn.
15th row Ch1, 1sc in each of next 6[7:9]sc, *1 fan in A, using MC, 1sc in each of next 3sc, rep from *, ending last rep with 6[7:9]sc in MC. Turn.
16th row Ch1, using MC, 1sc in each of next 6[7:9]sc changing to A with last yo of last st, *using A, 1sc in each of next 9sc of fan changing to MC with last yo of last sc, using MC, 1sc in each of next 3sc changing to A with last yo of last sc, rep from *, ending last rep with 6[7:9]sc in MC. Turn.
17th-28th rows As 3rd-14th rows.
Last 28 rows form fan pat and are rep throughout.
Cont in fan pat until 7 rows of fans

have been completed from beg, ending with a 2nd pat row.
Work 4 rows in sc, using MC only. Fasten off.

Neck and shoulder shaping

Next row Using hook and MC and with RS facing, skip first 9[9:10]sc and rejoin yarn to next sc with a sl st, ch1, 1sc in same place as sl st, 1sc in each of next 28sc. Turn, leaving rem sts unworked.

Next row Ch1, (insert hook in next sc, yo and draw a loop through) twice, yo and draw through all 3 loops on hook — called 2sc tog —, 1sc in each of next 18sc. Turn, leaving rem sts unworked.

Next row Sl st over first 9sc, 1sc in each of next 8sc, 2sc tog. Fasten off.
With RS facing, skip center 17[19:21]sc, rejoin MC to next st and work 2nd shoulder in the same way reversing shaping.

► FRONT

Using hook and MC, ch94[96:100]. Work base and first row as for back. 93[95:99]sc.
Work 3[5:7] rows more in sc.
Beg fan pat as foll:

1st pat row As for 15th pat row of back.

2nd pat row As for 16th pat row of back.

3rd-14th rows As for 3rd-14th rows of back.

15th row As for first row of back.

16th row As for 2nd row of back.

17th-28th rows As for 3rd-14th rows of back.

Last 28 rows form fan pat and are rep throughout.

Cont in fan pat until 5 rows of fans have been completed from beg, ending with a 2nd pat row.
Work one row in sc, using MC only.

Neck slit

Next row (WS) Using MC, ch1, 1sc in each sc to center sc. Turn, leaving rem 47[48:50]sc unworked.
Keeping to fan pat as set, cont on these 46[47:49]sc until one more row of fans has been completed, omitting first fan at neck edge and ending with a WS row.
Work 10 rows more in sc, using MC only. Fasten off.

Neck shaping

Next row (RS) Using hook and MC and with RS facing, skip first 5[6:7]sc at neck edge and rejoin yarn to next sc with a sl st, ch1, 1sc in same place as sl st, 1sc in each sc to end. Turn.
Cont in fan pat, dec one st at neck edge on next 5 rows. 36[36:37]sc.
Work in fan pat without shaping until front has same number of rows as back to shoulder shaping, so ending at neck edge.

Shoulder shaping

Next row (RS) Using MC, ch1, 1sc in each of first 27sc. Turn, leaving rem 9[9:10]sc unworked.
Next row Sl st over first 9sc, 1sc in each sc to end. Turn.
Next row Ch1, 1sc in each of first 9sc. Fasten off.
Using hook and MC and with WS facing, skip center st and rejoin yarn to next sc with a sl st, ch1, 1sc in same place as sl st, 1sc in each sc to end.
Complete 2nd side of neck in the same way, reversing shaping.

▶ RIGHT SLEEVE

Right side of sleeve

Using hook and MC, ch29[29:30].
Work base and first rows as for back. 28[28:29]sc.
2nd row (WS) Work in sc, inc 4[6:6] sts evenly across row. Turn. 32[34:35]sc.
Work 3 rows in sc without shaping.
6th row (WS) Work in sc, inc one st at end of row (side edge). Turn.
**Cont in sc, inc one st at side edge on every 3rd row twice. 35[37:38]sc.
Work 2 rows without shaping, so ending with a WS row.** Do not break off yarn. Set aside right side of sleeve.

Left side of sleeve

Using hook and MC, ch11[11:12].
Work base and first rows as for right side of sleeve. 10[10:11]sc.
2nd row (WS) Work in sc, inc 2 sts evenly across row. Turn. 12[12:13]sc.
Work 3 rows in sc without shaping.
6th row Work in sc, inc one st at beg of row (side edge).
Work as for right side of sleeve from ** to **. 15[15:16]sc. Fasten off.

Join sleeve

Join right and left sides of sleeve as foll:
Next row With RS facing, cont on right side of sleeve, ch1, 2sc in first sc, work in sc to end, ch1, cont in sc across left side of sleeve to last sc, 2sc in last sc. Turn.
Next row Ch1, 1sc in each sc to ch1, 1sc in ch1, 1sc in each sc to end. Turn. 53[55:57]sc.
Work one row without shaping.
Inc one st at each end of next row. 55[57:59]sc.
Beg fan pat as foll:
Next row (RS) Using MC, ch1, 1sc in each of first 5[6:7]sc, *1 fan in A, using MC, 1sc in each of next 3sc, rep from *, ending last rep with 5[6:7]sc in MC. Turn.
Cont in fan pat as set for back *and at the same time* shape sleeve by inc one st at each end of every 3rd row 0[4:8] times, then every 4th row 12[9:6] times (counting from last inc row), adding fans as sleeve widens. 79[83:87]sc.
Work 2[3:4] rows without shaping. Fasten off.

▶ LEFT SLEEVE

Left side of sleeve

Using hook and MC, ch29[29:30].
Work base-5th rows as for right side of right sleeve. 32[34:35]sc.
6th row (WS) Work in sc, inc one st at beg of row (side edge). Turn.
Work as for right side of right sleeve from ** to **. Fasten off.
Set left side of sleeve aside.

Right side of sleeve

Using hook and MC, ch11[11:12].
Work base-5th rows as for left side of right sleeve. 12[12:13]sc.
6th row (WS) Work in sc, inc one st at end of row (side edge). Turn.
Work as for right side of right sleeve from ** to **. 15[15:16]sc.
Do not break off yarn.

Join sleeve

Join right and left sides and complete as for right sleeve.

▶ COLLAR

Sew shoulder seams.
Note: When working stripe rib pat, carry color not in use *loosely* across top of previous row, working all sts over it. To make sure that carried yarn does not shorten width of row pull collar gently widthwise at end of each row.
Using hook and MC, ch15. Work base row as for back. 14sc.
**Beg stripe rib pat as foll:
1st row (RS) Using A, ch1, working in *back* loops only, 1sc in each sc to end. Turn.
2nd row (RS) Using MC, ch1, working in back loops only, 1sc in each sc to last 2sc, 2sc tog. Turn.
Rep last 2 rows 3 times more. 10sc.
Work 3 rows in stripe rib pat without shaping. Rep 2nd row.** 9sc.
Work 3 rows without shaping. Mark last row. Rep 2nd row.
Cont in stripe rib pat on these 8sc until collar fits from center front to center

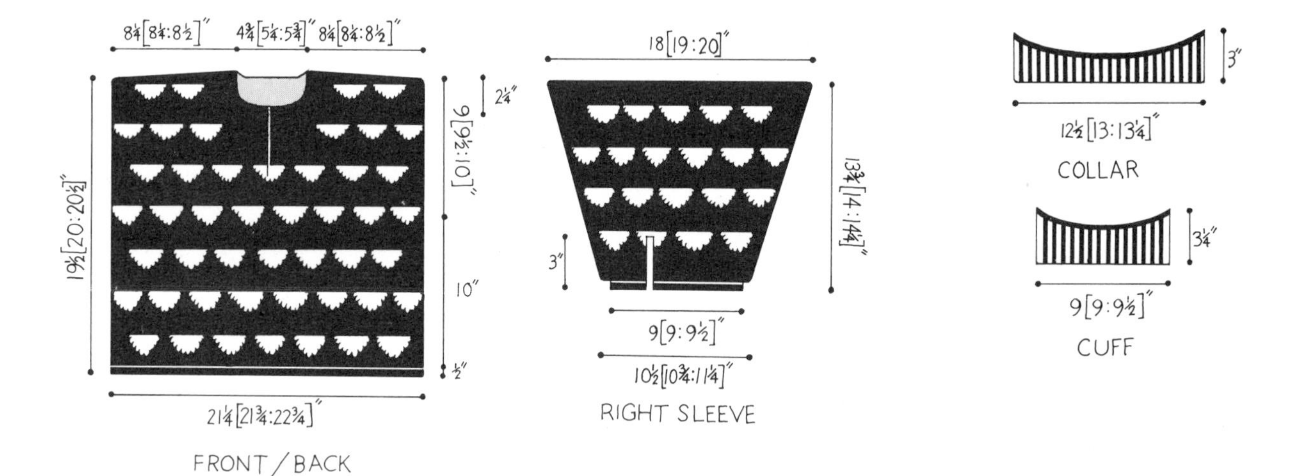

back, placing *shaped edge* of collar along neck edge, ending with a stripe in A. Mark last row as center back.
Cont in stripe rib pat, work same number of rows as between 2 markers, so ending with a row in MC at shaped edge.
Next row Using A, ch1, 2sc in first sc, work in pat to end. Turn. 9sc.
Cont in stripe rib pat, inc one st at beg of every 4th row twice, then at beg of every other row 3 times. 14sc.
Work one row without shaping.
Fasten off.

▶ CUFFS (make 2)

Using hook and MC, ch16.
Work base row as for back. 15sc.
Work as for collar from ** to **. 10sc.
Mark last row in A.
Cont in stripe rib pat until cuff measures 4¼[4¼:4¾]" from beg, ending with a stripe in A. Mark last row as center of cuff.
Cont in stripe rib pat, work same number of rows as between 2 markers, so ending with a row in MC at shaped edge.
Next row Using A, ch1, 2sc in first sc, work in pat to end. Turn. 11sc.
Cont in stripe rib pat, inc one st at beg of 4th row, then at beg of every other row 3 times. 15sc.
Work one row without shaping.
Fasten off.

▶ KNITTED ROLLED EDGINGS

Back edging
Using knitting needles and B and with RS facing, pick up and K7 sts for every 5 foundation ch along lower edge of back (see page 115).
Knit one row. Purl one row.
Rep from * to * once more.
Bind off tightly in knit.
Front edging
Work as for back edging.
Collar edging
Using knitting needles and B and with RS facing, pick up and K3 sts for every 2 row ends all along *straight* edge of collar. Complete edging as for back edging.
Cuff edgings
Work as for collar edging, but pick up sts along *shaped* edge.

▶ FINISHING

Do not press. Mark positions for sleeves on back and front 9[9½:10]" from shoulder seams. Sew sleeves between markers. Join sleeve and side seams.
Weave in all loose ends.
Sew on collar with RS of shaped edge of collar facing WS of neck edge and neck edge slightly overlapping collar.
Neck edging
Using hook and B and with RS facing work a row of sc evenly along short edge of collar, beg at left side of collar and working in folded rolled edge and then in sps between sc (not in foundation ch), cont in sc around slit edge (working 2sc in end of slit) and along short end of right side of collar. Fasten off.
With RS facing, rejoin B to beg of last row and work a 2nd row in sl st, inserting hook through both loops of top of each sc of previous row. Fasten off.
If desired, insert length of millinery wire through edging at short edges of collar to stiffen. Bend ends at WS and secure in place with B.
Sew button in place on left side of neck slit and work a ch for button loop on opposite side.
Cuff and sleeve slit edging
Using hook and B, work a row of sc evenly along sleeve slit, working 2sc in end of slit. Using hook and B, work a row of sc evenly along short ends of cuff. Fasten off. Work a 2nd row in sl st as for neck edging.
Pin cuff to sleeve with WS of cuff facing RS of sleeve.
Using hook and B, work 39[39:41]sc evenly along sleeve edge, working through cuff and foundation ch of sleeve with each sc. Fasten off.
Sew a button to each sleeve slit and work button loop opposite as for neck.

LEAVES

Slubbed cotton yarn in single crochet produces a firm fabric for this colorful T-shaped top. This design can be varied by making a top without the sleeves, designing your own motifs or omitting the motifs.

▶ SIZES

To fit 32[34:36:38-40]"/81[86:91:96-102]cm bust.
Note: Figures for larger sizes are in brackets. If there is only one set of figures, it applies to all sizes.
See diagram for finished measurements.

▶ MATERIALS

See page 118 for further yarn information
Use a medium weight slubbed cotton yarn (approx 109yd per 1¾oz):
17½[17½:19¼]oz in main color MC (yellow)
5¼oz in contrasting color A (turquoise)
5¼[7:7:8¾]oz in contrasting color B (white)
Size H crochet hook *or size to obtain correct gauge*
One pair of size 6 knitting needles

▶ GAUGE

16sc and 20 rows to 4" over pat using size H hook.
To save time, take time to check gauge.

Note: When working leaves, do not carry colors across back of work, but use a separate bobbin of yarn for each block of color (see page 112). When working from chart, read odd-numbered rows from right to left and even-numbered rows from left to right. Always change to new color with last yo of previous st.

▶ BACK

Using hook and MC, ch85[89:93:97].
Base row 1sc in 2nd ch from hook, 1sc in each ch to end. Turn.
84[88:92:96]sc.
1st row Ch1, 1sc in each sc to end. Turn.
Work 0[0:2:2] rows in sc. Cont in sc foll chart, beg with 3rd[1st:1st:1st] row of chart.**
When 113th row of chart has been completed, work neck shaping as foll:
Neck shaping
Next row (WS) Work first 24[26:28:30] sts in pat. Turn, leaving rem sts unworked.
Dec one st at neck edge on next row and then at neck edge on every foll row 3 times in all. 21[23:25:27]sc.
Work one row without shaping. Fasten off.
With WS facing, return to rem sts, skip next 36sc for center back neck, rejoin MC to rem sts and work in pat to end.
Work 2nd side of neck to match first side, reversing shaping. Fasten off.

▶ FRONT

Work as for back to **. When 102nd row of chart has been completed, work neck shaping as foll:
Neck shaping
Next row (RS) Work first 29[31:33:35] sts in pat. Turn, leaving rem sts unworked.
Dec 2 sts at neck edge on next 2 rows, then one st at neck edge on next row and 3 foll alternate rows.
21[23:25:27]sc.
Cont without shaping until front measures same as back to shoulder.
Fasten off.
With RS facing, return to rem sts, skip next 26sc for center front neck, rejoin MC to rem sts and work in pat to end.
Complete to match first side, reversing shaping.

▶ SLEEVES (make 2)

Using hook and MC, ch61[65:69:69].
Work base and first rows as for back.
60[64:68:68]sc.
Cont in sc foll chart for sleeve, beg with first row of chart and inc one st at each end of 7th row and then every foll 8th row until there are 66[70:74:74] sts.
When 30th row of chart has been completed, work without shaping until sleeve measures 6¾" from beg or desired sleeve length. Fasten off.

▶ BACK RIB

Using knitting needles and MC and with RS facing, pick up and K108[112:116:120] sts evenly along lower edge of back (see page 115).
Beg rib as foll:
1st rib row *K2, P2, rep from * to end.
Last row forms rib pat. Cont until rib measures 1". Bind off loosely in rib.

▶ FRONT RIB

Work as for back rib.

▶ SLEEVE EDGING

Using knitting needles and MC and with RS facing, pick up and K60[64:68:68] sts evenly along lower edge of sleeve. Work for 1" in K2, P2 rib as for back rib.

▶ NECKBAND
Join right shoulder seam. Using knitting needles and MC and with RS facing, pick up and K132 sts evenly around neck edge. Work for 1" in K2, P2 rib as for back rib.

▶ FINISHING
Weave in all loose ends. Join left shoulder and neckband seam. Mark positions for sleeves on back and front 8¼[8¾:9¼:9¼]" from shoulder seam. Sew on sleeves between markers. Join sleeve and side seams. Press seams lightly on WS with warm iron.

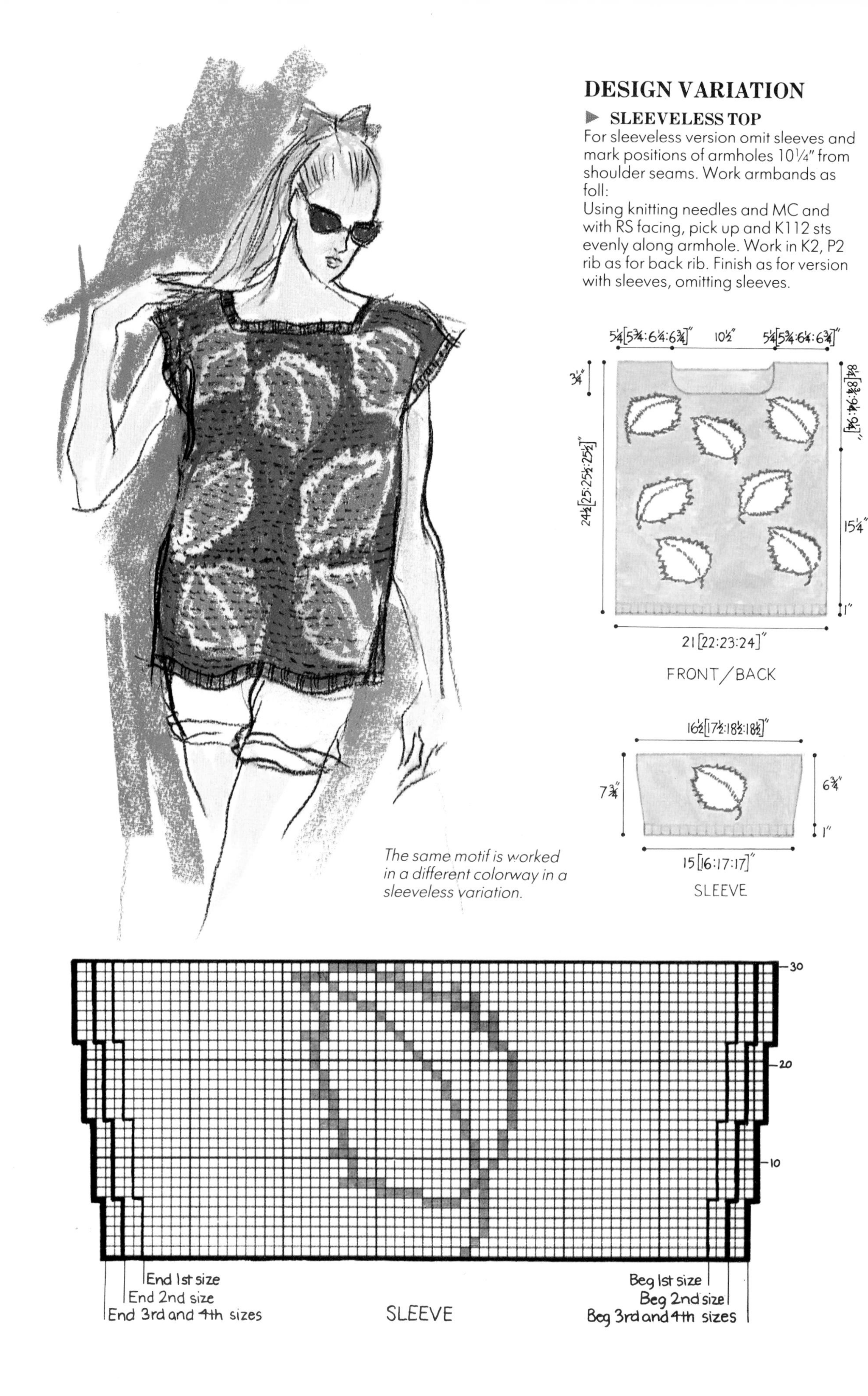

DESIGN VARIATION

▶ SLEEVELESS TOP

For sleeveless version omit sleeves and mark positions of armholes 10¼" from shoulder seams. Work armbands as foll:

Using knitting needles and MC and with RS facing, pick up and K112 sts evenly along armhole. Work in K2, P2 rib as for back rib. Finish as for version with sleeves, omitting sleeves.

The same motif is worked in a different colorway in a sleeveless variation.

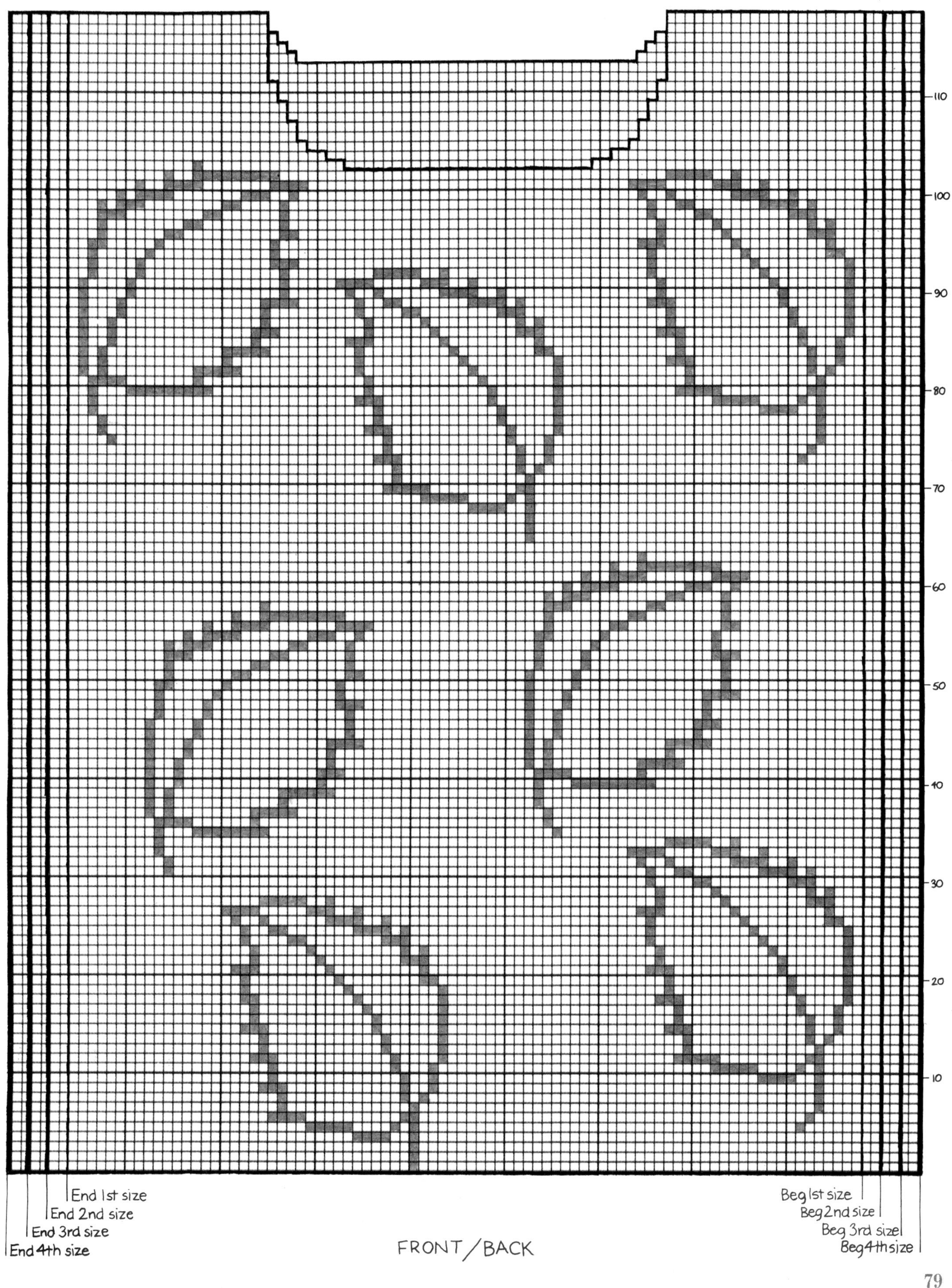
110
100
90
80
70
60
50
40
30
20
10
End 1st size
End 2nd size
End 3rd size
End 4th size
Beg 1st size
Beg 2nd size
Beg 3rd size
Beg 4th size

FRONT/BACK

DIAMONDS

Varying the heights of the stitches in each row creates the diamond shapes in this design so that you are only working with one color and one ball of yarn at a time. For a cooler and more youthful top, work the cropped version on page 82.

▶ SIZES

To fit 32-34[36-38]"/81-86[91-96]cm bust.

Note: Figures for larger size are in brackets. If there is only one set of figures, it applies to both sizes.

See diagram for finished measurements.

▶ MATERIALS

See page 118 for further yarn information

Use a lightweight cotton yarn (approx 202yd per 1¾oz):

6¼[8]oz in each of 2 colors A (green) and B (pale blue)

1oz in C (turquoise)

Size D crochet hook *or size to obtain correct gauge*

4 buttons

▶ GAUGE

22 sts and 17 rows to 4" over diamond pat using size D hook.

To save time, take time to check gauge.

Note: To check gauge ch32 and work base-5th rows of back or foll symbol chart. Cont in pat until sample measures 5". Before measuring gauge, block swatch using damp cloth and warm iron.

▶ BACK

Using A, ch104[116].

Base row 1sc in 2nd ch from hook, *1hdc in next ch, 1dc in next ch, 1tr in next ch, 1dc in next ch, 1hdc in next ch, 1sc in next ch, rep from * to end. Turn. 103[115] sts.

1st row Using B, ch3, skip first sc, *1dc in next st, 1hdc in next st, ch1, skip next st (tr), 1hdc in next st, 1dc in next st, 1tr in next st, rep from * to end. Turn. 103[115] sts, counting first ch3 as first st.

2nd row Using B, ch3, skip first tr, *1dc in next st, 1hdc in next st, 1sc in top of tr skipped in last row working over ch1 worked in last row, 1hdc in next st, 1dc in next st, 1tr in next st, rep from *, working last tr in 3rd of ch3. Turn.

3rd row Using A, ch1, 1sc in first st, *1hdc in next st, 1dc in next st, 1tr in top of tr 2 rows below (in same place as sc in last row), 1dc in next st, 1hdc in next st, ch1, skip next st (tr), rep from *, omitting ch1 at end of last rep and working 1sc in 3rd of ch3. Turn.

4th row Using A, ch1, 1sc in first st, *1hdc in next st, 1dc in next st, 1tr in next st, 1dc in next st, 1hdc in next st, 1sc in top of tr skipped in last row, rep from *, working last sc in sc at end of row. Turn.

5th row Using B, ch3, skip first sc, *1dc in next st, 1hdc in next st, ch1, skip next st (tr), 1hdc in next st, 1dc in next st, 1tr in top of tr 2 rows below (in same place as sc in last row), rep from *, working last tr in sc at end of row. Turn.

Rep 2nd-5th rows to form diamond pat. **Cont in pat until 34[38] rows have been worked from beg counting base row, so ending with a 5th pat row.

Armhole shaping

Next row Using B, ch1, 1 sl st in each of first 3 sts, 1sc in top of tr skipped in last row, rep from * of 4th row to last 3 sts. Turn, leaving last 3 sts unworked. 97[109] sts.

Next row Using A, as 5th row.

Next row Using A, as 2nd row.

Next row Using B, as 3rd row.

Next row Using B, as 4th row.

Cont in pat as now set until 34 rows have been worked from beg of armhole, so ending with a 5th pat row in A.

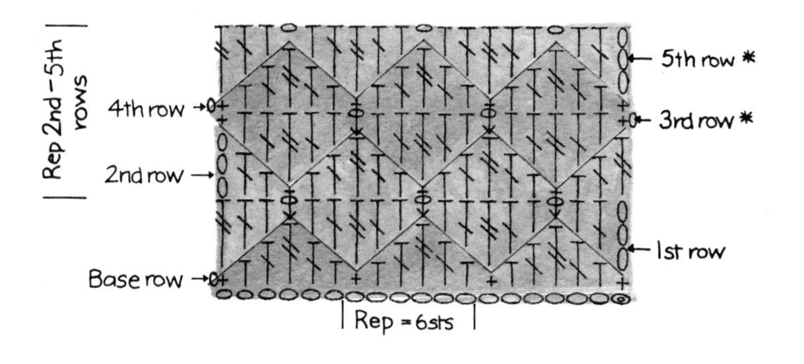

Foundation ch=multiple of 6ch plus 2 extra.

* In 3rd and 5th rows work tr in top of tr 2 rows below.

= 1 sc in tr skipped in row below. (See page 117 for other crochet symbols.)

Neck shaping

Next row Using A, ch3, skip first tr, rep from * of 2nd row 4[5] times, 1dc in next st, 1hdc in next st, 1sc in top of tr skipped in last row. Turn, leaving rem sts unworked. 4[5] diamonds. Fasten off A.

Next row Skip first 3 sts and rejoin B to first tr of last row with a sl st, ch1, 1sc in same tr, rep from * of 3rd row to end. Turn.

Next row Using B, as 4th row.

Next row Using A, as 5th row. Fasten off.

Work 2nd side of neck as for first side, reversing shaping.

▶ LEFT FRONT

Using A, ch56[62] and work base and first rows as for back. Turn. 55[61] sts. Cont in pat as for back until left front has same number of rows as back to armhole.

Armhole shaping

Next row Using B, ch1, sl st in each of first 3 sts, 1sc in top of tr skipped in last row, rep from * of 4th row of back to last 3 sts, 1hdc in next st, 1dc in next st, 1tr in last st. Turn. 52[58] sts.

Next row Using A, ch1, 1sc in first st, rep from * of 3rd row of back to last 3 sts, 1hdc in next st, 1dc in next st, 1tr in last st. Turn.

Next row Using A, ch3, skip first tr, rep from * of 2nd row of back to last 3 sts, 1dc in next st, 1hdc in next st, 1sc in last st. Turn.

Next row Using B, ch3, skip first sc, rep from * of 5th row of back to last 3 sts, 1dc in next st, 1hdc in next st, 1sc in last st. Turn.

Next row Using B, ch1, 1sc in first st, rep from * of 4th row of back to last 3 sts, 1hdc in next st, 1dc in next st, 1tr in last st. Turn.

Rep last 4 rows to form diamond pat. Cont in pat until 24[20] rows have been worked from beg of armhole, so ending in the middle of a row of diamonds in B.

Neck shaping

Next row Using B, ch1, 1sc in first st, rep from * of 4th row of back over first 5[6] diamonds. Turn, leaving rem sts unworked. 5[6] diamonds. Fasten off B.

Next row Skip first 3 sts and rejoin A to first tr of last row with a sl st, ch1, 1sc in same tr, 1hdc in next st, 1dc in next st, 1tr in top of tr 2 rows below, rep from * of 5th row of back to end. Turn.

Next row Using A, ch3, skip first tr, 1dc in next st, 1hdc in next st, 1sc in top of tr skipped in last row, rep from * of 4th row of back to end. Turn. Fasten off A.

Next row Skip first 3 sts and rejoin B to first tr of last row with a sl st, ch1, 1sc in same tr, rep from * of 3rd row of back to end. Turn. 4[5] diamonds.

Cont in pat until left front has same number of rows as back to shoulder. Fasten off.

▶ RIGHT FRONT

Work as for left front until 6 rows have been worked from beg counting base row, so ending with 5th pat row. Set aside right front and using a separate length of B, ch5 and fasten off. Cont on right front as foll:

Next row Using B, ch3, skip first tr, 1dc in next st, 1hdc in next st, 1sc in top of tr skipped in last row, pick up separate ch in B and work 1hdc in first ch, 1dc in next ch, 1tr in next ch, 1dc in next ch, 1hdc in last ch, skip 5 sts of last row and work 1sc in top of next tr skipped in last row, work in pat to end. Turn. Work 15 rows in pat, then rep buttonhole row and cont in this way working a buttonhole on every 16th row until there are 4 buttonholes *and at the same time* work as for left front, reversing armhole and neck shaping.

▶ FINISHING

Weave in all loose ends. Press pieces on WS with a damp cloth and a warm iron, blocking to correct measurements. Join shoulder and side seams.

Edging

Using B and with RS facing, work a row of sc evenly up right front around neck and down left front, working 3sc at corners. Using C and with RS facing, beg at right side seam and work a row of sc evenly along lower edge of right front (working 2sc for every 3 foundation ch), cont in sc up right front, around neck, down left front and around lower edge of left front and back as for lower edge of right front, working 3sc in corners. Join with a sl st to first sc, turn, ch1, insert hook from front to back and to front again around first sc, yo and draw through both loops on hook — called sc around post (see page 110) —, cont around edging working 1sc around post of each sc and 2sc around post of st at each corner. Join with a sl st to first sc of row and fasten off.

Using B and with RS facing, work a row of sc evenly around armhole edge. Change to C and join with a sl st to first st, ch1, 1sc in each sc to end, join with a sl st to first sc, turn, ch1, 1sc around post of each sc, join with a sl st to first sc. Fasten off.

Press seams and edging on WS with a damp cloth and a warm iron. Sew on buttons opposite buttonholes.

A cooler, cropped top is produced by shortening the design and altering the colorway.

DESIGN VARIATION

▶ CROPPED TOP

For a cropped top work back to **, then cont in pat until 18[22] rows have been worked from beg counting base row, so ending with a 5th pat row. Work armhole shaping and complete back as for longer version. Work left and right fronts foll instructions, but working 3 buttonholes instead of 4. Finish as for longer version.

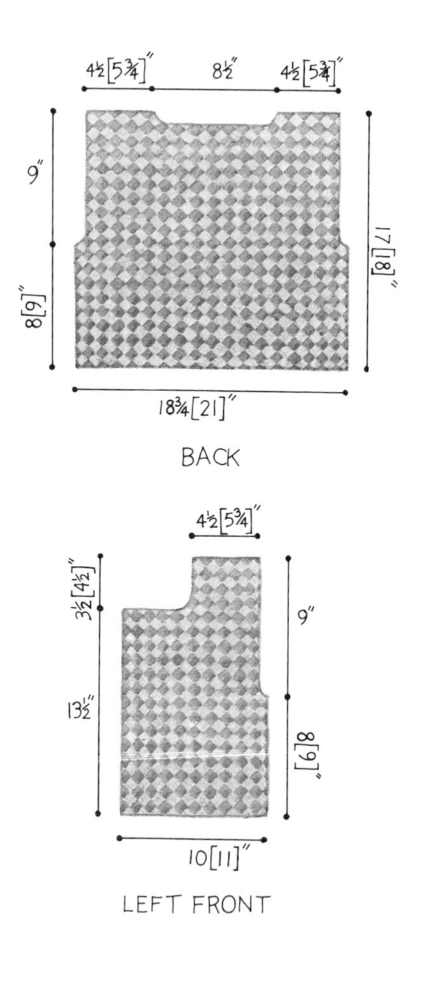

COLOR BLOCKS

Perfect for using leftover yarns, this charted top is worked in half doubles using smooth yarns and mohair. Follow the chart or create your own design after copying the outline onto graph paper, drawing in shapes and coloring them with crayons to see the final effect.

▶ SIZES

To fit 32[34-36:38-40]"/81[86-91:96-102]cm bust.

Note: Figures for larger sizes are in brackets. If there is only one set of figures, it applies to all sizes.

See diagram for finished measurements.

▶ MATERIALS

See page 118 for further yarn information

Use a lightweight wool yarn (approx 73yd per 1oz) and a lightweight mohair (approx 170yd per 1¾oz):

2[2:3]oz lightweight wool yarn in each of 4 colors A (yellow), B (coral), C (beige) and D (pale pink)

2oz lightweight wool yarn in each of 3 colors E (orange), F (pink) and H (pale yellow)

1oz lightweight wool yarn in each of 2 colors I (dusty rose) and G (pale orange)
3½[3½:5¼]oz lightweight mohair J (light green)
Sizes H and I crochet hooks *or sizes to obtain correct gauges*

▶ GAUGE

15hdc and 13 rows to 4" over color pat using size H hook.
15sc and 14 rows to 4" over rib pat using J and size I hook.
To save time, take time to check gauge.

Note: Use a separate bobbin of yarn for each block of color. When changing colors, change to new color with last yo of previous hdc keeping yarn on WS (see page 112). Read odd-numbered chart rows (RS) from right to left and even-numbered rows from left to right.

▶ BACK

Using smaller hook and A, ch66[68:70], then change to B and ch16[18:20].
Base row (WS) Using B, 1hdc in 3rd ch from hook, 1hdc in each of next 12[14:16]ch changing to A with last yo of last st, using A 1hdc in each ch to end. Turn. 80[84:88]hdc.
1st row (RS) Using A, ch2, 1hdc in each of first 67[69:71]hdc, using B 1hdc in each hdc to end. Turn.
Foll chart for color pat and beg with 2nd chart row, cont in hdc as for last row until 35th chart row has been completed.
Armhole shaping
Next row (36th chart row) Work over first 2 sts in sl st, ch2, work in pat to last 2 sts. Turn, leaving rem 2 sts unworked. 76[80:84]hdc.
Cont armhole shaping foll chart and working single decs at beg of row as foll: ch2, yo and insert hook in first hdc, yo and draw a loop through, yo and insert hook in next hdc, yo and draw a loop through, yo and draw through all 5 loops on hook — called 2hdc tog. Work decs at end of row by working 2hdc tog over last 2 sts.
When armhole shaping has been completed, work without shaping on rem 70[72:74]hdc foll chart until 68th[70th:72nd] chart row has been completed. Work neck and shoulder shaping as indicated. Fasten off.

▶ FRONT

Work as for back until 60th chart row has been completed. Work neck and then shoulder shaping as indicated. Fasten off.

▶ COLLAR

Sew shoulder seams.
Using larger hook and J, ch11.
Base row 1sc in 2nd ch from hook, 1sc in each ch to end. Turn. 10sc.
1st row Ch1, working in *back* loops only, work 1sc in each sc to end. Turn.
Last row forms rib pat and is rep throughout. Cont in rib pat until collar, slightly stretched, fits around neck edge. Fasten off.

▶ BACK RIB

Using larger hook and J, ch6 and work base and first rows as for collar. 5sc.
Cont in rib pat until rib fits across lower edge of back. Fasten off.

▶ FRONT RIB

Work as for back rib.

▶ ARMHOLE BANDS (make 2)

Using larger hook and J, ch6 and work base and first rows as for collar. 5sc.
Cont in rib pat until band, slightly stretched, fits around armhole. Fasten off.

▶ FINISHING

Do not press. Weave in all loose ends.
Using smaller hook and matching colors, work a row of sc evenly around neck edge and armhole. Sew armhole bands to armholes. Sew on front and back ribs. Join side seams. Join collar seam and sew collar in place to neck edge, lining collar seam up with left shoulder seam.

DESIGN VARIATION

▶ TOP WITHOUT RIBBING

For a simpler version of the sleeveless top omit crochet ribs, so that armholes and neck are edged with a single row of sc only.

Removing the ribbing and using a different colorway produces a simple variation.

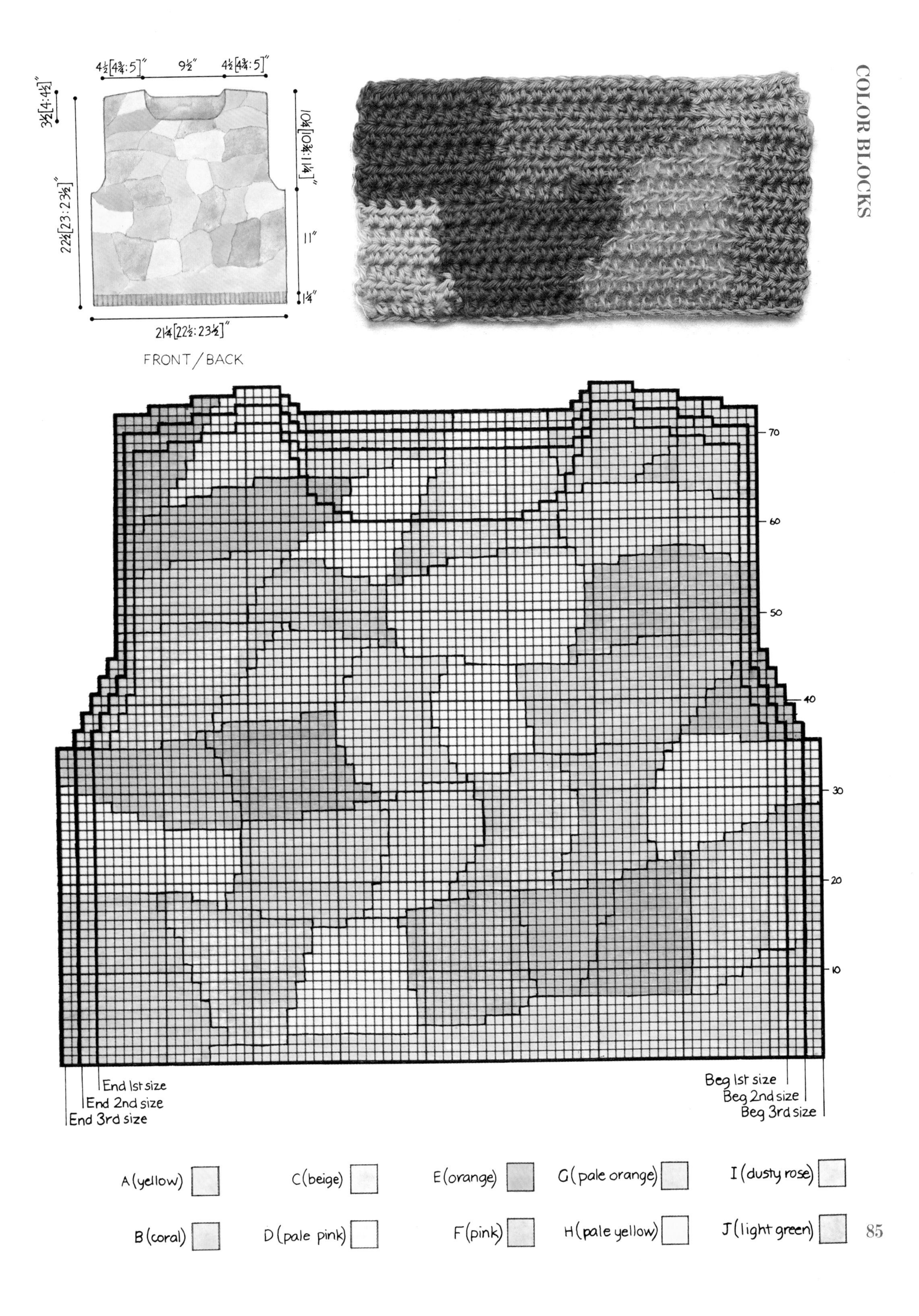
4½[4¾:5]"
9½"
4½[4¾:5]"
3½[4:4½]"
10¼[10¾:11¼]"
22¼[23:23½]"
11"
1¼"
21¼[22½:23½]"
FRONT / BACK
70
60
50
40
30
20
10
End 1st size
End 2nd size
End 3rd size
Beg 1st size
Beg 2nd size
Beg 3rd size
A (yellow)
B (coral)
C (beige)
D (pale pink)
E (orange)
F (pink)
G (pale orange)
H (pale yellow)
I (dusty rose)
J (light green)

WINTER FLOWERS

Hardly distinguishable from knitted stockinette stitch, Afghan crochet knit stitch produces a warm fabric. With front pockets, long sleeves and a stand-up collar, this jacket is worked in panels using a simple charted motif and sewn together afterward.

► SIZES

To fit 32[34:36]"/81[86:91]cm bust.
Note: Figures for larger sizes are in brackets. If there is only one set of figures, it applies to all sizes.
See diagram for finished measurements.

► MATERIALS

See page 118 for further yarn information
Use a lightweight wool yarn (approx 73yd per 1oz):
8[10:12]oz in A (beige)
5oz in B (blue)

15[17:20]oz in C (gray)
4oz in D (white)
Size J Afghan crochet hook *or size to obtain correct gauge.*
Size F crochet hook
Hooks and eyes for fastening
Shoulder pads (optional)

▶ GAUGE

17 sts and 20 loop rows to 4" over Afghan crochet knit st worked in one color only and using size J Afghan hook.

17 sts and 18 loop rows to 4" over Afghan crochet knit st worked in color pat using size J Afghan hook.
24 sts and 24 rows to 4" over seed pat using size F crochet hook.
To save time, take time to check gauge.

Note: Back, fronts and sleeves are made in panels which are sewn tog. When working with 2 colors in a row, strand color not in use loosely across back of work. To avoid long, loose strands at back of work twist yarns every 4 or 5 sts *or* in foll row work under and over loose strands by inserting hook above and below strands after every 4 or 5 sts (see page 116).

▶ BACK

Panel 1
Using Afghan hook and A, ch26. Beg Afghan knit st as foll:
Base row Insert hook in 2nd ch from hook, yo and draw a loop through, *insert hook in next ch, yo and draw a loop through, rep from * to end of ch. Do not turn at end of rows. 26 loops on hook.
1st row (return row) Yo and draw through first loop on hook, *yo and draw through next 2 loops on hook, rep from * until there is one loop on hook (this forms first loop of next row).
2nd row (loop row) Skip first vertical loop in row below and insert hook from front to back through 2nd vertical loop (under the chain), yo and draw a loop through, *insert hook through next vertical loop, yo and draw a loop through, rep from * to end.
Note: To form a firm edge, insert hook through center of last loop at edge making sure that there are 2 vertical strands of yarn on hook at extreme left-hand edge.
Last 2 rows form Afghan knit st and are rep throughout. Cont in Afghan knit st until 3 loop rows more are completed, ending with a return row. Work first row of chart as foll:
Next row Using A, work as for loop row until there are 9 loops on hook, using B draw up next 7 loops, using A draw up next 10 loops. (See Note above.)
Next row Using A, yo and draw through first loop on hook, (yo and draw through next 2 loops on hook) 9

times, using B (yo and draw through next 2 loops on hook) 7 times, using A (yo and draw through next 2 loops on hook) 9 times.
Cont in this way, foll chart for loop rows (reading chart rows from right to left) and always drawing through a loop in a matching color on return row, until 18 chart rows are completed, ending with a return row.
** Using A only, work 5 loop rows in pat, ending with a return row.
Work 18 chart rows, ending with a return row.**
Rep from ** to ** twice more. 4 motifs complete.
Using A only, work in pat until panel measures 21¼[21¾:22]" from beg, ending with a return row.

Shoulder shaping

Next row Work as for loop row until there are 21 loops on hook, leaving rem sts unworked.
Work a return row on these sts. Dec 5 sts at end of next 3 loop rows in the same way, ending with a return row. 6 sts rem. Fasten off.

Panel 2

Using Afghan hook and C, ch24[26:28]. Work base-2nd rows as for panel 1. 24[26:28] sts. Cont in Afghan knit st until 3 loop rows more are completed, ending with a return row. Work next 18 rows foll chart and using C and D.
Using C only work 5 loop rows in pat, ending with a return row. Work 18 chart rows, ending with a return row.
Rep from *** to *** twice more. 4 motifs complete.
Using C only, work in pat until panel 2 has same number of loop rows as panel 1 to beg of shoulder shaping, ending with a return row.

Neck shaping

Using C, work first side of neck as foll:
****Next row** Work as for loop row until there are 4 loops on hook, leaving rem sts unworked.
Work a return row on these sts.
Next row Work as for loop row until 2 loops are on hook, skip next st and draw up a loop in last st.
Work a return row. Work one loop and one return row without shaping. Dec one st at end of next loop row. 2 loops on hook. Yo and draw through 2 loops on hook. Fasten off.
Using C and with RS facing, draw up a

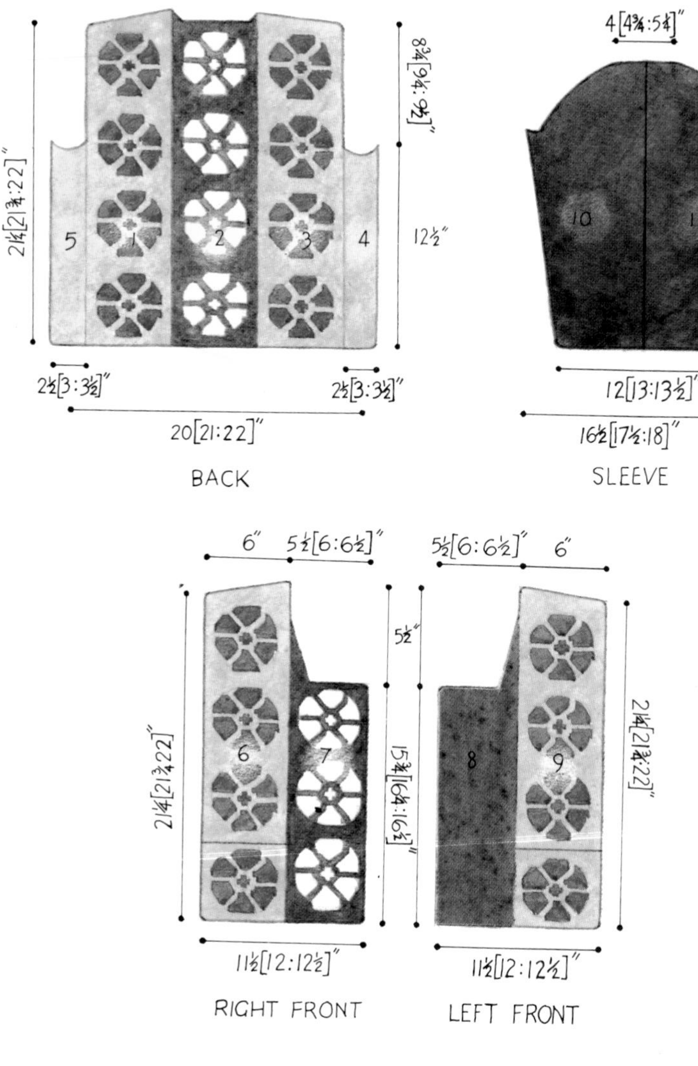

loop in last 4 sts of row and work a return row.
Next row Skip first 2 vertical loops in row below and work as for loop row across last 2 sts. 3 loops on hook.
Work a return row. Work one loop and one return row without shaping.
Dec one st in the same way at beg of next loop row. 2 loops on hook. Yo and draw a loop through 2 loops on hook. Fasten off.****

Panel 3

Work as for panel 1, reversing shoulder shaping by working decs at beg of row instead of end of row.

Panel 4

Using Afghan hook and A, ch11[13:15]. Work base-2nd rows as for panel 1. 11[13:15] sts. Cont in Afghan knit st, using A only, until panel measures 12½" from beg, ending with a return row.

Armhole shaping

Work as for panel 2 from **** to ****.

Panel 5

Work as for panel 4.

▶ RIGHT FRONT

Panel 6

Work as for panel 1 of back until first motif is complete, ending with a return row. Using A only, work one more loop and return row. Using ordinary crochet hook and A, ch1, 1sc in each vertical loop. Fasten off. This forms pocket.
Using Afghan hook and A, ch26 and work as for panel 1, omitting first motif, until panel 6 measures same as panel 1 to 2nd motif.
Complete as for panel 1.

Panel 7

Work as for panel 2 of back until 3 motifs have been completed, then cont without shaping, using C only, until panel measures 15¾[16¼:16½]" from beg, ending with a return row. Break off C and fasten off.

Neck shaping

Next row Skip first 17[19:21] vertical loops in last row and using C, draw up a loop in each of last 7 sts.
Cont in Afghan knit st until 2 more loop rows have been completed, ending with a return row.
Next row Skip first 2 vertical loops in row below and work as for loop row across last 5 sts. 6 loops on hook.
Work 3 loop rows without shaping, ending with a return row. Dec one st at neck edge on next loop row and then on every 4th loop row 4 times in all. 2 sts. Work 2 loop rows more on these 2 sts, drawing through 2 loops on hook at end of 2nd loop row. Fasten off.

▶ LEFT FRONT

Panel 8

Using C, ch24[26:28] and work base-2nd rows as for panel 2. 24[26:28] sts. Work in Afghan knit st, omitting motifs, until panel 8 measures same as panel 7 to neck shaping, ending with a return row.

Neck shaping

Next row Work as for loop row until there are 7 loops on hook.

Work a return row and complete neck shaping as for right front, reversing shaping.

Panel 9

Work as for panel 6, reversing shoulder shaping by working decs at beg of rows instead of end of row.

▶ SLEEVES (make 2)

Panel 10

Using C, ch26[28:29]. Work base- 2nd rows as for panel 1. Cont in Afghan knit st, inc one st at end of every 7th loop row 9 times in all. 35[37:38] sts.

Note: Work inc by inserting hook under ch between last 2 sts of row and drawing a loop through to make an extra st, then working last (edge) st in usual way.

Work without shaping until panel measures 14[14½:15]" from beg, ending with a return row.

Cap shaping

Next row Work as for loop row until there are 32[34:35] loops on hook, leaving rem sts unworked.

Work a return row. Dec one st at end of every alternate loop row 4 times, then one st at end of every loop row 10 times, then 2 sts at end of every loop row 5 times, ending with a return row. 8[10:11] sts.

Work one more loop and return row. Fasten off.

Panel 11

Work as for panel 10, reversing shaping by working incs and decs at beg of loop rows instead of at end.

▶ COLLAR

Using crochet hook and C, ch133.

Base row 1sc in 3rd ch from hook, *ch1, skip 1ch, 1sc in next ch, rep from * to end. Turn. 132 sts, counting each sc, each ch1 sp and turning ch as one st.

1st row Ch2, skip first sc, *1sc in next ch sp, ch1, rep from *, ending with 1sc in ch2 sp at end. Turn.

Rep last row to form seed pat.

Cont in seed pat until collar measures 1¾" from beg. Work one row in sc, working in each sc and each ch sp, then work one row in sl st, inserting hook under both loops at top of sc. Fasten off.

Edging

Using D, ch133. Work base and first rows as for collar. Cont in seed pat until edging measures 1".

Finish as for collar.

▶ CUFFS (make 2)

Using C, ch67[71:73]. Work base and first rows as for collar. 66[70:72] sts.

Cont in seed pat until cuff measures 1¾" from beg. Finish as for collar.

Edging

Using D, ch67[71:73]. Work as for cuff until edging measures 1".

Finish as for collar.

▶ FINISHING

Pin all Afghan crochet pieces to correct measurements face down on a padded surface. Press on WS with a warm iron and damp cloth.

Pin pockets in place on panels 6 and 9. Sew panels tog foll diagram. Work seam by overlapping last st of one panel over first st of adjacent panel and working a running st through both layers in a matching color. When joining panels 6 and 9, work through pockets and linings.

Join shoulder, sleeve and side seams. Set in sleeves.

Edging

Using crochet hook and C, work a row of sc evenly along horizontal straight edge at base of neck shaping on left front, down left front, then along lower edge changing to A when necessary to match colors, up right front and across base of neck, working 3sc at 4 corners and working through both thicknesses at base of pockets. Turn and work a 2nd row of sc in first.

Fasten off.

Sew edgings to collar and cuffs, overlapping so that edging protrudes ¾". Sew cuff seam. Sew on collar. Sew on cuffs, gathering lower sleeve to fit. Sew on hooks and eyes to fasten front. Sew in shoulder pads if desired. Press seams lightly on WS.

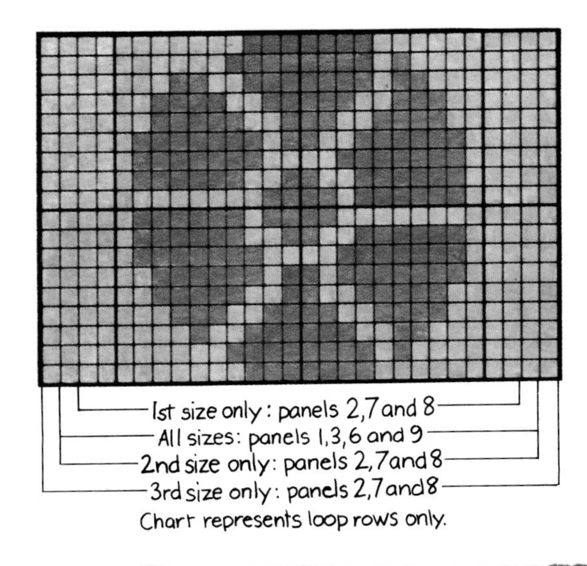

BOBBLED FAIR ISLE

Double crochet bobbles and Afghan stitch fans give this pretty jacket the look of Fair Isle knitting. The contrast of shiny mercerized cotton and soft wool adds texture to the crochet fabric.

▶ SIZES

To fit 32[34:36:38]"/81[86:91:96]cm bust.

Note: Figures for larger sizes are in brackets. If there is only one set of figures, it applies to all sizes.

See diagram for finished measurements.

▶ MATERIALS

See page 118 for further yarn information

Use a lightweight wool yarn (approx 218yd per $1\frac{3}{4}$oz) and a lightweight cotton yarn (approx 202yd per $1\frac{3}{4}$oz):

7[$8\frac{3}{4}$:$8\frac{3}{4}$]oz lightweight wool yarn in A (white)

$3\frac{1}{2}$[$5\frac{1}{4}$:$5\frac{1}{4}$]oz lightweight wool yarn in B (dusty pink)

$1\frac{3}{4}$oz lightweight wool yarn in each of C (gray green) and D (pale gray)

$3\frac{1}{2}$oz lightweight cotton yarn in E (pale aqua)

$1\frac{3}{4}$oz lightweight cotton yarn in each of F (pale lilac), G (cherry) and H (pink)

Sizes F, G and H crochet hooks *or sizes to obtain correct gauges*

Shoulder pads (optional)

▶ GAUGE

21 sts to 4" and 32 row pat rep to $7\frac{1}{2}$" over color pat using size G hook for fan rows and size F hook for all other pat rows.

21 sts and 22 rows to 4" over seed pat using size H hook (for sleeves).

To save time, take time to check gauge (see Note above).

Note: When working sc in color pat, always insert hook through both loops of the top of the sc of the last row in the usual way except where specifically stated otherwise. When changing colors in a row, change to new color with last yo of previous sc thus closing last st with new color (see page 112).

To check gauge over color pat ch28, using A and size F hook. Work one row in sc. 27sc. Then work first-34th rows of color pat. To check gauge over seed pat ch27, using A and size H hook. Work base-first rows of seed pat as for beg of back. Then cont in seed pat until piece measures 5".

▶ BACK

Using size G hook and A, ch111[117:123:129]. Beg seed pat as foll:

Base row 1sc in 3rd ch from hook, *ch1, skip 1ch, 1sc in next ch, rep from * to end. Turn. 110[116:122:128] sts, counting each sc, each ch sp and turning ch as one st.

1st row Ch2, 1sc in first ch sp, ch1, 1sc in next ch sp, rep from *, ending with ch1, 1sc in ch2 sp at end. Turn.

Last row forms seed pat.

2nd-5th rows Rep first row 4 times more.

6th row Using size F hook, ch1, 2sc in first sc, *1sc in next ch sp, 1sc in next sc, rep from *, ending with 1sc in ch2 sp at end. Turn. 111[117:123:129]sc.

This completes seed pat edging.

Beg color pat as foll:

1st pat row (fan row) (RS) Using size G hook and B, ch1, skip first sc, (insert

hook in next sc, yo and draw a loop through) 3 times — 4 loops on hook, yo and draw through 1 loop on hook, (yo and draw through 2 loops on hook) 3 times — 4 Afghan sts made, draw E through loop and drop and tighten B, ch4, skip first ch and draw up a loop *loosely* in each of rem E chs, draw up a loop *loosely* in each of first 3 Afghan sts inserting hook from right to left through vertical bar of each st and leaving last Afghan st unworked — 7 loops on hook, yo and draw through all 7 loops (fan), ch1 for eye, *draw B through loop and drop and tighten E, draw up a loop in eye of fan just made, 1 loop in back of last loop of fan, 1 loop in vertical bar of last unworked Afghan st, 1 loop in each of next 3sc — 7 loops on hook, yo and draw through 1 loop on hook, (yo and draw through 2 loops on hook) 6 times — 7 Afghan sts made, draw E through loop and drop B, draw up a loop in each of first 6 vertical bars of Afghan sts, yo and draw through all 7 loops on hook, ch1 for eye, rep from *, ending draw B through loop and drop E, draw up a loop in eye of fan just made, 1 loop in back of last loop of fan, 1 loop in vertical bar of last unworked Afghan st, 1 loop in each of last 2sc — 6 loops on hook, yo and draw through 1 loop on hook, (yo and draw through 2 loops on hook) 5 times — 6 Afghan sts made, draw E through loop and drop B, draw up a loop in each of last 6 vertical bars of Afghan sts, yo and draw through all 7 loops on hook, ch1, draw B through loop and drop E. Turn.

2nd row Using size F hook and B, ch1, 1sc in eye of first fan, *1sc in top loop of same fan, 1sc in top of next Afghan st, 1sc in eye of next fan, rep from *, ending with 1sc in top loop of last fan, 1sc in top of E ch. Turn. 111[117:123:129]sc.

Note: Always count sts at end of last row to make sure that there are correct number of sts.

Cont with size F hook until next fan row is reached.

3rd and 4th rows Using F, ch1, 1sc in each sc to end. Turn.

5th row Using A, ch1, working in *back* loops only, 1sc in each sc to end. Turn.

6th row Using A, ch1, 1sc in first sc, *1sc in next sc but inserting hook through *front* loop only, 1sc in each of next 3sc, rep from *, ending with 1sc in each rem sc to end. Turn.

7th row (bobble row) Using A, ch1, 1sc in each sc to first of skipped loops of last row, changing to G with last yo of last sc, *skip sc above skipped loop, (yo, insert hook from bottom to top through skipped loop, yo and draw a loop through, yo and draw through 2 loops on hook) 5 times — 6 loops on hook, drop G and using A draw through all 6 loops on hook — called bobble —, carrying G across top of last row and working all sts over it, work 1sc in each of next 3sc, rep from *, ending last rep with 1sc in last sc. Turn.

8th row Using A, ch1, 1sc in each sc and each bobble. Turn.

9th and 10th rows As 3rd and 4th rows.

11th row As first row of color pat, but inserting hook through *back* loops only when working in sc of last row.

12th row As 2nd row.

13th row Using C, ch1, 1sc in each of next 2sc changing to A with last yo of last sc, using A, 1sc in each of next 2sc changing to C with last yo of last sc, cont in this way working 2sc in C and 2sc in A alternately until row is complete. Turn.

14th-16th rows Ch1, work all sc in A in C and all sc in C in A, thus reversing positions of C and A in each row. Turn.

17th and 18th rows As first and 2nd rows of color pat.

19th and 20th rows Using H, work in sc. Turn.

21st row Using D, work in sc working in *back* loops only. Turn.

22nd and 23rd rows As 6th and 7th rows.
24th row Using D, as 8th row.
25th-26th rows As 19th and 20th rows.
27th-34th rows As 11th-18th rows.
Rep 3rd-34th color pat rows to form color pat.
Cont in color pat until back measures 27[27½:28:28½]" from beg. Fasten off.

▶ **FRONTS** (make 2)
Using size G hook and A, ch43[45:49:51] and work base and first rows as for seed pat on back. 42[44:48:50] sts. Work 2nd-6th rows as for seed pat on back inc one st on 6th row for *2nd and 4th sizes only.* 42[45:48:51]sc.
Beg with first color pat row of back, complete as for back.

▶ **SLEEVES** (make 2)
Using size H hook and A, ch57 and work base and first rows as for seed pat on back. 56 sts.
**Work 6[5:5:5] rows more in seed pat.
Next row (inc row) Ch2, 1sc in first sc, ch1, 1sc in first ch sp, work in pat across row, ending with (1sc, ch1, 1sc) all in ch2 sp. Turn. 4 sts increased.** 60 sts.
Rep from ** to ** 11[12:13:13] times more. 104[108:112:112] sts. Work in seed pat without shaping until sleeve measures 17¾" from beg or desired sleeve length. Fasten off.

▶ **FRONT BANDS** (make 2)
Using size H hook and A, ch161[163:165:167] and work base and first rows as for seed pat on back. 160[162:164:166] sts. Work 4 rows more in seed pat. Fasten off.

▶ **FINISHING**
Do not press. Weave in all loose ends. Join shoulder seams leaving 6¼" free at center back for back neck. Sew on front bands from lower edge of fronts to center back neck. Sew seam of band at center back. Mark positions of sleeves 10[10¼:10¾]" from shoulder seams. Sew on sleeves between markers. Join side and sleeve seams. Press seams lightly on WS with warm iron. If desired, sew in shoulder pads.

DESIGN VARIATIONS

▶ **VEST**
For a vest work back and fronts as for cardigan. For armbands ch117 and work as for front band. Finish as for cardigan, omitting sleeves and leaving 11" open from shoulder seams for armbands. Join armband seam and sew in place.

▶ **PULLOVER**
For a pullover work back and front alike. Finish as for cardigan omitting front bands and leaving 11" open for neck. Then make neckband as for a single armband. Join neckband seam and sew in place.

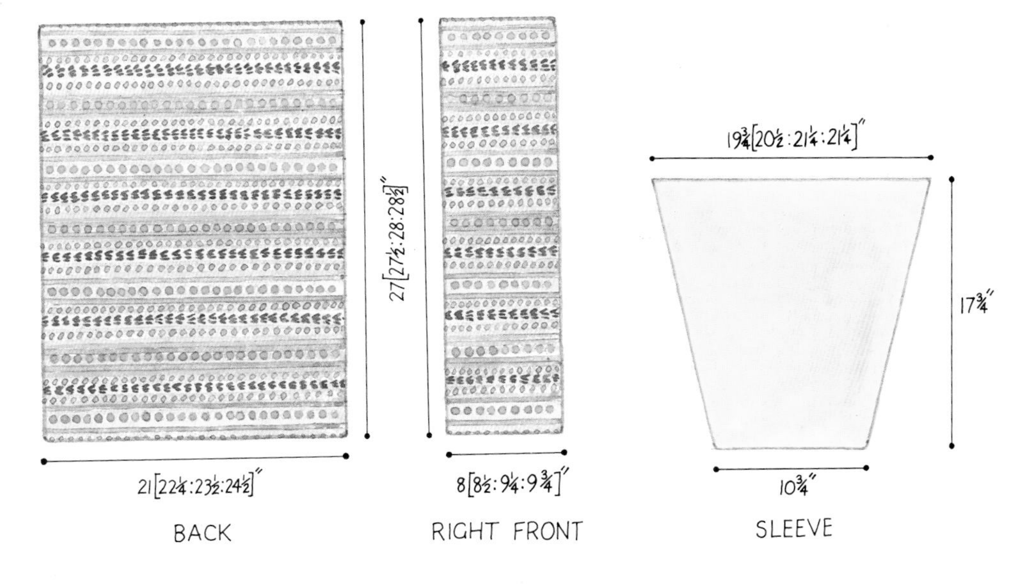

WAVES & CHECKS

The patterns on this sweater, crocheted in a slubbed cotton yarn, are made by varying the stitch heights and by using overlapping, elongated single crochet which means only one color is used in each row. A design variation can be made from this pattern by omitting the sleeves.

▶ SIZES

To fit 32[34:36:38]"/81[86:91:96]cm bust.

Note: Figures for larger sizes are in brackets. If there is only one set of figures, it applies to all sizes.

See diagram for finished measurements.

▶ MATERIALS

See page 118 for further yarn information

Use a medium weight slubbed cotton yarn (109yd per 1¾oz):
12¼[12¼:14:15¾]oz in A (lilac)
5¼[5¼:7:7]oz in each of B (light blue) and D (pink)
7[8¾:8¾:8¾]oz in C (purple)
3½oz in E (coral)
Size H crochet hook *or size to obtain correct gauge*

▶ GAUGE

16 sts to 4" over pat and 18 rows of pat rep to 3½" using size H hook.
18sc and 20 rows to 4" over rib pat using size H hook.
To save time, take time to check gauge.

Note: To check gauge ch20 and work base-18th rows of back foll instructions for first size. Make sure that the elongated sc sts are worked *loosely* so that they do not pull the fabric tog.

▶ BACK

Using A, ch80[84:88:92].
Base row Using A, 1sc in 2nd ch from hook, 1sc in each sc to end. Turn. 79[83:87:91]sc.
1st row Using A, ch1, 1sc in each sc to end. Turn.
2nd row As first row.
3rd row Using B, ch1, 1sc in each of first 3sc, working next 2 sts through rows below, insert hook from front through top of sc 2 rows below next sc, yo and draw a loop through pulling loop up to height of previous row so that fabric is not pulled tog, yo and draw through 2 loops on hook — called 1sc in next sc 2 rows below —, *1sc in each of next 2sc, (1sc in next sc 2 rows below) twice, rep from *, ending with 1sc in each of last 2sc. Turn.
4th row Using B, as first row.
5th row Using A, as first row.
6th row Using A, ch1, 1sc in first sc, 1sc in next sc 2 rows below, *1sc in each of next 2sc, (1sc in next sc 2 rows below) twice, rep from *, ending with 1sc in last sc. Turn.
Using C, work 4 rows in sc.
11th row Using D, ch1, 1sc in first sc, *1sc in next sc one row below, 1sc in next sc 2 rows below, 1sc in next sc 3 rows below, 1sc in next sc 2 rows below, 1sc in next sc one row below, 1sc in next sc, rep from * to last sc, 1sc in last sc. Turn.
Using D, work 3 rows in sc.
15th row Using C, as for 11th row.
Using C, work one row in sc.
17th row Using B, ch1, 1sc in first st, *1hdc in next st, 1dc in next st, 1tr in next st, 1dc in next st, 1hdc in next st, 1sc in next st, rep from *, ending with 0[1:1:0]hdc in next st, 0[1:1:0]dc in next st, 0[1:0:0]tr in next st, 0[1:0:0]dc in next st. Turn.
18th row Using E, ch5[2:2:5], skip first st, 0[1:0:0]sc in next st, 0[1:0:0]hdc in next st, 0[1:1:0]dc in next st, 0[1:1:0]tr in next st, *1dc in next st, 1hdc in next st, 1sc in next st, 1hdc in next st, 1dc in next st, 1tr in next st, rep from * to end, working last st in turning ch. Turn.
19th row Using A, as first row working last sc in turning ch.
2nd-19th rows form pat and are repeated throughout.
Cont in pat until back measures 20¾[21¼:21¾:22¼]" from beg.
Fasten off.

▶ FRONT

Work as for back until front measures 9¼[9¾:10¼:10¾]" from beg.

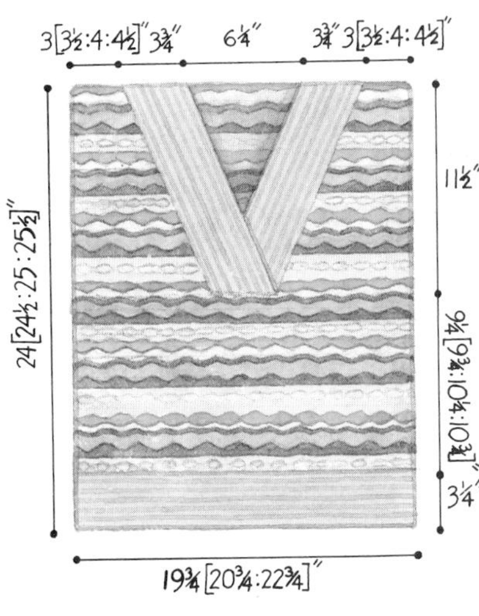

FRONT/BACK

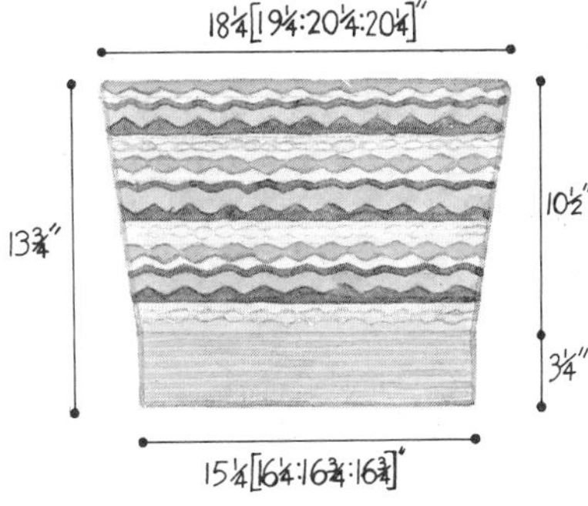

SLEEVE

Neck shaping
Keeping to pat as set, beg neck shaping as foll:
Next row Work in pat across first 32[34:36:38] sts. Turn, leaving rem sts unworked.
Cont on these sts, dec one st at neck edge on every 2nd and 3rd rows alternately 10 times in all. 22[24:26:28] sts. Dec one st at neck edge every 3rd row 10 times. 12[14:16:18] sts.
Cont without shaping until front measures same as back to shoulder. Fasten off. Skip center 15 sts and work in pat across last 32[34:36:38] sts. Work 2nd side of neck as for first side, reversing shaping.

▶ SLEEVES (make 2)
Using A, ch62[66:68:68] and work base-2nd rows as for back. 61[65:67:67]sc.
3rd row Using B, ch1, 1sc in each of first 3sc, *(1sc in next sc 2 rows below) twice, 1sc in each of next 2sc, rep from *, ending with 1[1:0:0]sc in sc 2 rows below next sc, 1[1:0:0]sc in next sc. Turn.
Cont working in pat as for back *and at the same time* inc one st at each end of 7th row and then every 8th[8th:7th:7th] row 6[6:7:7] times in all. 73[77:81:81] sts.
Cont in pat without shaping until sleeve measures 10½" from beg. Fasten off.

▶ BACK RIB
Using A, ch87[92:96:101].
Base row 1sc in 2nd ch from hook, 1sc in each ch to end. Turn. 86[91:95:100]sc.
1st row Ch1, working in *back* loops only throughout, 1sc in each sc to end. Turn.
Rep last row to form rib pat. Work 14 rows more in rib pat. Fasten off.

▶ FRONT RIB
Work as for back rib.

▶ NECKBANDS (make 2)
Using A, ch56 and work base and first rows as for back rib. 55sc.
***2nd row** Ch1, 2sc in first sc, 1sc in each sc to last 2sc, (insert hook in next sc, yo and draw a loop through) twice — called 2sc tog. Turn.
Rep first row 3 times.*
Rep from * to * twice more, rep 2nd row once, rep first row once. Fasten off.

▶ SLEEVE BANDS (make 2)
Using A, ch67[73:76:76] and work base and first rows as for back rib. 66[72:75:75]sc. Work 14 rows more in rib as for back rib. Fasten off.

▶ FINISHING
Do not press. Weave in all loose ends. Join shoulder seams. Sew ribs to back and front. Sew sleeve bands to sleeves. Mark positions for sleeves 9[9½:10:10]" from shoulder seams. Sew on sleeves between markers. Join side and sleeve seams. Sew neckbands in place overlapping right neckband over left neckband at center front. Press lightly on WS, avoiding ribs.

DESIGN VARIATION

▶ SLEEVELESS TOP
For a sleeveless top follow instructions omitting sleeves and sleevebands. For armhole bands ch92 and work base and first rows as for back rib. Work in rib pat for 6 rows more and fasten off. Sew armhole band seams. Finish as for version with sleeves, omitting sleeves and leaving 10¼" from shoulder seams open for armholes. Sew on armhole bands.

A sleeveless variation makes a loose summer vest in crisp contrasting tones of black, white and gray.

OPENWORK

OPENWORK

Crochet lace is probably the most well-known crochet fabric and it is still popular as bedspreads, tablecloths and edgings for sheets and pillowcases. Using lace collars and cuffs on garments goes in and out of fashion but there are other equally effective ways of using crochet openwork for sweaters. The advantage of working open crochet stitches rather than solid stitches is that the resulting fabric is lighter and provides an attractive drape. It is best to stick to the stitches that are not too transparent unless you really want a see-through effect.

▶ ADDING COLOR

Most crocheters are conditioned to think of lacy fabrics in white or ecru cotton yarn, unaware of how stunning a splash of color can be. There is no need to restrict openwork to smooth cotton. Fuzzier yarns such as chenille or mohair are particularly striking for widely spaced stitches because the fibers extend in the open holes. Variations on the bobbled zigzag patterns on *Bobbled lace* (page 103) are given here (3 and 5). They translate easily onto the simple top because the top is merely two rectangles and requires no neck or armhole shaping. The pattern with vertical stripes (4) is for more advanced crocheters. Each vertical stripe is worked with a separate length of yarn. A simpler way to introduce color is with horizontal stripes so that each color is worked over two rows (5).

▶ MOTIFS ON FILET

Filet crochet should not be seen as merely curtain fabric. Color patterns or motifs can transform a simple filet net into a perfect fashion fabric. Again stripes are the simplest color design. The net ground is also an ideal base for weaving (see page 113) or for applied motifs. The motifs here (1), worked onto a striped filet net, are little rectangles in surface slip stitch (see page 111). Motifs can be charted and worked into the basic net fabric (2). Both of these designs are alternatives for the checkered pattern on *Chenille checkers* (page 106).

▶ BOBBLES ON FILET

Contrasting bobble patterns on filet (4) are designed by charting bobble shapes or outlines onto a graph paper so that each square represents a chain space. The bobbles are worked in the center of the space. The sample shown here is another possible design variation for *Chenille checkers* (page 106).

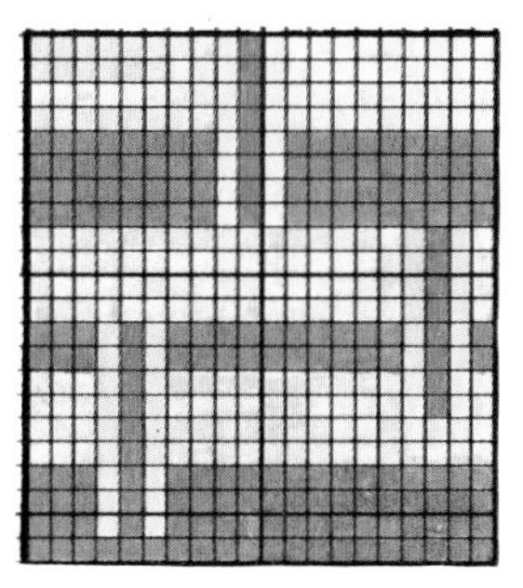

1 Worked in hdc filet net (see symbol chart) with added sl st motifs following chart above for stripe sequence and placement of sl st motifs. Each square represents a ch space.

2 Worked in hdc filet net (see symbol chart) following chart above for colors. Each square represents a ch space.

1

2

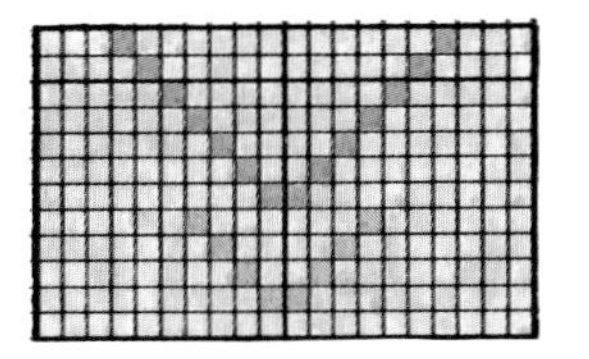

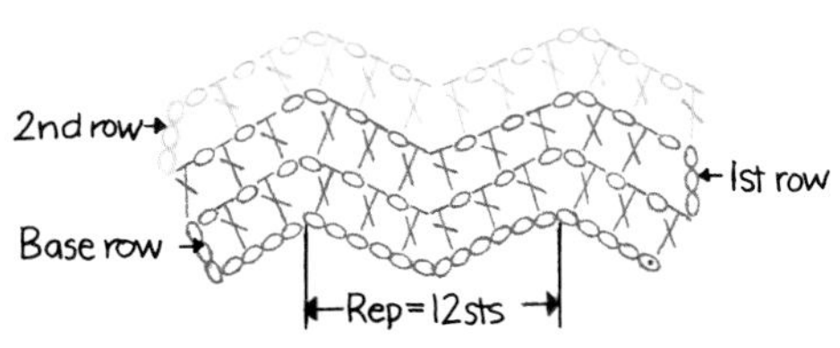

Foundation ch = multiple of 12ch plus one.

5 Repeat 2nd row to form pat, working 2 rows in each color alternately. Weave 4 strands of a contrasting yarn up centre of every other zigzag.

3 Worked in hdc filet net (see symbol chart) with bobbles following chart above for placement of bobbles. Each square represents a ch space or a bobble. (See page 111 for bobbles.)

Symbol chart for filet net (1, 2 and 3)

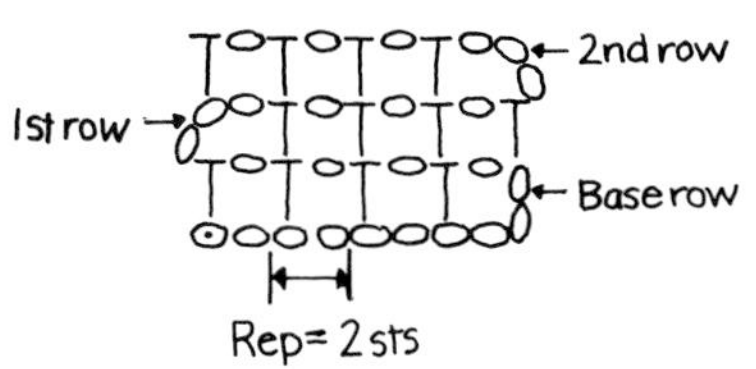

Foundation ch = odd number of ch.
Rep 2nd row to form pat.

4 See page 103 for symbol chart to work openwork zigzag pat with bobbles. Use a separate ball of yarn for each zigzag to form vertical stripes and use a short length of contrasting color for each bobble.

5

3

4

SCALLOPED LACE

This soft mohair sweater is very quick to make. It is worked in a combination of doubles, single crochet and chain stitches which form a simple openwork pattern. The sweater can be worn with or without the cowl neck, which is made separately.

▶ SIZES

To fit 32[34-36:38-40]"/81[86-91:96-102]cm bust.

Note: Figures for larger sizes are in brackets. If there is only one set of figures, it applies to all sizes.

See diagram for finished measurements.

▶ MATERIALS

See page 118 for further yarn information

Use a lightweight silk and mohair yarn (approx 66yd per 3/4oz):

8 1/4[9:10 1/2]oz in main color MC (white)

2 1/4[2 1/4:3]oz in each of 3 contrasting colors A (yellow), B (pink) and C (pale lilac)

Sizes F and G crochet hooks *or sizes to obtain correct gauges*

▶ GAUGE

6 V sts (or six ch4 spaces) and 11 rows to 4" over lace pat using size F hook. 18sc and 18 rows to 4" over rib pat using size G hook.
To save time, take time to check gauge (see Note below).

Note: Back, front and sleeves are worked in rows which progress from side seam to side seam instead of from lower edge to top in the usual way. To check gauge ch26 using MC and work base-2nd rows of back or foll symbol chart. Cont in pat until work measures 5".

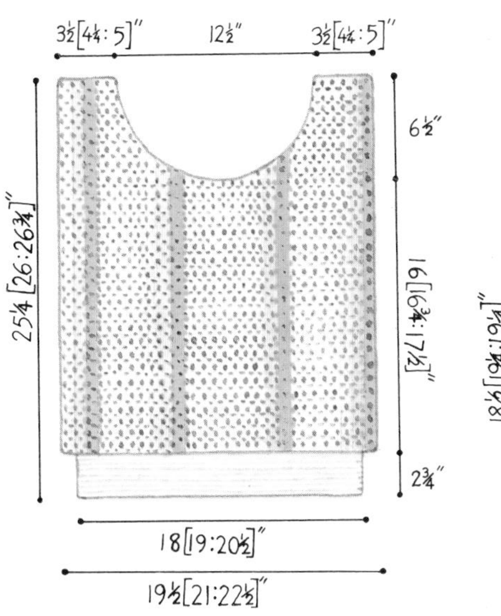

FRONT/BACK

▶ BACK AND FRONT (alike)

Using smaller hook and MC, ch104[107:110] and beg at side seam as foll:
Base row 1sc in 2nd ch from hook, *ch4, skip 2ch, 1sc in next ch, rep from * to end. Turn. 34[35:36] ch4 spaces.
1st row Using A, ch5, 1dc in first ch4 sp, *(1dc, ch1, 1dc — called V st) all in next ch4 sp, rep from * to end. Turn. 34[35:36] V sts, counting ch5 and first dc as first V st.
2nd row Using A, ch1, 1sc in first dc, ch4, 1sc in sp between first 2 V sts, *ch4, 1sc in sp between next 2 V sts, rep from *, ending last rep with 1sc in ch5 sp. Turn.
Last 2 rows form lace pat. Cont in lace pat, working next 2 rows in B, then 2 rows in C and 3[5:7] rows in MC.

Neck shaping

Using MC, beg to shape neck as foll:
Next row Work sl st loosely across top of first 2 V sts, 1sc in sp between 2nd and 3rd V sts, work in pat to end. Turn. Two ch4 sps decreased. 32[33:34] ch4 sps.
Next row Work in pat to last ch4 sp. Turn. One V st decreased. 31[32:33] V sts.

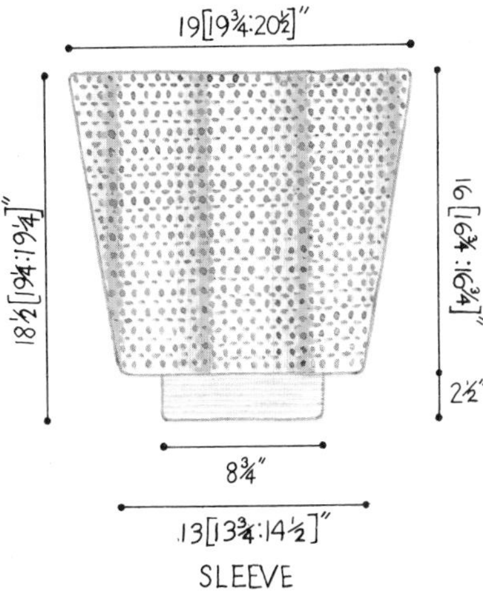

SLEEVE

Rep last 2 rows once more. 28[29:30] V sts.
Next row Work sl st loosely across top of first V st, 1sc in sp between first and 2nd V sts, work in pat to end. Turn. 27[28:29] ch4 sps.
Next row Using A, work in pat without dec. Turn.
Rep last 2 rows 3 times more, working in stripes of one row A, 2 rows B, 2 rows C and one row MC. 24[25:26] V sts.
Using MC, work 11 rows in pat without shaping. Work one row A.
Next row Using A, ch4, 1sc in 2nd ch from hook, ch4, skip ch2, 1sc in first dc, work in pat to end. Turn. One ch4 sp increased. 25[26:27] ch4 sps.
Next row Using B, work in pat without inc. Turn.
Rep last 2 rows twice more, working one row B, 2 rows C and one row MC. 27[28:29] V sts.
Using MC, cont to shape neck as foll:
Next row Inc one ch4 sp at beg of row, work in pat to end. Turn.
Next row Work in pat to end of row, then work one more V st in last ch4 sp. Turn. 29[30:31] V sts.
Next row Ch7, 1sc in 2nd ch from hook, ch4, skip 2ch, 1sc in next ch, ch4, 1sc in first dc, work in pat to end. Turn. 31[32:33] ch4 sps.
Rep last 2 rows once more. 34[35:36] ch4 sps.
Cont in pat without shaping, working 2[4:6] rows MC, then 2 rows A, 2 rows B, 2 rows C and one row MC. Fasten off.

▶ SLEEVES (make 2)

Using smaller hook and C, ch14[17:17] and work base row as for back. 4[5:5] ch4 sps.
1st row Using B, ch5, 1dc in first ch4 sp, *1 V st in next ch4 sp, rep from * to end, then work 1 more V st in last ch4 sp. Turn. 5[6:6] V sts.
2nd row Using B, ch13, 1sc in 2nd ch from hook, (ch4, skip 2ch, 1sc in next ch) 3 times, ch4, 1sc in first dc, work in pat to end. Turn. 9[10:10] ch4 sps.
Rep last 2 rows 3 times more, working 2 rows A and 4 rows MC. 24[25:25] ch4 sps.
Cont in pat without shaping, working 6 rows more MC, 2 rows C, 2 rows B, 2

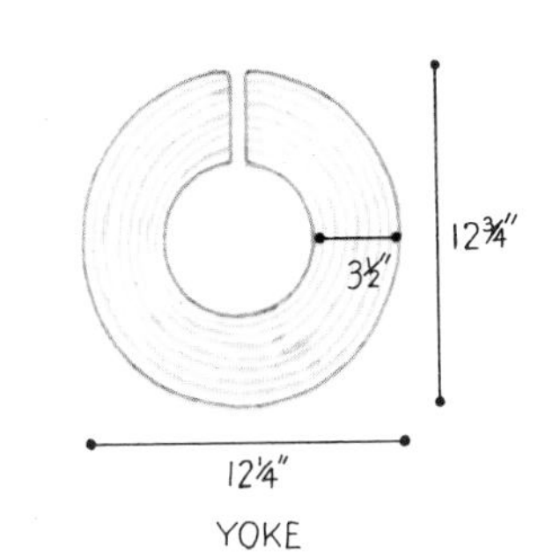

YOKE

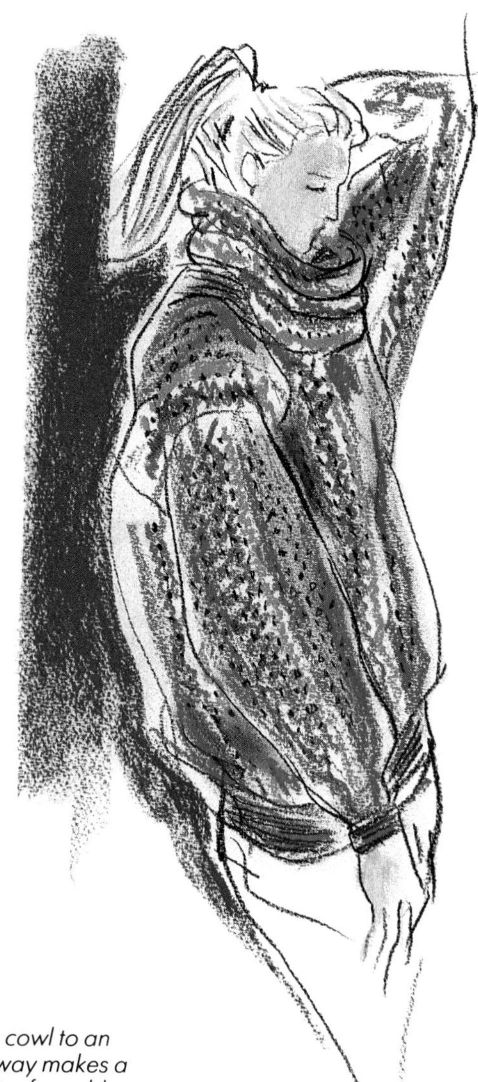

The addition of a cowl to an alternative colorway makes a softly snug sweater for colder days.

rows A, 10[12:14] rows MC, 2 rows C, 2 rows B, 2 rows A and 7 rows MC, so ending with a V st row.
Using MC, beg shaping 2nd side of sleeve as foll:
Next row Work sl st loosely across top of first 4 V sts, 1sc in sp between 4th and 5th V sts, work in pat to end. Turn. 20[21:21] ch4 sps.
Next row Work in pat to last ch4 sp. Turn. 19[20:20] V sts.
Rep last 2 rows 3 times more, working one row more MC, 2 rows C, 2 rows B, one row A. Fasten off.

▶ BACK RIB
Using larger hook and MC, ch82[87:93].
Base row 1sc in 2nd ch from hook, 1sc in each ch to end. Turn. 81[86:92]sc.
1st row (WS) Ch1, working in *front* loop only of each sc, 1sc in each sc to end. Turn.
2nd row (RS) Ch1, working in *back* loop only of each sc, 1sc in each sc to end. Turn.
Last 2 rows form rib pat. Work in rib pat until rib measures 2¾" from beg. Fasten off.

▶ FRONT RIB
Work as for back rib.

▶ CUFFS (make 2)
Using larger hook and MC, ch40. Work base-2nd rows as for back rib. 39sc. Cont in rib pat until cuff measures 2½" from beg. Fasten off.

▶ YOKE
Using larger hook and MC, ch179 and work base and first rows as for back rib. 178sc.
2nd row (RS) Ch1, working in *back* loop only of each sc, 1sc in each of first 10sc, (insert hook in next sc, yo and draw a loop through) twice, yo and draw through all 3 loops on hook — called 2sc tog —, *1sc in each of next 10sc, 2sc tog*, rep from * to * 12 times more, 1sc in each sc to end. Turn. 164sc.
3rd row As first row.
4th row Ch1, working in *back* loop only of each sc, 1sc in each sc dec 14 sts evenly across row. Turn. 150sc.
Rep last 2 rows 5 times more. 80sc.
Next row As first row.
Fasten off.

▶ COWL
Using smaller hook and MC, ch95.
Work base row as for back rib. 94sc.
****1st row** Using A, ch5, 1dc in first sc, *skip 2sc, (1dc, ch1, 1dc) all in next sc, rep from * to end. Turn. 32 V sts.
2nd row Using A, as for 2nd row of back. Turn.
3rd row Using B, ch5, 1dc in first ch4 sp, *(1dc, ch2, 1dc — called V st) all in next ch4 sp, rep from * to end. Turn.
4th row Using B, ch1, 1sc in first dc, ch5, 1sc in sp between first 2 V sts, *ch5, 1sc in sp between next 2 V sts, rep from *, ending last rep with 1sc in ch5 sp. Turn.
Rep last 2 rows 3 times more, working V sts in ch5 sps and working 2 rows more in B, then 4 rows in C.
Next row Using MC, ch3, 1sc in first ch5 sp, *3sc in next ch5 sp, rep from * to end. 94sc.
Using MC, work one row in sc.**
Rep from ** to ** 2 times more.
Next row Using MC, ch3, skip first 2sc, 1dc in each of next 2sc, *skip next sc, 1dc in each of next 2sc, rep from * to end.
Work one row in sc. Fasten off.

▶ FINISHING
Do not press. Join shoulder seams. Mark positions of sleeves 9½[9¾:10¼]" from shoulder seams. Sew on sleeves between markers. Sew on cuffs and back and front ribs, easing in fullness. Join side and sleeve seams. Sew center back yoke seam. Sew yoke to neck edge with seam at center back.
Using smaller hook and A and with RS facing, work one row of sc evenly around neck edge. Join with a sl st to first sc. Fasten off.
Join cowl seam.

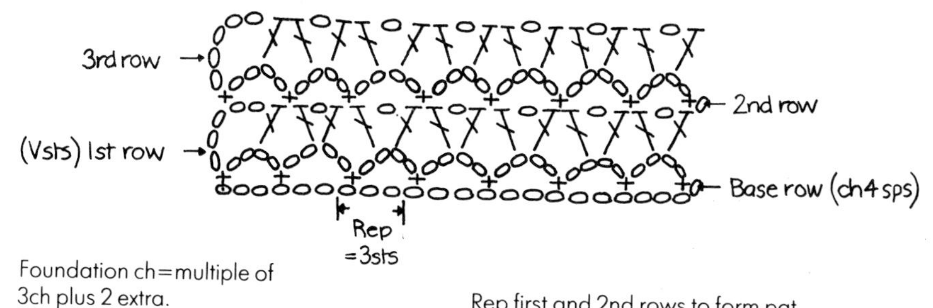

Foundation ch=multiple of 3ch plus 2 extra.

Rep first and 2nd rows to form pat.

BOBBLED LACE

Double crochet bobbles dot the openwork zigzags of this loose-fitting off-the-shoulder tunic. The simple lace pattern is worn over a body-hugging crochet rib top with a high neckline which snaps together.

▶ SIZES

To fit 32-34[36:38-40]"/81-86[91:96-102]cm bust.

Note: Figures for larger sizes are in brackets. If there is only one set of figures, it applies to all sizes.

See diagram for finished measurements.

▶ MATERIALS

See page 118 for further yarn information

Use a lightweight cotton yarn (approx 202yd per 1¾oz):

14[16:17½]oz for lace top

10[11½:13½]oz for ribbed top

Size E crochet hook *or size to obtain correct gauges*

Snaps

▶ GAUGE

20dc to 3½" over lace pat using size E hook.

23sc and 30 rows to 4" over rib pat using size E hook.

To save time, take time to check gauge.

Note: Back and front of ribbed top are worked in rows which progress from side seam to side seam instead of from lower edge to top in the usual way. To check gauge ch36 and work base-4th rows of back or foll symbol chart. Cont in pat until sample measures 5".

LACE TOP

▶ BACK AND FRONT (alike)

Ch132[144:156].

Base row 1dc in 4th ch from hook, 1dc in each of next 3ch, ch2, 1dc in each of next 5ch, *skip 2ch, 1dc in each of next 5ch, ch2, 1dc in each of next 5ch, rep from * to end. Turn. 110[120:130]dc, counting turning ch as first dc.

1st row (RS) Ch4, skip first 3dc and work 1dc in 4th dc, ch1, skip next dc, 1dc in first of next 2ch, ch1; 5dc in same ch as last dc was worked, remove hook and insert through top of first dc of 5dc group, draw working loop through — called bobble —, *ch1, 1dc in next ch, (ch1, skip next dc, 1dc in next dc) twice, skip next 2dc, (1dc in next dc, ch1, skip next dc) twice, 1dc in first of next 2ch, ch1, 1 bobble in same ch as last dc, rep from *, ending with ch1, 1dc in next ch, ch1, skip next dc, 1dc in next dc, ch1, skip last 2dc, 1dc in 3rd of ch3. Turn.

2nd row Ch3, skip first dc and first ch1 sp, (1dc in next dc, 1dc in next ch1 sp) twice, *ch2, skip st at top of bobble, (1dc in next ch1 sp, 1dc in next dc) twice, 1dc in next ch1 sp, skip next 2dc, (1dc in next ch1 sp, 1dc in next dc) twice, 1dc in next ch1 sp, rep from *, ending with ch2, skip st at top of bobble, (1dc in next ch1 sp, 1dc in next dc) twice, 1dc in 3rd of ch4. Turn.

3rd row Ch3, skip first 2dc, 1dc in each of next 3dc, *1dc in first of next 2ch, ch1, 1 bobble in same ch as last dc, ch1, 1dc in next ch, 1dc in each of next 4dc, skip 2dc, 1dc in each of next 4dc, rep from *, ending with 1dc in first of next 2ch, ch1, 1 bobble in same ch as last dc, ch1, 1dc in next ch, 1dc in each of next 3dc, skip last dc, 1dc in 3rd of ch4. Turn.

4th row Ch3, skip first 2dc, 1dc in each of next 3dc, *1dc in next ch1 sp, ch2, skip st at top of bobble, 1dc in next ch1 sp, 1dc in each of next 4dc, skip next 2dc, 1dc in each of next 4dc, rep from *, ending with 1dc in next ch1 sp, ch2, skip st at top of bobble, 1dc in next ch1 sp, 1dc in each of next 3dc, skip last dc, 1dc in 3rd of ch3. Turn.

First-4th rows form lace pat. Cont in lace pat until work measures 22[22¾:23½]" from beg, ending with a 2nd or a 4th row.

Work a finishing row as foll:

Last row (RS) Ch3, skip first dc, 1dc in next dc, 1hdc in each of next 2dc, 1sc in next dc, 1sc in ch2 sp, *1sc in next dc, 1hdc in each of next 2dc, 1dc in each of next 4dc, 1hdc in each of next 2dc, 1sc in next dc, 1sc in ch2 sp, rep from *, ending with 1sc in next dc, 1hdc in each of next 2dc, 1dc in last dc, 1dc in 3rd of ch3. Fasten off.

▶ FINISHING

Do not press. Join shoulder seams, leaving 12½" open at center for neck opening. Join side seams, leaving 8½[9:9½]" open at top for armholes. Work a row of sc evenly around armholes, join with a sl st to first sc and fasten off.

RIBBED TOP

▶ BACK

Side shaping

** Ch10 and beg shaped piece at underarm as foll:

Base row (RS) 1sc in 2nd ch from hook, 1sc in each ch to end. Turn. 9sc.

1st row (WS) Ch9, 1sc in 2nd ch from

5th row

4th row

3rd row

2nd row

1st row

Base row

bobble (see first row of instructions)

Foundation ch = multiple of 12ch.

Rep 1st-4th rows to form pat.

5¼[5¼:5½]"

2¼[2¼:2¾]"

7¾[8¼:9]"

16½[17¾:18¾]"

22¼[22¾:23½]"

14½"

14½[15½:16¾]"

17¾[18½:19½]"

FRONT/BACK

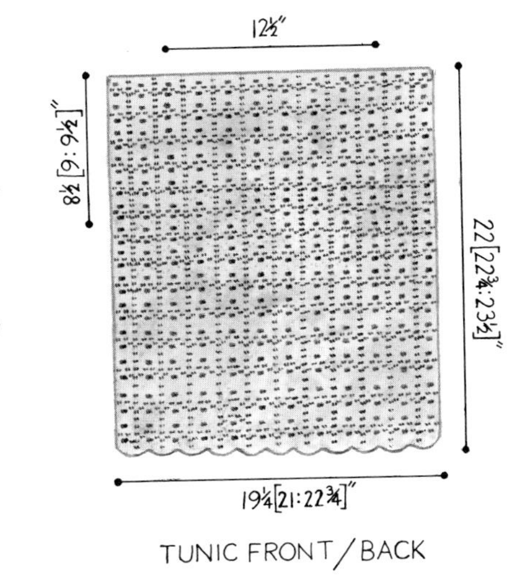

TUNIC FRONT/BACK

hook, 1sc in each of next 7ch, working in *back* loops only work 1sc in each sc to end. Turn. 17sc.
2nd row Ch1, working in *back* loops only, work 1sc in each sc to end. Turn.
Rib pat is formed by working sc in *back* loops only throughout. Cont in rib pat as foll:
3rd row As first row. 25sc.
4th row As 2nd row.
Rep last 2 rows once more, so ending with a RS row. 33sc. Break off yarn and set piece aside.
Ch17 and work base row as for first piece. 16sc.
Next row (WS) As 2nd row.
Next row (RS) Ch5, 1sc in 2nd ch from hook, 1sc in each of next 3ch, work in rib pat to end. Turn. 20sc.
Rep last 2 rows 3 times more. 32sc.
Joining and armhole shaping
Join to first piece as foll:
Next row (WS) Work in rib pat to end, do not turn, ch19, then cont in rib pat across first piece. Turn.
Next row (RS) Ch1, 2sc in first sc (armhole edge), work in rib pat to end, working 1sc in each ch. Turn. 85sc.
Work one row without shaping.
Next row Ch1, 2sc in first sc, work in rib pat to end. Turn. 86sc.
Work one row without shaping.
Rep last 2 rows 0[2:2] times more, so ending at armhole edge. 86[88:88]sc.
Inc one st at armhole edge on next and every foll row 20[20:24] times in all, so ending at armhole edge.
106[108:112]sc.
Next row Ch1, 2sc in each of first 2sc, work in rib pat to end. Turn.
108[110:114]sc.
Next row Work in pat to last 2sc, 2sc in each of last 2sc. Turn. 110[112:116]sc.
Rep last 2 rows 3 times more, so ending at armhole edge.
122[124:128]sc.
Next row Ch8[8:9], 1sc in 2nd ch from hook, 1sc in each of next 6[6:7]ch, work in pat to end. Turn.
129[131:136]sc.
Work one row without shaping. Break off yarn.**
Neck shaping
Next row Skip first 3[3:4]sc and rejoin yarn to next sc with a sl st, ch1, 1sc in same place as sl st, work in pat to end. Turn. 126[128:132]sc.
Next row Work in pat to last 2sc, (insert hook in next sc, yo and draw a loop through) twice, yo and draw through all 3 loops on hook — called 2sc tog. Turn. 125[127:131]sc.

Next row Ch1, 2sc tog, work in pat to end. Turn. 124[126:130]sc.
Work 35[35:37] rows without shaping, so ending at neck edge. Inc one st at neck edge on next 2 rows.
126[128:132]sc.
Next row Ch4[4:5], 1sc in 2nd ch from hook, 1sc in each of next 2[2:3]ch, work in pat to end. Turn.
129[131:136]sc.
***Work one row without shaping.
Break off yarn.
Armhole shaping
Next row Skip first 7[7:8]sc and rejoin yarn to next sc with a sl st, ch1, 1sc in same place as sl st, work in pat to end. Turn. 122[124:128]sc.
Next row Work in pat to last 4sc, (2sc tog) twice. Turn. 120[122:126]sc.
Next row Ch1, (2sc tog) twice, work in pat to end. Turn. 118[120:124]sc.
Rep last 2 rows 3 times more.
106[108:112]sc.
Dec one st at armhole edge on next and every foll row 20[20:24] times in all. 86[88:88]sc.
Work one row without shaping. Dec one st at armhole edge on next and every foll alternate row 2[4:4] times in all, so ending at lower edge. 84sc.
Side shaping
Next row Work in pat over first 32sc. Turn, leaving rem sts unworked.
Work one row on these 32sc.
Next row Work in pat over first 28sc. Turn, leaving rem sts unworked.
Cont working 4sc less on every alternate row until there are 16sc.
Fasten off.
With RS facing, skip 19 center sc and rejoin yarn to next sc with a sl st, ch1, 1sc in same place as sl st, work in pat to end. Turn.
Next row Work in pat over first 25sc. Turn, leaving rem sts unworked.
Work one row on these 25sc.
Next row Work in pat over first 17sc. Turn, leaving rem sts unworked.
Work one row on these 17sc.
Next row Work in pat over first 9sc.
Fasten off.***

▶ FRONT

Work as for back from ** to **.
Neck shaping
Next row Skip first 9[9:10]sc and rejoin yarn to next sc with a sl st, work in pat to end. Turn. 120[122:126]sc.
Dec one st at neck edge on next 2 rows. 118[120:124]sc.
Work one row without shaping.
Dec one st at neck edge on next row.
Rep last 2 rows twice more.
115[117:121]sc.
Work 25 rows without shaping.
Inc one st at neck edge on next and every foll alternate row 4 times in all.
119[121:125]sc.
Inc one st at neck edge on next row, so ending at neck edge. 120[122:126]sc.

Next row Ch10[10:11], 1sc in 2nd ch from hook, 1sc in each of next 8[8:9]ch, work in pat to end. Turn. 129[131:136]sc.
Complete as for back from *** to ***.

▶ FINISHING

Do not press. Join side seams. With RS facing and beg at right side seam, work sc evenly up right back armhole, along back neck easing in neck to correct width, down left back armhole, up left front armhole, along front neck easing in neck to correct width and down right front armhole, working 2sc in corners of straps. Join to first sc with a sl st and fasten off. With RS facing, rejoin yarn with a sl st to beg of back neck edge, ch1, work 1sc around post of each sc from the front along neck edge, turn, ch1, work 1sc around post of each sc from back along neck edge (see page 114). Fasten off.
Work a rolled edging in the same way along front neck edge.
Sew snaps to ends of straps.

CHENILLE CHECKERS

Chenille cotton in half double filet net is worked here in overlapping blocks of color. If you prefer not to crochet with bobbins, you could work a plain filet net in stripes or a solid color. A simple single crochet rib is worked around the sleeves and lower edge and on the elegant wide collar.

▶ SIZES

To fit 32[34:36-38]"/81[86:91-96]cm bust.

Note: Figures for larger sizes are in brackets. If there is only one set of figures, it applies to all sizes.

See diagram for finished measurements.

▶ MATERIALS

See page 118 for further yarn information

Use a lightweight cotton chenille yarn (approx 175yd per 1¾oz):

8¾[8¾:10½]oz in A (brown)

3½[3½:5¼]oz in B (rust)

3½[5¼:7]oz in C (steel gray)

Sizes E and F crochet hooks *or size to obtain correct gauge*

▶ GAUGE

10 spaces and 13 rows to 4" over filet color pat using size E hook.

To save time, take time to check gauge.

Note: When working filet color pat do not carry colors across row, but use a separate bobbin of yarn for each square of color (see page 112). When working from chart, read odd-numbered rows (RS) from right to left and even-numbered rows (WS) from left to right.

▶ BACK

Using smaller hook and A, ch97[105:113].

Beg filet color pat as foll:

Base row 1hdc in 5th ch from hook, *ch1, skip 1ch, 1hdc in next ch, rep from * to end. 47[51:55] spaces.

First size only:

1st row (RS) Using A, ch3 *loosely*, skip first hdc, 1hdc in next hdc, (ch1, 1hdc in next hdc) 5 times, *using B (ch1, 1hdc in next hdc) 9 times, using A (ch1, 1hdc in next hdc) 7 times*, rep from * to * once more, then using B (ch1, 1hdc in next hdc) 8 times, ch1, 1hdc in 2nd of ch3. Turn. 47 spaces.

2nd row Using B, ch3 *loosely*, skip first hdc, 1hdc in next hdc, (ch1, 1hdc in next hdc) 7 times, *using A (ch1, 1hdc in next hdc) 7 times, using B (ch1, 1hdc in next hdc) 9 times*, rep from * to * once more, then using A (ch1, 1hdc in next hdc) 6 times, ch1, 1hdc in 2nd of ch3. Turn.

3rd row Using A, ch3 *loosely*, skip first hdc, 1hdc in next hdc, ch1, 1hdc in next hdc, (1hdc in next ch sp, 1hdc in next hdc) twice thus forming 2 blocks, (ch1, 1hdc in next hdc) twice, *using B (ch1, 1hdc in next hdc) 3 times, (1hdc in next ch sp, 1hdc in next hdc) 4 times thus forming 4 blocks, (ch1, 1hdc in next hdc) twice, using A (ch1, 1hdc in next hdc) 3 times, (1hdc in next ch sp, 1hdc

in next hdc) twice thus forming 2 blocks, (ch1, 1hdc in next hdc) twice*, rep from * to * once more, then using B (ch1, 1hdc in next hdc) 3 times, (1hdc in next ch sp, 1hdc in next hdc) 4 times, ch1, 1hdc in next hdc, ch1, 1hdc in 2nd of ch3. Turn.

2nd size only:

1st row (RS) Using B, ch3 *loosely*, skip first hdc, 1hdc in first hdc, *using A (ch1, 1hdc in next hdc) 7 times, using B (ch1, 1hdc in next hdc) 9 times*, rep from * to * twice more, then using A, ch1, 1hdc in next hdc, ch1, 1hdc in 2nd of ch3. Turn. 51 spaces.

2nd row Using A, ch3 *loosely*, skip first hdc, 1hdc in next hdc, *using B (ch1, 1hdc in next hdc) 9 times, using A (ch1, 1hdc in next hdc) 7 times*, rep from * to * twice more, then using B, ch1, 1hdc in next hdc, ch1, 1hdc in 2nd of ch3. Turn.

3rd row Using B, ch3 *loosely*, skip first hdc, 1hdc in next hdc, *using A (ch1, 1hdc in next hdc) 3 times, (1hdc in next ch sp, 1hdc in next hdc) twice thus forming 2 blocks, (ch1, 1hdc in next hdc) twice, using B (ch1, 1hdc in next hdc) 3 times, (1hdc in next ch sp, 1hdc in next hdc) 4 times thus forming 4 blocks, (ch1, 1hdc in next hdc) twice*, rep from * to * twice more, then using A, ch1, 1hdc in next hdc, ch1, 1hdc in 2nd of ch3. Turn.

3rd size:

1st row (RS) Using B, ch3 *loosely*, skip first hdc, 1hdc in next hdc, (ch1, 1hdc in next hdc) twice, rep from * to * of first row for 2nd size 3 times in all, then using A (ch1, 1hdc in next hdc) 3 times, ch1, 1hdc in 2nd of ch3. Turn. 55 spaces.

2nd row Using A, ch3 *loosely*, skip first hdc, 1hdc in next hdc, (ch1, 1hdc in next hdc) twice, rep from * to * of 2nd row for 2nd size 3 times in all, then using B (ch1, 1hdc in next hdc) 3 times, ch1, 1hdc in 2nd of ch3. Turn.

3rd row Using B, ch3 *loosely*, skip first hdc, 1hdc in next hdc, (ch1, 1hdc in next hdc) twice, rep from * to * of 3rd row for 2nd size 3 times in all, then using A (ch1, 1hdc in next hdc) 3 times, ch1, 1hdc in 2nd of ch3. Turn.

All sizes:

Cont in filet color pat as set, foll chart and beg with 4th row of chart. When 30th chart row has been completed, beg with first row again. Work in pat, rep first-30th rows of chart, until back measures approx 21½[22:22½]" from beg.

Neck shaping

Next row Work in pat across first 13[15:17] spaces, counting each block or space. Turn, leaving rem sts unworked.

Work one more row in pat on these sts. Fasten off.

Work 2nd side of neck in the same way.

▶ FRONT

Work as for back until front measures 17¾[18¼:18¾]" from beg.

Neck shaping

Next row Work in pat across first 19[21:23] spaces, counting each block or space. Turn, leaving rem sts unworked.

Keeping pat correct, dec 2 spaces at beg of next row (by working sl st over first 2 spaces), then dec one space at beg of every other row (neck edge) 4 times. 13[15:17] spaces.
Work without shaping until front measures same as back to shoulder. Fasten off.
Work 2nd side of neck in the same way, reversing shaping.

▶ SLEEVES (make 2)

Using smaller hook and A, ch69[73:77]. Work base row as for back. 33[35:37] spaces.

First size only:

1st row (RS) Using B, ch3 *loosely*, skip first hdc, 1hdc in next hdc, (ch1, 1hdc in next hdc) 7 times, using A (ch1, 1hdc in next hdc) 7 times, using B (ch1, 1hdc in next hdc) 9 times, using A (ch1, 1hdc in next hdc) 7 times, then using B, ch1, 1hdc in next hdc, ch1, 1hdc in 2nd of ch3. Turn. 33 spaces.

2nd size only:

1st row (RS) Using B, ch3 *loosely*, skip first hdc, 1hdc in next hdc, (ch1, 1hdc in next hdc) 8 times, using A (ch1, 1hdc in next hdc) 7 times, *using B (ch1, 1hdc in next hdc) 9 times, using A (ch1, 1hdc in next hdc) 7 times*, using B (ch1, 1hdc in next hdc) twice, ch1, 1hdc in 2nd of ch3. Turn. 35 spaces.

3rd size only:

1st row (RS) Using A, ch3 *loosely*, skip first hdc, 1hdc in next hdc, rep from * to * of first row for 2nd size twice, then using B (ch1, 1hdc in next hdc) 3 times, ch1, 1hdc in 2nd of ch3. Turn. 37 spaces.

All sizes:

Cont in filet color pat as set, foll chart and beg with 2nd row of chart *and at the same time* shape sides as foll:
**Work 4 rows without shaping, inc one space at end of next 2 rows (by working 1hdc, ch1, 1hdc in 2nd of ch3 at end of row). ** Rep from ** to ** 5 times more. 45[47:49] spaces.
Work in pat without shaping until sleeve measures 12½" from beg. Fasten off.

▶ BACK RIB

Using larger hook and A, ch9.
Base row 1sc in 2nd ch from hook, 1sc in each ch to end. Turn. 8sc.
1st row Ch1, working in *back* loops only, 1sc in each sc to end. Turn.
Rep last row to form rib pat. Cont in rib pat until rib fits across lower edge of back. Fasten off.

▶ FRONT RIB

Work as for back rib.

▶ SLEEVE RIBS (make 2)

Using smaller hook and A, work 1sc in each foundation chain across lower sleeve edge to slightly draw in width. Fasten off.
Work sleeve rib as for back rib until rib, slightly stretched, fits across lower sleeve edge. Fasten off.

▶ COLLAR

Join shoulder seams. Using smaller hook and A, work a round of sc evenly around neck edge and join with a sl st to first sc. Fasten off.
Using larger hook and A, ch15 and work base and first rows as for back rib. 14sc. Cont in rib pat until collar measures approx 36" unstretched. Fasten off.

▶ FINISHING

Do not press. Darn in all loose ends. Sew on back, front and sleeve ribs. Mark positions of sleeves 9[9¼:9¾]" from shoulder seams. Sew on sleeves between markers. Join side and sleeve seams. Sew on collar, beg at center front and easing in fullness at curves.

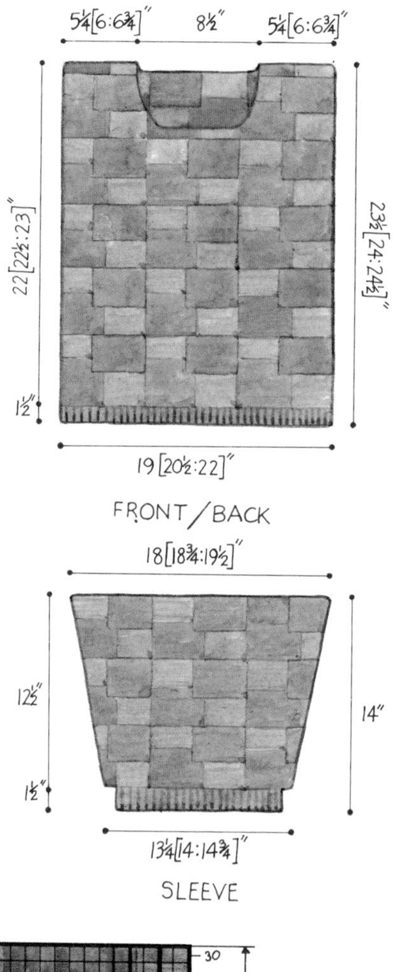

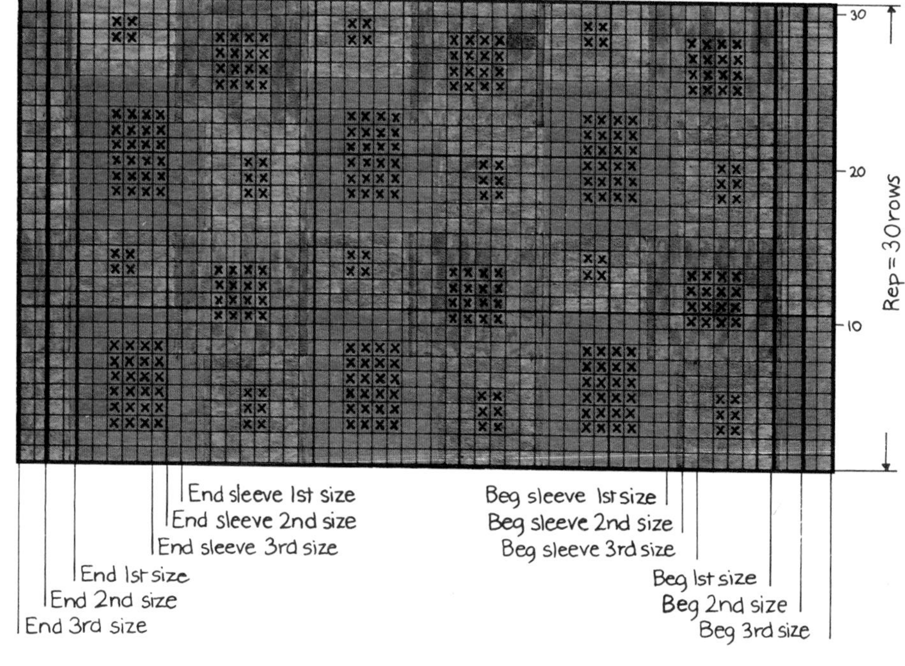

☐ one space ☒ one block

APPENDIX

CROCHET TIPS

Here are some tips that even an experienced crocheter is well advised to read before beginning any of the sweaters in this book!

► WHAT SIZE TO MAKE?

After choosing the sweater you want to make, you must first decide which size to follow. Sizes are given according to bust measurement, but it is wise to consider a few factors before choosing to work the size which covers your bust measurement. The designer sizes garments according to the way a particular design should fit an "average" shape. Most of us do not have a perfectly "average" shape, however. For instance, if you know your shoulder width is narrow compared to your bust measurement, you may decide to work a smaller size than recommended — or vice versa. Likewise if your hip measurement is more than 4" larger than your bust measurement, you may need a size larger than the recommended one. It's a good idea to measure the width of a similar sweater in your wardrobe and compare it to the one given on the measurement diagram provided.

► CHOOSING YARNS

Once you have chosen which size to crochet, you can purchase your yarn. It is wise to buy the yarn specified in the pattern instructions (see page 118). If this is not possible, choose a comparable yarn. Stick to the same type of yarn. Then compare the thickness of the substitute to the life-size photograph of the strand of yarn given on page 119. If in doubt, take the book to your yarn shop and purchase only one ball of comparable yarn to test it by making a gauge swatch. Calculate the total length of yarn you will need; the weight per yard varies drastically between different yarns due to their fiber content.

► CHECKING GAUGE

Once you have your yarn, you are ready to begin. It can never be repeated enough to a crocheter — **check your gauge before beginning.** If you can't achieve the correct gauge with the hook size specified, you *must* change your hook size or your sweater will not come out to the correct size. Keep in mind that the hook size in the instructions is only a *guideline*. The frustration of working halfway up a back before realizing it is a few inches wider or narrower than it should be is a common experience for many crocheters. Remember you will be *saving time if you take time to check your gauge.*

Making a gauge swatch

Using the specified yarn, hook size and stitch pattern, work a piece which measures at least 6" by 6". Lay the piece on a flat surface. In order not to stretch the fabric inadvertently do not smooth it into place but let it settle into its natural shape. With pins, mark out 4" across the fabric. Then count the number of stitches between the pins. Do the same to count the number of rows. The side edges of the crochet fabric are usually less tight, so measure

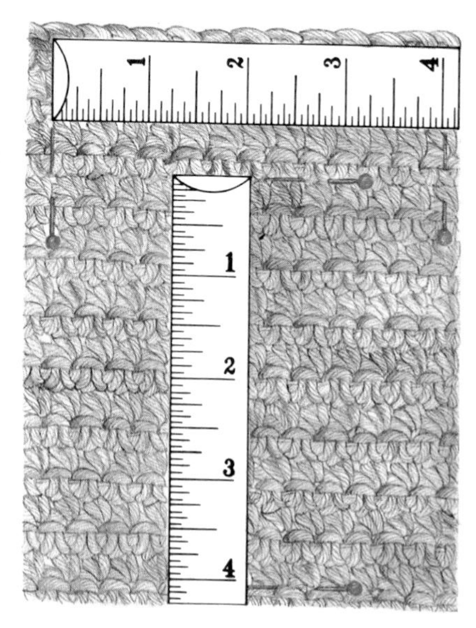

rows down the center of the sample. Be sure to count half stitches and rows too.

* If you have too many stitches or rows per 4" then make another sample with a larger hook.

* Too few stitches and rows per 4" means a smaller hook is needed. *Keep testing until you are sure which hook size is best for you.* You will not regret the time spent.

► TOP TEN TIPS

Follow these important tips to improve your crochet tenfold!

- Always *check your gauge* before beginning.
- Choose which size to make by comparing the diagram measurements to a similar sweater you have that *fits you comfortably.*
- When using a substitute yarn *buy one ball to start with* so that you can check its suitability first.
- Remember when substituting yarn to *match yardage and not weight* when deciding on amounts.
- *Measure your crochet pieces frequently* while crocheting to make sure your gauge is not altering.
- *Recount stitches* after every few rows to avoid losing stitches.
- If the pattern instructions state *"at the same time"*, read the whole sentence before proceeding.
- When measuring lengths *do not stretch the fabric* and *measure up the center* of the piece.
- Use an *edge to edge seaming technique* whenever possible to avoid bulky seams.
- Keep a yarn label for pressing and washing requirements.

TEXTURE TECHNIQUES

There are many crochet techniques that create raised effects. The most obvious and pronounced are the various types of bobbles. Other more subtle textures are also shown here.

► WORKING AROUND POSTS

This technique is often used in combination with other types of stitches, but it can also be used on its own to produce a textured surface much in the way that knit and purl

1

2

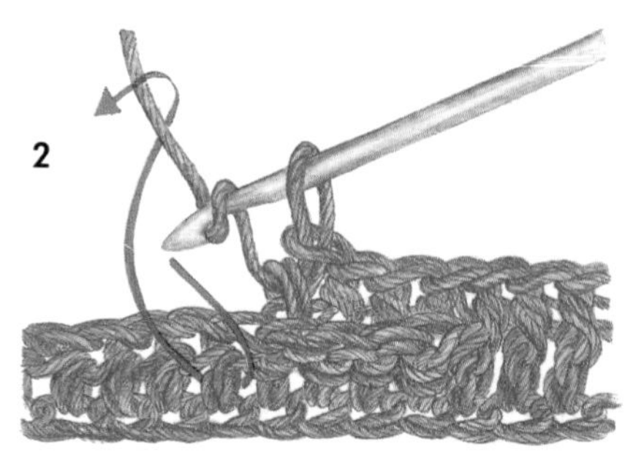

stitches form shapes in traditional Guernsey sweaters. An example of this method worked in half doubles is shown on the cotton design on page 64. Rolled edging and ribbing can also be made by working around the post of single crochet and double crochet stitches respectively (see page 114).

1 Make a base row of hdc. Ch2 to count as the first hdc. To work around the post from the front of the work, yo and insert the hook from front to back between the first and 2nd stitches, then behind the 2nd stitch and back to the front between the 2nd and 3rd stitches. Complete hdc as usual.

2 To work around the post from the back of the work, yo and insert the hook from back to front between the stitch being worked and the previous stitch, then in front of the stitch and to the back between the next two stitches. Complete the hdc in the usual way.

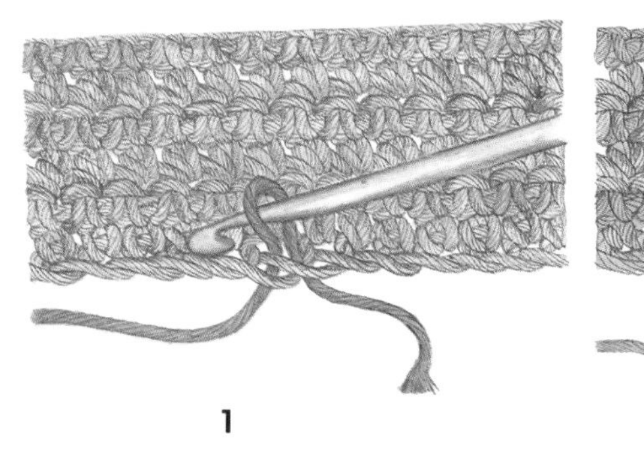

1

2

▶ SURFACE SLIP STITCH

Surface slip stitch is formed in exactly the same way as chain stitch embroidery, but a crochet hook is used instead of a needle. It is a perfect way to add narrow vertical or horizontal stripes in a contrasting color to plaids (as seen in the designs on pages 32 and 41). It is also sometimes used to make mock cables. The technique needs a little practice for the beginner but it is well worth the effort. Slip stitch crochet can be worked on any crochet ground, but when learning the technique start on a firm fabric such as single crochet.

1 When beginning at the lower edge of the crochet fabric, insert the hook from front to back through the foundation ch. Then holding the yarn at the back of the work throughout, yo and draw a loop through to the front. Leave a loose end long enough (approximately 4") to weave in on the wrong side later. Remember to work loosely as you proceed so that the fabric does not pull together.

2 Keeping the loop on the hook, insert the hook between the first two rows. Yo and draw a loop through the fabric and the loop on the hook. Continue in this way, always inserting the hook between the following two rows. For a horizontal stripe work between the stitches instead of the rows.

▶ CHAIN STITCH EMBROIDERY

This stitch is interchangeable with surface slip stitch. Although it is slower to work than the crochet technique, it is much easier. Unlike surface slip stitch it is not possible to work from a continuous strand of yarn, so begin by threading a blunt-ended needle with a strand of yarn approximately 20" long. For a thicker chain use two or three strands.

Fasten the yarn to the back of the work and bring the needle through to the front at the appropriate position. Reinsert the needle back through the hole where it was first brought through, then to the front again between the

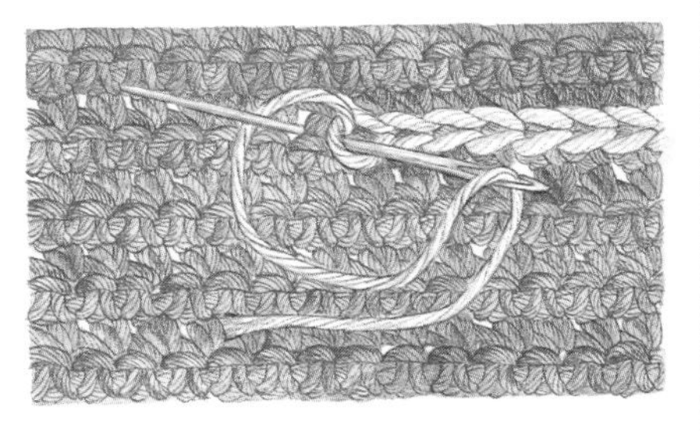

next two stitches (or rows), keeping the loop of yarn at the front under the point of the needle. Continue in this way inserting the needle to the back through the previous hole and to the front again a between the next two stitches.

This detail from the jacket on page 32 shows the white stripes which can be worked in slip stitch or chain stitch.

▶ BOBBLES

There are several ways to make the round, raised textures called bobbles, puff stitches or popcorns. The technique that makes the most pronounced effect is shown here. This type of bobble with slight variations has been used on the designs on pages 54, 57 and 103. This bobble is worked on a half double crochet ground and is made up of five stitches, but the bobble can easily be reduced or enlarged by decreasing or increasing the size of stitches or the number of stitches.

Work to the position of the bobble and then work 1hdc, 3dc, 1hdc all in the next stitch. Remove the hook from the loop, drawing the loop out slightly so that it will not unravel. Reinsert the

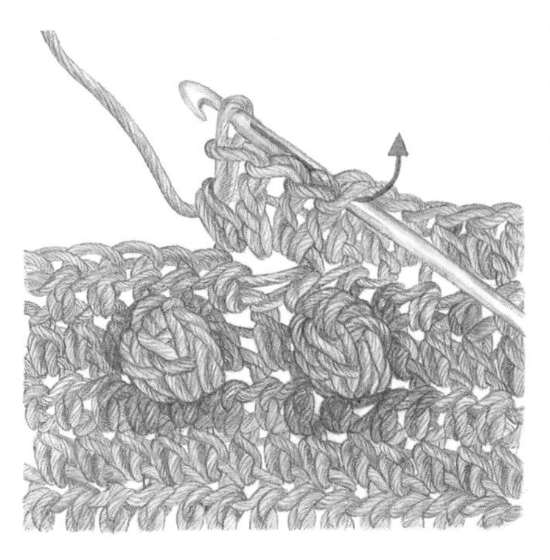

hook in the top of the first hdc of the group of five stitches. Then draw the working loop through and continue in hdc until the next bobble is reached.

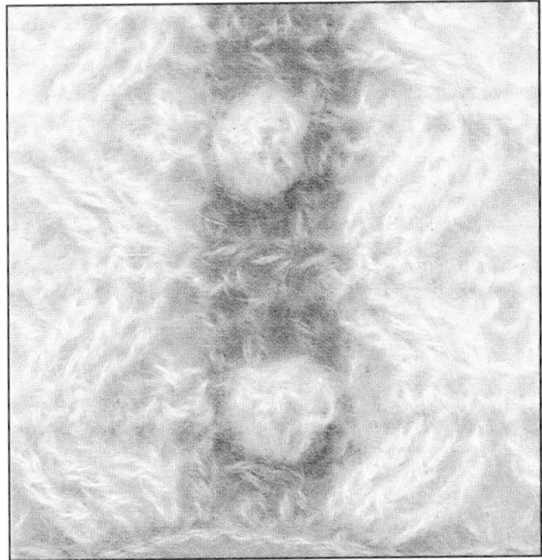

Bobbles are worked between the cables on the vest on page 54. Bobbles and cables in a contrasting color emphasize the texture.

COLOR PATTERNS

Crochet is at its most exciting when the basic stitches are worked in a contrast of stunning colors and beautiful fibers. The basic color pattern techniques shown here are so simple to grasp that they are within reach of the most inexperienced crocheter.

▶ CHANGING COLORS

The most versatile method of working crochet color patterns is called "colorwork". Each color is used for as many stitches as indicated in the instructions or on the chart. Successful results in colorwork crochet are dependent upon knowing the correct method for changing from one color to another in a row.

The pattern chosen here to illustrate color changes is a simple check. When working with only two colors in a row, the color not in use can either be carried along the top of the row below and worked over, or stranded loosely across the back of the work.

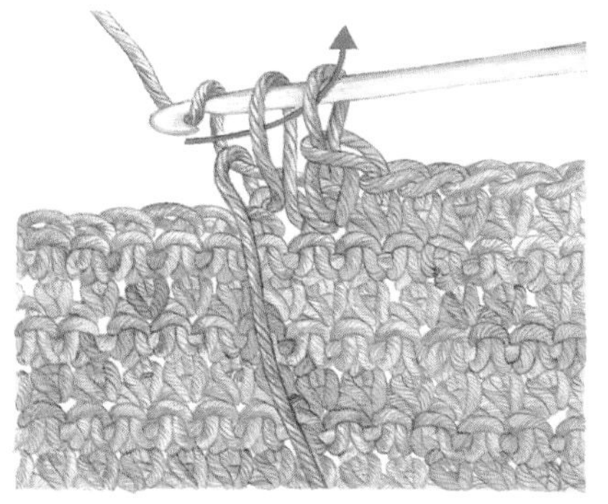

Single crochet
When the design being worked is in sc, work to the last stitch in the first color. Insert the hook in the next stitch, yo and draw a loop through. Drop the first color and using the second color, yo and draw a loop through. Always change to the new contrasting color in this way — by working the last yo of the previous stitch in the new contrasting color.

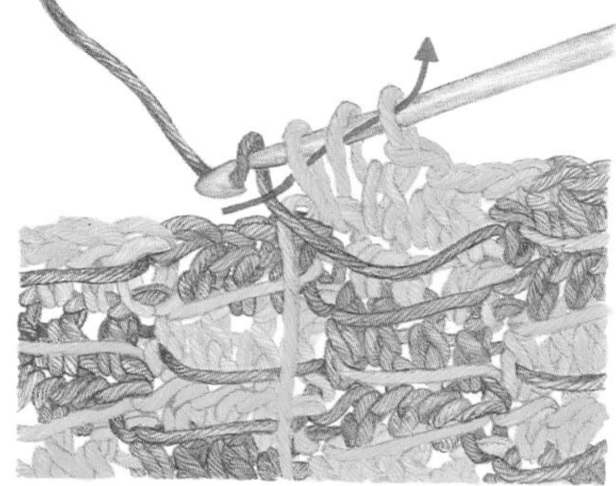

Half double crochet
Change colors on hdc in the same way as for sc by working the last yo of the previous stitch in the new color, so that the stitch before the new color starts is "closed" by the new color. The work is shown here on the wrong side and the yarn not in use is being stranded across the back of the fabric. Always drop the color not in use to the wrong side of the work.

Double
For double colorwork, the new color is also used to close the previous stitch before beginning the new color. When the color not in use is carried across the top of the previous row and worked over as shown here, the crochet fabric is reversible. Do not pull the new color too tightly when picking it up to use again or your work will become too narrow.

▶ BLOCKS OF COLOR

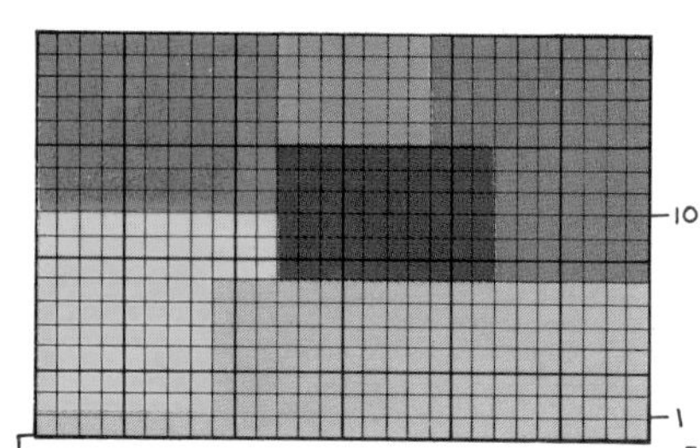

Any number of color designs can be charted on graph paper and then translated into crochet. When there are only two colors used in each row and both colors are used alternately across the row, they can both be carried across the row. But if isolated motifs or large blocks of several colors are being worked, then separate balls or bobbins of each color are needed. In this way each section uses its own separate source of yarn which is picked up and used when that section is reached. Plastic bobbins are worthwhile purchases as you can control the flow of yarn from them and avoid tangled balls.

1 Wind a long length of each color onto a bobbin. Work the crochet following the chart square by square.

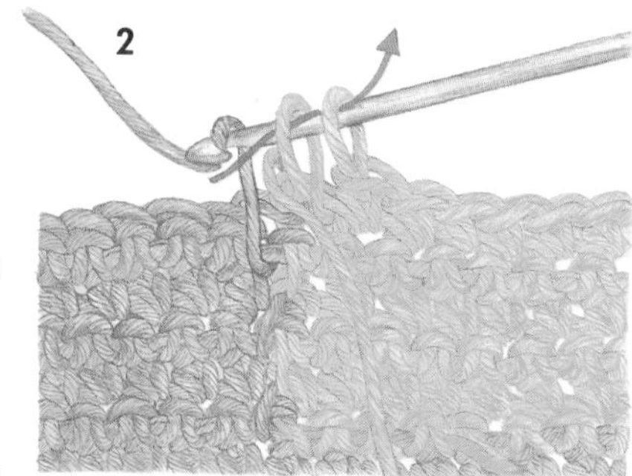

Odd-numbered rows (RS) are read from right to left and even-numbered rows (WS) from left to right.

2 When changing colors drop the first color to the wrong side of the work, and work the last yo of the previous stitch with the new color.

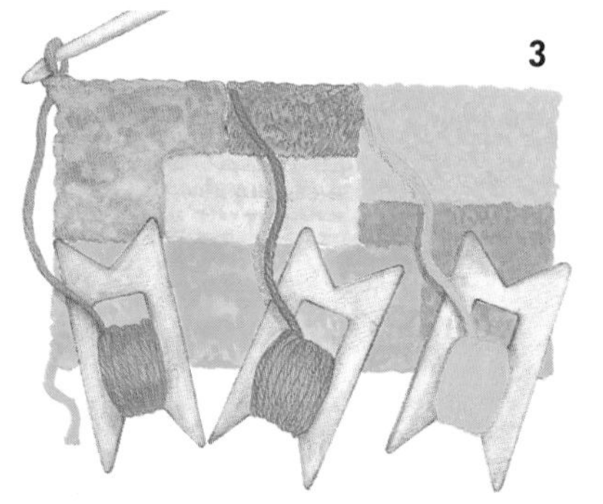

3 The bobbins hang at the back of the work and the yarn is unwound as it is used. If you do not want to weave in loose ends when the piece is completed, you can work over the ends when changing to a new block of color.

This is a detail from Color Blocks on page 83. The color pattern on the vest is worked using a separate bobbin of yarn for each color.

▶ WEAVING CROCHET

Some color pattern techniques involve the combination of different basic crochet stitches. Colorful plaids and tweeds, for example, can be made by weaving onto a ground of filet crochet net (see page 48).

To weave onto a striped hdc filet net, take three or four strands of yarn threaded through a blunt-ended needle. The strands should be long enough to work the number of vertical rows to be woven in that color plus approximately 12" extra for adjusting and weaving in the ends. Beginning at the lower right-hand edge of the piece, pass the needle through the foundation ch under the first ch space, leaving a 6" loose end at the beginning. Then weave *loosely* in and out of the spaces toward the top of the fabric.

At the top of the fabric pass the needle through the ch above the last ch space. Then insert the needle through the ch above the next ch space to the left. Weave down the fabric working *over* the rows worked *under* in the last vertical stripe and vice versa. When the vertical stripes in the first color are complete, continue with the next color and so on. After weaving the entire piece, smooth out the woven strands, matching the measurements of the piece to the garment diagram. Weave in the loose ends.

▶ ELONGATED STITCHES

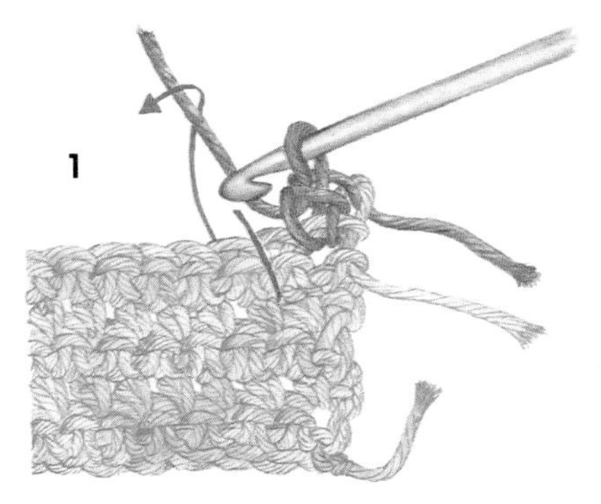

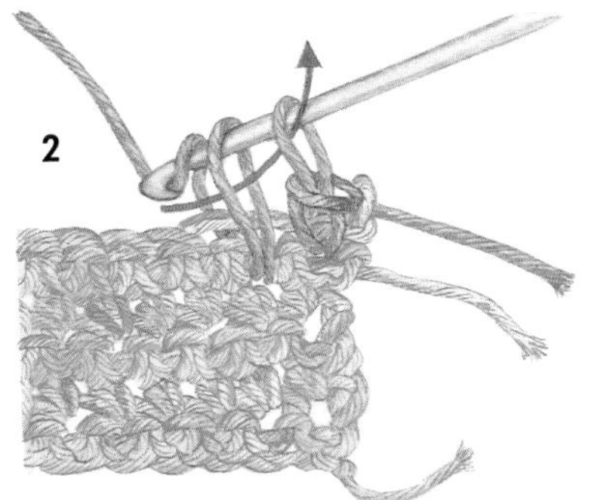

A very easy way to make color patterns or isolated motifs is with elongated single crochet. The stitches form long V shapes on the front and the back of the crochet fabric and are especially effective when worked in a yarn which contrasts in texture with the background. Many shapes can be formed with the elongated stitches and instructions for a triangle shape are given here.

1 This is worked onto a base of several rows of sc. At the beginning of the pattern row change to the new color or different textured yarn, ch1 and work 1sc in the first stitch. Insert the hook from the front to the back through the top of the stitch one row below the next stitch and yo.

2 Draw a loop through the fabric extending it up as high as the previous stitch and working *loosely* so that the background is not pulled together. Complete the sc in the usual way.

3 Work an elongated sc in the top of the stitch two rows below the next stitch, then one three rows below the next stitch and four rows below the next stitch. Continue working in this way, counting stitches carefully across the previous row.

CROCHET EDGINGS

Remember that the success of a crochet garment depends on its neat, even edgings. There is no sense in making beautiful crochet pieces and topping them off with careless finishes. Take your time with edgings and you will have a garment to be proud of.

▶ SINGLE CROCHET EDGING

The simplest and most common crochet edging is the single crochet edging. Instructions usually call for single crochet to be worked "evenly along the edge". Unfortunately there is no steadfast rule that will determine exactly how many stitches to work along an edge, so the only answer is to experiment until a smooth finish is achieved. If too few stitches are worked, the edge will pull together and if too many are worked, the edge will curl. Keep trying until you get it right. It helps to lay the work flat as you go to check for tightness.

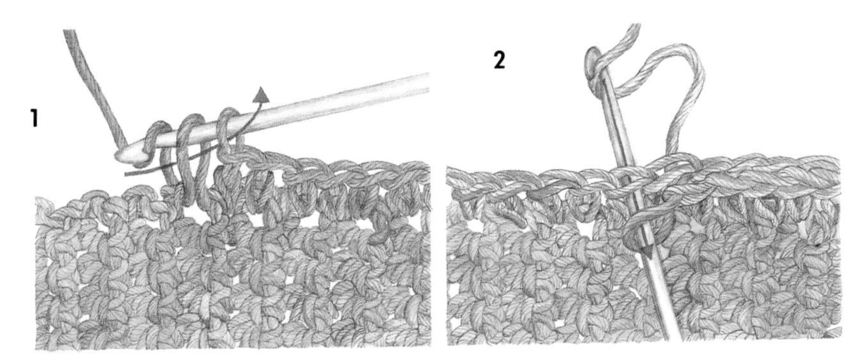

1 Join the yarn to the fabric with a sl st, inserting the hook through the edge of the fabric, yo and draw a loop through. Ch1 and then work a sc in the same place as the sl st was worked. Continue along the edge in sc.

2 For a firmer finish work a round of sl st *loosely* over the first round of sc. Work each sl st by inserting the hook under *both* loops at the top of each sc, yo and draw a loop through the sc and the loop on the hook.

▶ ROLLED EDGING

This interesting edging gives a very attractive finish to your crochet garment. It has more body than a simple single crochet edging and is made by working single crochet around the posts of the stitches in the previous row. Shown here worked in rows, the rolled edging can also be worked in *rounds* in which case the right side would always be facing and the stitches would be worked around the post from the *front* in every round. The number of rows or rounds worked depends on how wide the edging is to be. Two rounds are sufficient to form an edging which will roll to the right side of the fabric and cover the base row.

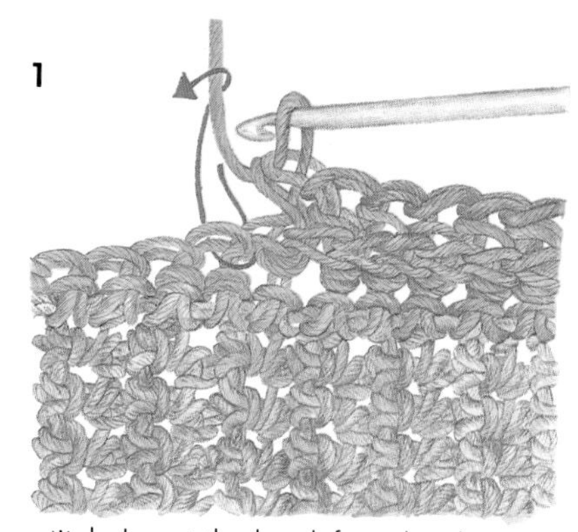

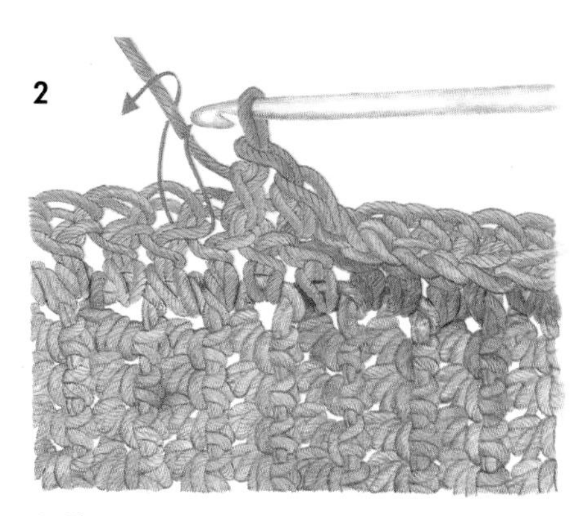

1 Begin with a row of sc along the right side of the fabric. If you are working in rows, turn the work at the end of the row. Ch1 and work 1sc in the first stitch. Insert the hook from back to front through the space before the next stitch, around the next stitch and from front to back through the next space. Draw a loop through and complete the sc in the usual way. Continue working a sc around the post of each stitch from the back to the end of the row, working 1sc in the last stitch. Turn the work so that the right side is facing again.

2 Ch1 and work 1sc in the first stitch. Insert the hook from front to back through the space before the next stitch, around the next stitch and from back to front through the next space. Draw a loop through and complete the sc in the usual way. Continue working a sc around the post of each stitch from the front to the end, working 1sc in the last stitch. For a deeper edge, increase the number of rows.

▶ SINGLE CROCHET RIB

Crochet rib is ideal for a wider edging. The single crochet rib was developed to imitate knitted ribbing and although it is not nearly as elastic as the knitted version it is as close an approximation as is possible with crochet. Often the rib is worked in a strip and turned sideways to form the base for the first row of the back, front or sleeves. Generally it is better to add this ribbing after the garment pieces are completed; you can then adjust the length of the ribbing.

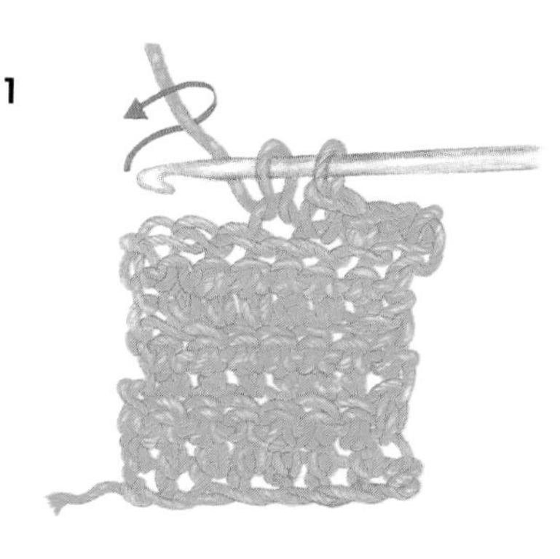

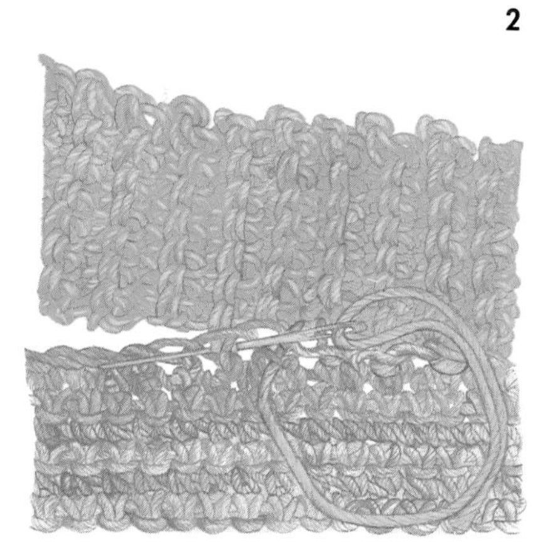

1 Work the base row in sc to the width required for the depth of the ribbing. *Turn and ch1. Inserting the hook under the *back* loop only at the top of each stitch, work in sc to the end of the row Repeat from * to form the ribbing, working the edge stitches tightly.

2 When the ribbing is the required length, fasten off. With the right side facing, sew the ribbing to the edge of the crochet fabric with a simple running stitch. If the ribbing is being added to the side edge of the crochet piece, work a sc edging onto the garment selvage first. Always place the garment edge over the ribbing while seaming.

▶ DOUBLE CROCHET RIBBING

The double crochet ribbing is not as elastic as the single crochet ribbing, but it produces raised horizontal "ribs" similar in appearance to knitted ribs. As the effect is purely decorative this technique should not be used where a snug or stretchy fabric is required. The relief texture is achieved by working doubles around the posts of the stitches of the previous row (see page 110). For double crochet ribbing at the base of the back, front or sleeves, work the ribbing to the required depth and then begin the main stitch pattern. For neck or armhole ribbing work the base row of double crochet directly onto the crochet fabric.

1 To begin, work a base row in dc. Turn and ch3 to count as the first stitch. Skip the first stitch in the row below, yo and insert the hook *from the front* around the next stitch. Complete the dc in the usual way. Work the next stitch around the dc *from the back*. Continue working one stitch around the post from the front and from the back alternately. Work 1hdc in the 3rd ch at the end.

2 Work the next row in the same way as the last row but working around the post from the back on stitches that were worked around the post from the front in the last row and vice versa. In this way the horizontal "ribs" are formed.

KNITTED EDGINGS

For any crocheter with basic knitting skills, knitted edgings offer an effective alternative to crochet edgings. Knitting will provide a softer and more flexible finished edge to the firmer and crisper crochet fabric.

▶ PICKING UP STITCHES

Before a knitted edging can be worked, stitches must be picked up along the edge of the crochet fabric. Stitches are either picked up along the foundation chain, the last row of stitches or along the row ends. The number of stitches to be picked up will be given in the instructions. These stitches should be dispersed *evenly* along the edge specified. One way to ensure that the stitches are picked up evenly is to divide the edge being worked into tenths, mark them with pins and then work one tenth of the stitches required across each section. With the right side facing insert the point of the knitting needle through the edge of the fabric and wrap the yarn around the needle. Draw the yarn through. The first loop is now on the

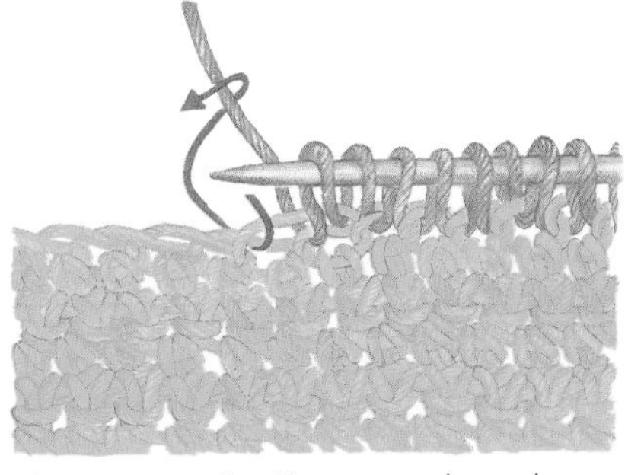

knitting needle. Continue along the edge of the fabric in the same way drawing through loops until there are the required number of stitches on the needle. Check that the stitches have been picked up evenly and redo if necessary.

▶ ROLLED EDGING

1

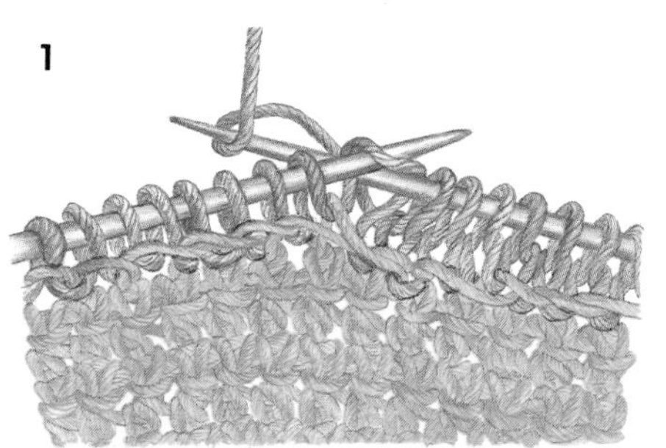

2

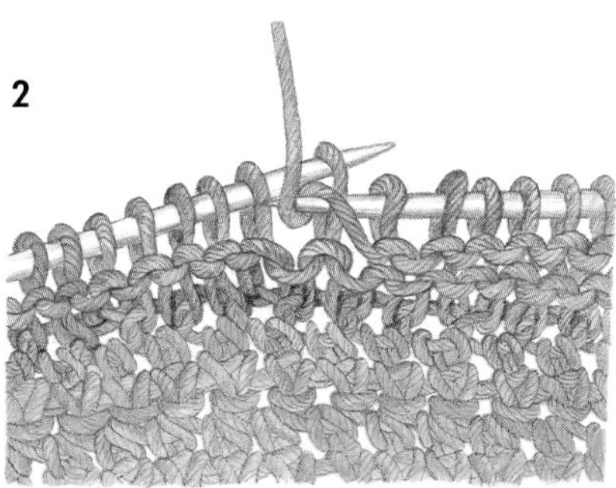

3

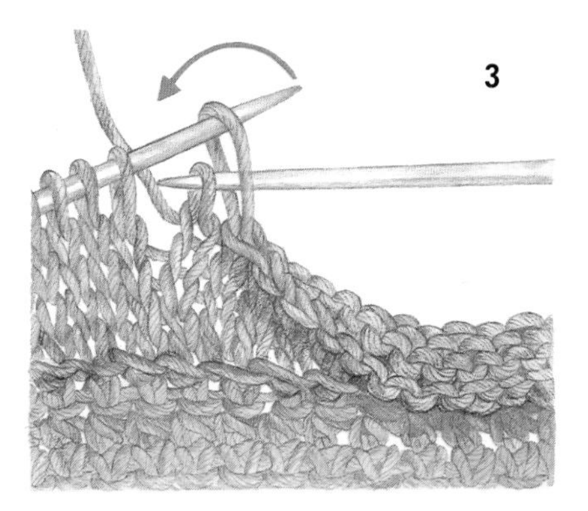

This edging forms a neat, rounded edge similar to a bold piping. It is an effective border for armholes, necklines and cuffs. Unlike crochet rolled edging, the knitted version is worked so that it rolls to the wrong side of the fabric instead of to the right side. It is worked in reverse stockinette stitch so that the first row is a knit row, the second row a purl row and so on until the edging is the required depth. The edging can be worked in rows or in rounds with a circular knitting needle. When worked in rounds, every row is purled and the right side is always facing. Pick up the required number of stitches along the edge of the fabric and hold the knitting needle with the loops in the left hand and the empty needle in the right hand ready to begin.

1 The edging here is worked in rows. To knit the first row, insert the right-hand needle from front to back through the front of the first loop. Wrap the yarn around the tip of the right-hand needle, draw the yarn through the loop to form a new loop on the right-hand needle, dropping the loop just worked through from the left-hand needle. Continue working knit stitches one at a time in this way to the end of the row.

2 Turn the work so that the right side is facing. To purl the 2nd row, insert the right-hand needle from right to left through the front of the first loop. Wrap the yarn around the tip of the right-hand needle and draw the yarn through the loop to form a new loop, dropping the loop just worked through from the left-hand needle. Continue working purl stitches in this way to the end of the row.

3 Work one more knit row followed by one more purl row. On the next row knit the first two stitches. Using the left-hand needle, pass the first stitch over the second and off the needle to bind off the first stitch. Knit the next stitch and bind off another stitch. Continue in this way to the end. When one stitch remains break off the yarn, leaving a long enough piece to weave in later. Draw the end through the loop to fasten off. The edging will roll to the wrong side of the fabric. There is no need to stitch the edging down to the wrong side. If it is not rolling firmly, unravel the bound-off row and bind off again more tightly.

▶ RIBBING

Knitted ribbing is more flexible and elastic than crochet ribbing. Begin the ribbing by picking up stitches along the edge of the crochet fabric. When picking up along a neckline, armhole or any rounded edge, pick up fewer stitches along the curved sections than along the straight sections so that the finished ribbing will lie flat around the curves.

1 On the first row knit one stitch and purl one stitch alternately to the end of the row. This creates an elastic rib called "K1, P1 rib".

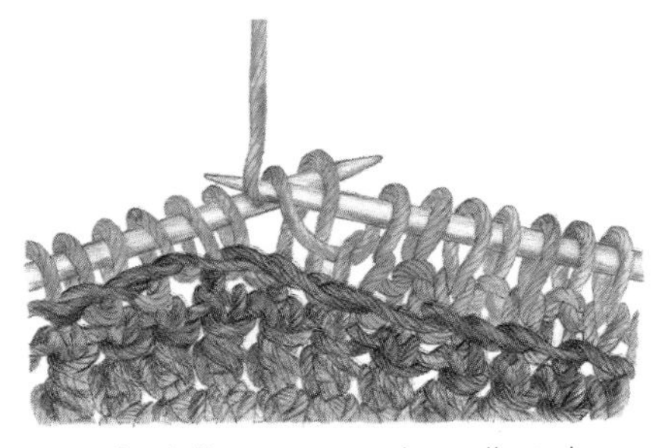

2 In the following rows knit all stitches purled in the last row and vice versa. Continue until the ribbing is the correct depth, then *bind off in rib* by knitting and purling stitches in the same way while binding off.

2

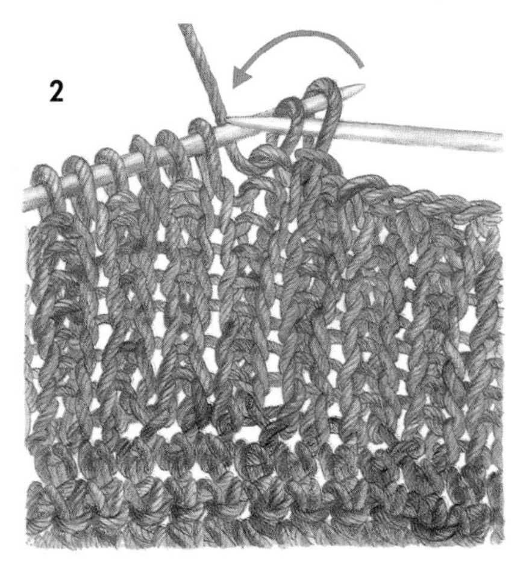

AFGHAN CROCHET

Afghan crochet is a cross between knitting and crochet and may have been the precursor to knitting. This kinship is most evident in Afghan crochet "knit" stitch.

▶ PLAIN STITCH

Afghan crochet is worked with a long hook with a knob on the end. The fabric is made by picking up loops all along the work, binding them off in the following row, then picking up loops again and so on. Because of the way all the loops must fit onto the hook the width of the fabric is limited by the length of the hook and the number of loops it can hold.

1 To work the basic stitch (plain stitch), begin with a foundation ch. Insert the hook into the second loop from the hook, yo and draw a loop through the ch. Continue in this way drawing up a loop through each ch to the end. Do not turn but work all rows with the right side facing.

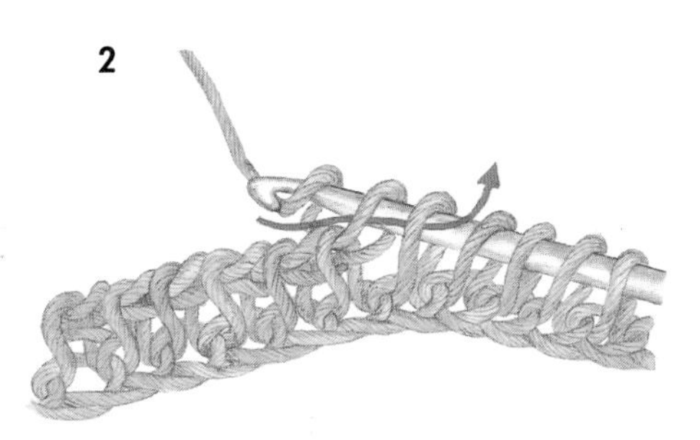

2 For the next row (the return row — right side facing) yo and draw a loop through the first loop on the hook. *Yo and draw a loop through the next two loops on the hook. Repeat from * until there is one loop left on the hook. This loop forms the first stitch of the next row.

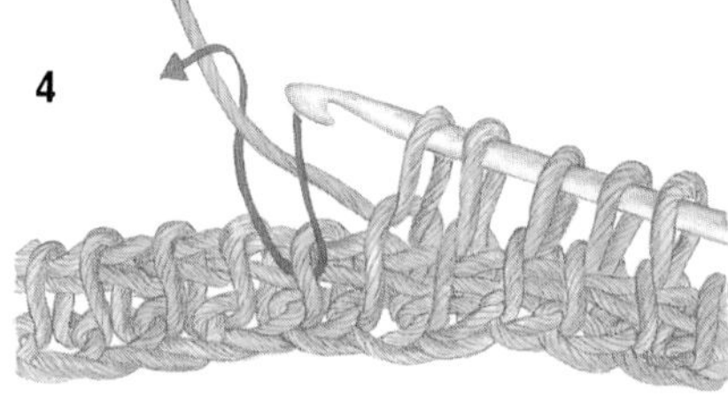

3 Skip the first vertical loop in the row below and insert the hook from right to left through the next vertical loop. Yo and draw a loop through. There are now two loops on the hook.

4 Continue in this way from right to left across the row. This row is called a loop row. Each loop row is followed by a return row.

5 At the end of each loop row be sure to insert the hook through the center of the last loop at the edge so that there are two vertical strands of yarn at the extreme left-hand edge.

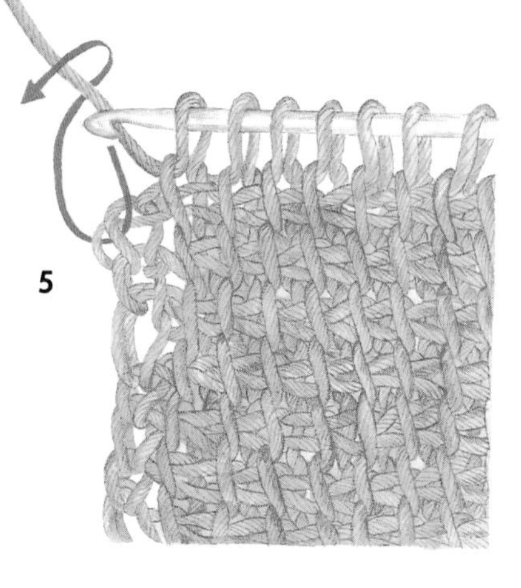

▶ KNIT STITCH

The return row of chain stitches is the only thing that separates Afghan knit stitch from knitting. Although the resulting Afghan fabric is thicker and less elastic than stockinette stitch, it still has an attractive feel and texture if worked on a large enough hook. After a knit stitch piece has been completed it should be pressed with a warm iron and a damp cloth to flatten the curl at the edges, so be sure to use a yarn that can be pressed.

1 Work the foundation ch and the first loop row and return row as for plain stitch. Then begin the next row by skipping the first vertical loop below and inserting the hook from front to back through the center of the next vertical loop. The hook should pass through the loop *under* the ch formed by the return row. Yo and draw a loop through.

2 Continue to the end of the row drawing a loop through each vertical loop in the same way. Work return and loop rows alternately to form the fabric. The last loop stitch of each loop row is worked as for plain stitch.

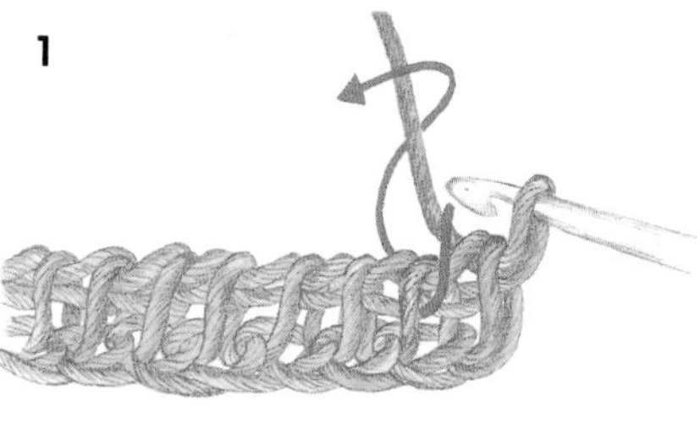

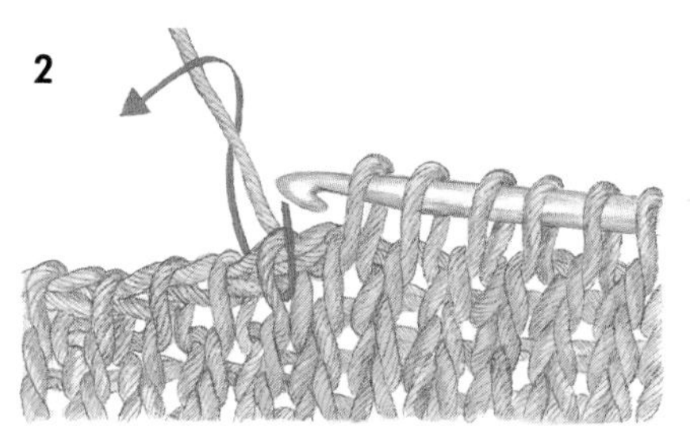

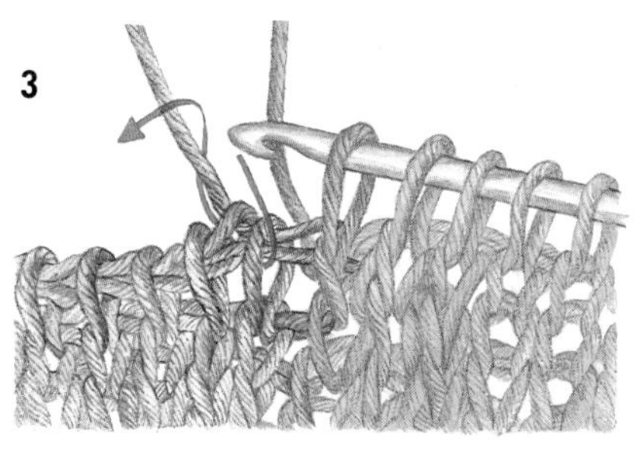

3 When working color patterns in knit stitch, change to the new color on a loop row where indicated in the instructions, dropping the first color to the back of the work. Use separate lengths of yarn if each color is used only in one area. If the colors alternate across the row, strand the color not in use *loosely* across the back of the work.

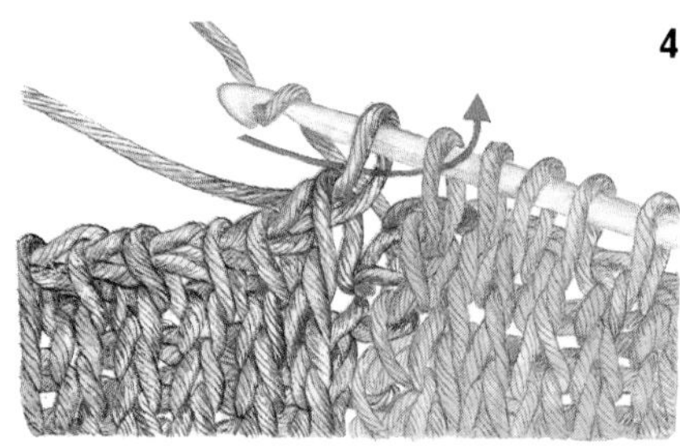

4 When working return rows on a color pattern, draw the matching color through each loop, changing colors when the first loop in a new color is reached. If the colors are used alternately across the row, strand the color not in use across the back as for loop rows. To avoid long, loose strands, work over and under them on the following row.

FINISHING

Painstaking execution of blocking and seaming will add professional polish to your crochet. If you put as much thought and patience into these finishing touches as you have into your crocheting, you will be well rewarded.

▶ BLOCKING AND PRESSING

Hesitate before applying an iron to your crochet pieces! First read the pattern instructions and the yarn label for advice. Some yarns will not react well to heat and will begin to melt down if mistreated, so heed the yarn label when it says *do not press* or shows the international symbol of a crossed-out iron. An iron with dots on it means that ironing won't damage the yarn: one dot means a cool iron should be used, two dots indicates a warm iron, and three dots a hot iron. Highly textured crochet fabrics should not be flattened by ironing. If you want to block your pieces into shape but they will not stand pressing, you can always wet block. This is done by pinning the pieces out on a padded surface and covering them with a damp towel. Leave to dry, then unpin. If pressing is indicated in your instructions and permitted on the yarn label, it is still important to treat your crochet fabric gently. Pin the pieces out with the right side facing down. Cover them with a damp (or dry cloth as directed and press separately, lifting the iron and not dragging it when you move it across the piece.

▶ EDGE TO EDGE SEAM

This type of seam produces a flat, invisible join. It is sometimes called overcasting. Use it wherever possible to avoid bulky seams. Thread a blunt-ended needle with a length of yarn. Then place the crochet pieces together with the right sides facing and line up the rows. Take special care when lining up stripes and plaids. Pin together at intervals if desired.

Work the seam by inserting the needle under one strand of yarn on one side and across to the other side.

▶ BACKSTITCH SEAM

This is sometimes necessary where the edge of the crochet piece has "stepped" increases or decreases. Work small, even backstitches as close to the edge as possible. Before beginning, secure the yarn to the edge of the fabric with a few short overcast stitches. Never use knots as they will unravel with wear. Work each stitch by reinserting the needle back through the fabric at the same place it emerged from the previous stitch and passing it through to the front a short distance away.

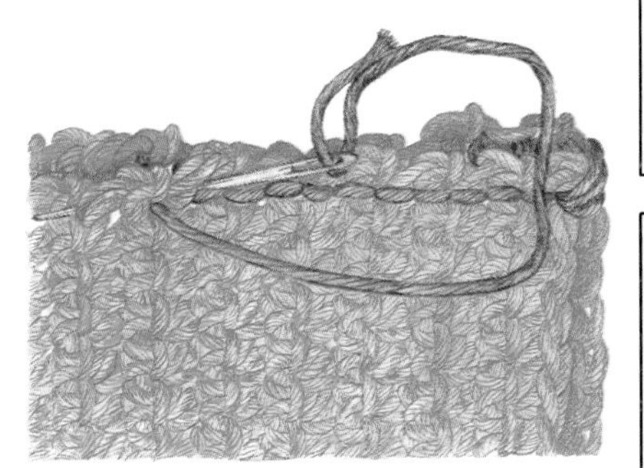

▶ SLIP STITCH SEAM

This is the quickest seaming method. Use a hook one or two sizes smaller than the hook used for the crochet fabric and work each stitch loosely. Single crochet stitch can also be used for a seam. It is more elastic but creates a bulkier edge. Insert the hook through both thicknesses and draw a loop through. *Insert the hook through again and draw a loop through the fabric and the loop on hook. Repeat from * until the length of seam is joined.

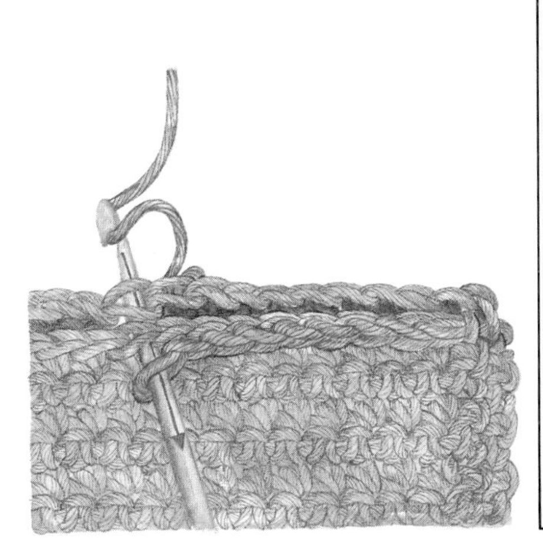

▶ ABBREVIATIONS

approx	approximately
beg	begin(ning)
ch	chain(s)
cm	centimeter(s)
cont	continu(e)(ing)
dc	double crochet
dec	decreas(e)(ing)
foll	follow(s)(ing)
hdc	half double crochet
"	inch(es)
inc	increas(e)(ing)
K	knit
mm	millimeter(s)
MC	main color
oz	ounce(s)
P	purl
pat(s)	pattern(s)
rem	remain(s)(ing)
rep	repeat(ing)
RS	right side(s)
sc	single crochet
sl st	slip stitch(es)
sp(s)	space(s)
st(s)	stitch(es)
tog	together
tr	triple
WS	wrong side(s)
yd	yards
yo	yarn over hook
*	repeat instructions following or between asterisks as many times as directed
()	repeat instructions inside parentheses as many times as directed

▶ CROCHET SYMBOLS

Crochet stitch patterns can be written in a shorthand of international symbols. Each type of stitch is represented by a symbol which resembles the shape or height of the stitch itself. There are numerous symbols for various types and combinations of stitches but only the basic stitch symbols have been used in this book and are given below.

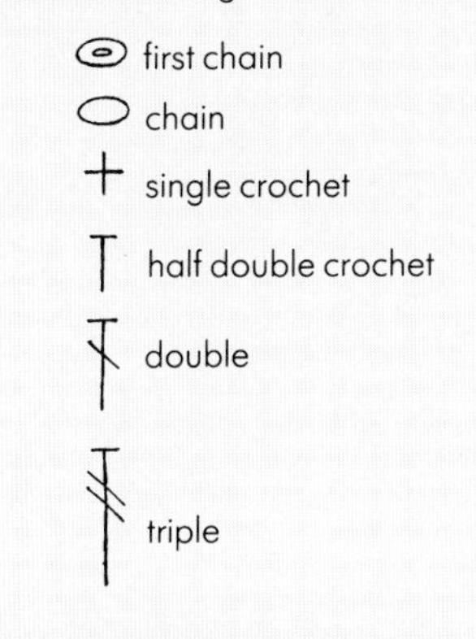

YARNS

These are life-size photographs of the yarns used for each of the sweaters in the book. The labels which describe the thicknesses of the yarns as *fine*, *lightweight* and *medium weight* are only meant as a general guideline. The brand names are those of the yarns used by the designer in crocheting the sweaters for this book. For best results, use these brands. If you are attempting to find a substitute, place the yarn next to the photograph to check that it is the same thickness. Always choose the same type of yarn as a substitute — i.e. choose another mohair for a mohair, a slub yarn for a slub yarn, a smooth yarn for a smooth yarn, etc. For information on how to calculate quantities when substituting a different yarn, see page 110.

Note: Fiber content is given in parentheses after each yarn name. The colors given in the instructions are purely descriptive and are meant to serve as a guide; they are not the same color names used by the yarn manufacturer.

page 12 Broad stripes
medium weight acrylic and rayon yarn — the specific brand used for this sweater has been discontinued

page 15 Striped panels
fine wool tweed yarn —
Rowan *Light Tweed* (wool)

page 18 Checked stripes
lightweight mohair —
Pingouin *Mohair 50*
(mohair/acrylic/wool)

page 22 Stripes on stripes
lightweight wool yarn —
Rowan *Lightweight DK* (wool)

page 26 Stripes & squares
lightweight cotton yarn —
MC and D = Rowan *Cabled Mercerized Cotton* (cotton)
lightweight metallic yarn —
A, B and C = Pingouin *Place Vendôme*
(viscose/polyester)

page 32 Bold block plaid
lightweight wool yarn —
G = Anny Blatt *No 4* (wool)
lightweight mohair —
A, B, C, D, E and F = Anny Blatt *Soft Anny* (kid mohair/polycholorid)

page 36 Tricolor check
lightweight cotton yarn —
Rowan *Cabled Mercerized Cotton*
(cotton)

page 38 Textured checks
lightweight wool yarn —
A, C, D, F, G and H = Rowan *Lightweight DK* (wool)
lightweight cotton knop yarn —
B and E = Scheepjeswol *Miranda*
(cotton/acrylic)

page 41 Check & plaid
lightweight cotton yarn —
F and G = Rowan *Cabled Mercerized Cotton* (cotton)
fine wool tweed yarn —
A, B, C, D and E = Rowan *Light Tweed*
(wool)

page 44 Buffalo plaid
fine wool tweed yarn —
Rowan *Light Tweed* (wool)

page 48 Woven plaid
lightweight cotton chenille —
Rowan *Fine Cotton Chenille* (cotton/polyester)

page 54 Cables
lightweight mohair —
Anny Blatt *Soft Anny* (kid mohair/polycholorid)

page 57 Zigzags
fine slubbed cotton and linen yarn —
Scheepjeswol *Linnen* (cotton/linen)

page 60 Clusters
lightweight wool and silk yarn —
Baruffa/Lane Borgosesia *Serilana*
(wool/silk)

page 64 Basketweave
lightweight cotton yarn —
Rowan *Cabled Mercerized Cotton*
(cotton)

page 72 Fans
medium weight wool yarn —
B = Rowan *Designer DK Wool* (wool)
lightweight cotton and viscose yarn —
A
lightweight cotton chenille —
MC = Rowan *Fine Cotton Chenille*
(cotton/polyester)

page 76 Leaves
medium weight slubbed cotton yarn —
Scheepjeswol *Granada* (cotton)

page 80 Diamonds
lightweight cotton yarn —
Rowan *Cabled Mercerized Cotton*
(cotton)

page 83 Color blocks
lightweight wool yarn —
A, B, C, D, E, F, G, H and I = Rowan *Lightweight DK* (wool)
lightweight mohair —
J = lightweight mohair, nylon and acrylic yarn

page 86 Winter flowers
lightweight wool yarn —
Rowan *Lightweight DK* (wool)

page 90 Bobbled Fair Isle
lightweight cotton yarn —
E = Pingouin *Fil D'Ecosse No 5*
(cotton)
F, G and H = Rowan *Cabled Mercerized Cotton* (cotton)
lightweight wool yarn —
A, B, C and D = Pingouin *Pingofine*
(acrylic/wool)

page 94 Waves & checks
medium weight slubbed cotton yarn —
Scheepjeswol *Granada* (cotton)

page 100 Scalloped lace
lightweight mohair and silk —
Pingouin *Mohair et Soie* (kid mohair/silk)

page 103 Bobbled lace
lightweight cotton yarn —
Rowan *Cabled Mercerized Cotton*
(cotton)

page 106 Chenille checkers
lightweight cotton chenille —
Rowan *Fine Cotton Chenille* (cotton/polyester)

page 12

page 15

page 18

page 22

page 26

page 32

page 36

page 38

page 41

page 44

page 48

page 54

page 57

page 60

page 64

page 72

page 76

page 80

page 83

page 86

page 90

page 94

page 100

page 103

page 106

YARN SUPPLIERS

For information about yarn availability, mail order and retail stores, contact the yarn companies.

ANNY BLATT
USA:
Anny Blatt
24770 Crestview Court
Farmington Hills, MI 48018

CANADA:
Anny Blatt
Diamond Yarns Inc
9697 St. Laurence Blvd
Montreal, Quebec H3L 2N1

UK:
Laines Anny Blatt (UK) Ltd
Bull Bridge
Ambergate, Derby DE5 2EY
Tel: 077385-6025

AUSTRALIA:
Anny Blatt AUST Pty Ltd
26 Punch Sreet
Artarmon, NSW 2064
Tel: (02) 439 4266

BARUFFA/LANE BORGOSESIA
USA:
Baruffa/Lane Borgosesia
RD2, Fields Lane
N. Salem, NY 10560

UK:
Serilana available from Maxwell Cartlidge Ltd

MAXWELL CARTLIDGE LTD
UK (only):
P.O. Box 33
Colchester
Essex

PINGOUIN
USA:
V. Hoover Promafil Corp
PO Box 100
Jamestown, SC 29453

CANADA:
Pingouin
Promafil Canada Ltée
1500 Jules Poitras
St. Laurent, PQ H4N 1X7

UK:
Pingouin
7-11 Lexington St
London W1R 4BU
Tel: 01-439 8891

AUSTRALIA:
Pingouin Aust Pty Ltd
4757 Collins Sreet
Alexandria NSW 2015

ROWAN
USA:
Rowan Yarns
Westminster Trading
5 Northern Boulevard
Amherst NH 03031
Tel: (603) 886 5041

UK:
Rowan Yarns
Green Lane Mill
Washpit, Holmfirth
Huddersfield HD7 1RW
West Yorkshire
Tel: 0484-686714

AUSTRALIA:
Sunspun Enterprises Pty
195 Canterbury Road
Canterbury
Vic 3126

NEW ZEALAND:
Creative Fashion Center
PO Box 45083
Epuni Railway
Lower Hutt

SCHEEPJESWOL
USA:
Scheepjeswol USA
155 Lafayette Ave
N. White Plains, NY 10603

CANADA:
Scheepjeswol (Canada) Ltd
400 Blvd Montée de Liesse
Montreal, Quebec H4T 1N8

UK:
Scheepjeswol
PO Box 48
No 7 Colemeadow Road
Redditch B98 9NZ
Tel: 0527-61056

NEW ZEALAND/AUSTRALIA:
Thorobred Scheepjeswol Ltd
300 Richmond Road
Grey Lynn, PO Box 52028
Kingsland, Auckland

ACKNOWLEDGMENTS

The author would like to thank Anne Farmer (Cambridgeshire Knitters) and her crocheters for their help in producing many sweaters for the book. She also thanks her mother Jean Myers Miller for introducing her to the joy of textiles and for making three of the sweaters with her usual needlework excellence.
The publishers would like to thank the following people for their help and advice in the production of this book: Suzi Read for checking the patterns; Barbara Jones (Artistic Licence) for hair and make-up; Sarah Gisborne (Models One-Plus) and Vanessa Spiro (Bookings) for the modelling; Fanny Rush for the styling for fashion photography; and *Accessorize* for all jewelry.

Editor Charyn Jones
Art Editor Louise Tucker

General Editor Pippa Rubinstein
Managing Editor Susan Berry
Art Director Debbie MacKinnon

Fashion Photography Julie Fisher
Still-life Photography Chris Crofton, Assistant Jayne Pearce

Step-by-step Illustration Lindsay Blow

Fashion Illustration Colin Barnes
Charts and measurement diagrams David Ashby